LIFE AT THE DAKOTA

STEPHEN BIRMINGHAM

LIFE AT THE DAKOTA

New York's Most Unusual Address

Guilford, Connecticut

An imprint of Rowman & Littlefield

Distributed by NATIONAL BOOK NETWORK

Copyright © 1979 by Stephen Birmingham (Random House)
First Lyons Press edition 2016

British Library Cataloguing in Publication Information available

Library of Congress Cataloging-in-Publication Data Available

The Random House edition of this book was previously cataloged by the Library of Congress as follows:

Birmingham, Stephen.
  Life at the Dakota.
  Includes index.
  1. New York (City). Dakota. 2. New York (City)—Social life and customs. 3. Social classes—New York (City) I. Title.
F128.8.D34   974.7'1   79-4800

ISBN 978-1-4930-2473-5 (pbk. : alk. paper)

Acknowledgments

A BOOK ABOUT an apartment house is, of necessity, a book about people, and there are a number of people at the Dakota whom I would like to thank for their impressions, memories, anecdotes and for sharing with me their feelings for the building. In particular, I am grateful to Miss Lauren Bacall, Mr. Ward Bennett, Mr. and Mrs. Henry Blanchard, Mr. and Mrs. Sanford Blank, Miss Adele Browning, Mr. George Davison-Ackley, Mr. Edward O. D. Downes, Mr. and Mrs. Lawrence Ellman, Mr. Peter Fink, Miss Roberta Flack, Miss Ruth Ford, Mr. Paul Goldberger, Miss Sheila Joan Herbert, Miss Anne Ives, Mrs. C. D. Jackson, Mr. Warner LeRoy, Mr. Richard Lukins, Mr. David Marlow, Mr. Jimmy Martin, Mr. and Mrs. Albert Maysles, Mr. and Mrs. Peter Nitze, Mrs. Pauline Pinto, Mr. Rex Reed, Mr. and Mrs. Wilbur L. Ross, Jr., Mr. and Mrs. Paul Segal, Dr. and Mrs. B. Scott Severns, Mr. Guedaliahou Shiva, Mr. and Mrs. Allen Staley, Mr. Anthony Victoria, Mr. Frederick Victoria, Mr. Michael Wager, Mr. and Mrs. Frederic Weinstein and Mrs. Dorothy P. West.

For the woman who is considered "the heart of the Dakota," Miss Winifred Bodkin, a special word of thanks.

I am also indebted to a number of others—former Dakotans as well as men and women who at one point or another have had the Dakota's interests at heart and helped determine its fortune—among them Mr. Ernest Gross, Miss Marya Mannes, Mr. George Beane, Mr. William Miller, Mr. William Quinlan, Mrs. Charles Quinlan, Mr. Louis J. Glickman, Mrs. W. Rodman Fay, and Mr. Stephen C. Clark. For making available to me their files on the Dakota's architectural and social history, I would like to thank especially Mr. Andrew Alpern, A.I.A., and the trustees and staff of the New York State Historical Society in Cooperstown, New York.

The finicky eye, intelligence and taste of my editor at Random House, Charlotte Leon Mayerson, has affected nearly every page that follows. And, as always, I must thank my friend and agent, Mrs. Carol Brandt, for her cool guidance of the project from the outset.

While all of these people contributed in some way to this book, I alone must hold myself accountable for any errors or shortcomings.

S. B.

Contents

Introduction

THERE IS A CASTLE in northern France that rises and falls against the horizon as one approaches it along the highway, driving westward from Épernay. The castle is the ancestral home of the Dukes of Montmort, and the rising and falling phenomenon is caused by the repeated gentle dips and elevations of the roadway. The castle appears on each incline, then disappears with each declivity, then reappears again. It sinks and surfaces many times before one finally reaches it, rather like a ship cresting and then vanishing across a rolling sea. Counting the appearances and disappearances of the Château Montmort is a favorite pastime of small children, as they return home to Paris with their parents after weekend picnics in the Champagne country.

But the curious thing about the rising and falling castle of Montmort is that each time it appears it not only seems larger, it also seems to change shape and form and outline, even color. New turrets appear, new wings, new towers. With each appearance the castle seems an entirely different building, with no relationship to the one the traveler has seen just moments before. In each appearance Château Montmort rearranges itself not subtly but dramatically, as though one had tapped the tube of a kaleidoscope and made the pieces of colored glass compose themselves into an entirely new pattern. The mystery of how the castle tricks and surprises the mind and eye is one of light and landscape and, perhaps, memory, though there is a tale in the region that each view of the castle is a mirage, a ghost, capable of emitting fluctuating, pulsating, changing images of itself, because when one arrives at Montmort at last, the castle is hardly visible.

The rising and falling castle might be a suitable metaphor for the Dakota apartments in New York. Not just because in the course of its nearly hundred-year history the Dakota has had its ups and downs, but because every aspect of the Dakota changes, depending upon the angle from which it is viewed, and also depending upon who is viewing it. No two visions of the Dakota are quite the same, and, because it is a building that has housed and continues to house a number of people, the Dakota has collected more than its share of visions.

Memory is as tricky an instrument as vision, and the Dakota houses many memories, no two quite alike. The Dakota has collected many stories, some of them improbable, many of them contradictory. Many of the Dakota's tales have strikingly different versions, depending on who is recalling them, depending upon how events were perceived. One cannot, therefore, approach the Dakota in terms of "getting down the facts." In a sense, the Dakota has no facts to offer, only impressions. So one must approach the Dakota rather as one would enter a funhouse Hall of Mirrors, full of wonder, watching the images and impressions change in shape and size and substance each time they appear.

At the same time, tracing the history of the Dakota and the people who have lived there is a little like examining the past of a small village in New Hampshire, a village which, on the surface, appears to have slept unchanged for a hundred years or more, and yet which, in human terms, has changed constantly. But this is a peculiar little village. For one thing, its neighbors abut each other vertically as well as horizontally. For another, it is a town whose residents have always been, for the most part, rich—at times chic, at times trend-setting, at times foolish, at times eccentric, always interesting.

But, for the most part, *rich.*

Part One

"CLARK'S FOLLY"

Oh, who of us would change a jot,
  Or even an iota—
We happy few whose happy lot
  Is Life in the Dakota? . . .

Where else, Oh fortress of delight,
  Inhabitants so famous
That every chronicle in sight
  Must write of us or frame us? . . .

Blessed be the roof that shelters us!
  With all our hearts we praise it,
And daily pray, unanimous,
  That nobody will raze it! . . .

FROM "Ballad of the Dakota"
BY Marya Mannes

Chapter 1

"An Era of Upholstery"

MODERN NEW YORKERS have grown accustomed to the experience of going around the corner to what was last week's favorite delicatessen only to discover that, this week, it has become a wig shop; or finding, where the little place that sold handbags used to be, just off Lexington, that the entire block has disappeared to make room for an office tower. Faced with yet another example of the fact that New York is a restless, ever-changing, never-finished city, New Yorkers simply shrug and go on about their business.

New York in the 1880's was already a city that seemed to have made up its mind that whatever existed was dispensable and replaceable, provided some more profitable use could be found for it. In the years following the Civil War, when great New York fortunes were being made—by men named Rockefeller, Harriman, Gould, Frick, Morgan, Schiff and Vanderbilt, among others—money had become New York's main industry, while the city's secondary pastime seemed to involve systematically turning New York's back upon its past. Anything of even mildly antiquarian or historic interest was the target of destruction, and anyone who deplored the way the city was remaking itself from a sleepy seaport into a bustling capital of finance was regarded as a hopeless sentimentalist. The past was not New York's concern; its concern was the future, and Progress. Buildings were flung up only to be torn down a few years later and replaced by newer, more modern structures. Any structure that didn't quite work or didn't quite pay was demolished to make room for something else that might. The modernization of New York, as it marched toward the twentieth century, was as reckless as it was relentless.

Already it seemed that New York was destined to become a city of towers, that it would grow upward as rapidly as it grew outward. In 1884, the year that the Dakota was completed, the architect Richard Morris Hunt had put the finishing touches on a huge new building on Park Row to house Whitelaw Reid's New York *Tribune*. The *Tribune* tower soared an unprecedented eleven stories into the sky and was topped by a tall campanile, but it was not to be New York's tallest building for long. A year later Bradford Lee Gilbert designed the Tower Building, to be erected at 50 Broadway. The Tower Building, which was to occupy a plot of land only twenty-one feet wide, was to rise to a startling thirteen stories, eclipsing the *Tribune* building in height. The doubters and naysayers confidently predicted that the building would never withstand a high gale. Gilbert was so confident of his structure's safety that he announced that he himself would occupy the topmost floors with his offices, but at least one neighbor in an adjoining building evacuated his property, certain that his building would be crushed by the weight of Gilbert's when inevitably it fell. In 1886, when the building had reached only ten stories, eighty-mile-an-hour winds struck the city and huge crowds gathered on Broadway—at a safe distance—to watch the Tower Building topple. Gilbert, in a panic, rushed downtown and climbed to the top of his building to see how it was doing. All night long the winds raged, and the Tower Building didn't even tremble. It remained standing until 1913, when it was demolished.

All at once the building of taller and yet taller buildings became a matter of competition. Joseph Pulitzer's new building for the *World* clocked in at fifteen stories and was surmounted with a cupola with a dazzling golden dome. Then came the American Surety Company's tower opposite Trinity Church—twenty stories high. As New York flexed its muscles for the future, there seemed to be no limit to how high a building could go.

At the same time, while all this building was going on, New Yorkers suffered from what a modern psychologist would label a poor self-image. New Yorkers who cared about such matters, and who had visited such European cities as London, Paris and Rome, were the first to admit that New York was becoming a not very pretty city and disparaged (according to a contemporary account) "this cramped horizontal gridiron of a town without . . . porticoes, fountains or perspectives, hide-bound in its deadly uniformity of mean ugliness." The rigid, block-by-block pattern of the new streets that were being laid out was considered boring, and the problem of naming the new streets seemed to have defeated the imagination. They were simply numbered, south to north for the streets, east to west for the perpendicular avenues. Sophisticated New Yorkers complained that their city had none of the exuberance and spectacle of Paris—no Place de l'Étoile, no Place de la Concorde, none of the monumental statuary, arches, bridges and vistas that Baron Hausmann had created. New York lacked the intimate, formal little squares of London's Mayfair and Belgravia. Instead of a Piccadilly or a Champs Élysées, New York had Broadway, and the most that could be said for Broadway was that it was very long. The fashionable area to live was now Murray Hill, on Madison Avenue north of Thirty-fourth Street, where a few years earlier gentlemen of fashion had gone quail hunting, though a few diehard families like the Astors still clung to their mansions on lower Fifth Avenue, between Washington and Madison Squares, even though that part of town was rapidly being taken over by "trade." But the houses of the rich, each trying to outdo the others in opulence and splash—and built in wildly varying architectural styles from Moorish to English Gothic to Italian Renaissance—were considered pretentious and embarrassing to the purists. New York seemed capable of creating everything but a style of its own.

New York, in the late nineteenth century, was also an astonishingly dirty city for a variety of reasons. Only about half of New York's families had bathrooms; the rest were served by outhouses. The Saturday-night bath had become a national ritual, but brushing one's teeth was unheard of. By 1885, some 250,000 horses—pulling carts, carriages, trolleys and public omnibuses—jammed New York's streets.

The clatter of horse-drawn traffic up and down Broadway continued night and day. Venturing out into the streets on foot was for the daring, and strollers encountered an obstacle course between piles of steaming dung which swarmed with flies. In hot, dry weather the horse manure in the streets quickly dried to a fine powder and swirled in the air as dust. Ladies wore heavy veils for shopping, not out of modesty or for fashion, but to keep this unlovely substance out of their mouths, eyes and noses. New York horses were driven until they expired, and as many as a hundred horses collapsed daily in the streets. It was often a matter of days before the carcasses could be hauled away, and the odor of decaying horseflesh added its own pungency to the city air. In the 1880's, meanwhile, New Yorkers were only beginning to get used to the luxury of paved streets in certain areas.

Forty-second Street had become the northernmost limit of fashionability; beyond that Fifth Avenue and its adjoining streets had a ragged, unfinished look. Still, though the metropolis consumed less than a third of the area that it does today, New York had already become a city of inconvenient and time-consuming distances. It took a Manhattan businessman anywhere from an hour to an hour and a half to get from his home to his place of work in the slow-moving traffic of the densely congested streets. In 1883, when finishing touches were being applied to the Dakota, the Brooklyn Bridge opened to great civic fanfare, after thirteen years in the building. (Like the builder of the Dakota, the designer of the bridge, John Roebling, would not live to see the completion of his great project.) The Brooklyn Bridge was not designed to appeal to the aesthetic sense. It was without the ornament, spontaneity or romance of bridges that crossed the Seine, the Arno or the Thames. Its beauty was in its stern, no-nonsense practicality—a utilitarian bridge in which every exposed cable slung from the two sturdy towers at either end clearly had a duty to perform: to support the roadbed. The bridge was designed to provide New Yorkers with the novelty, and the convenience, of driving across the East River instead of crossing it slowly by ferryboat. The bridge also dramatized New York's need for a public transportation system less cumbersome than the hansom cab and horse-drawn omnibus, and suddenly the phrase on everyone's lips was "rapid transit."

London had had a subway system since 1863, but New York had not yet gone underground for at least two reasons. For one thing, New York was built on solid rock, and tunneling through the Manhattan schist presented enormous engineering obstacles. For another, during the years when "Boss" Tweed had the city in his grip, Tweed and his "ring" controlled the surface transportation lines and wanted no competition. Still, a number of ambitious underground plans had been proposed. One was the "Beach Pneumatic Tunnel," a scheme by which a blast of air, blown out by a giant blowing machine at the rear of a car, would force an underground car along a track like a sailboat before a wind. It was an era of extravagant speculation and high-blown promise; the backers of the Pneumatic Tunnel claimed that it would carry passengers from one end of Manhattan to the other at the rate of 20,000 people per hour. A short experimental section of the Beach Pneumatic Tunnel was actually built under Broadway between Warren and Murray streets, a distance of one short block. This precursor of the jet age did not work well. It traversed the distance in more time than it took to walk it.

Still another proposal called for building an entire underground street below Broadway, complete with sidewalks, gas lamps, shops and stalls. This street would be wide enough for horse-drawn vehicles and would have a railroad track running down its center for steam-driven locomotives pulling trains. This project came to naught when John Jacob Astor III and other powerful landlords protested that the underground avenue would weaken the foundations of their buildings.

And so, instead of building down, New York built up, and elevated railroads began to sprout along Sixth Avenue, Third Avenue, Ninth Avenue and eventually Second Avenue. The four-car green-painted trains carried passengers uptown and downtown from daybreak to midnight at the astonishing speed of thirty miles an hour. Though certainly convenient, the elevated trains were not an unmixed blessing. They were bumpy and noisy—horses reared in fright at the approach of each clattering locomotive—and they were not without danger. Newspapers filled with accounts of accidents and of trains that had jumped their tracks and threatened to dump their passengers into the street some thirty feet below. One hair-raising turn on the Ninth Avenue line seemed particularly hazardous. The engineers, it seemed, believed that the proper way to accomplish this turn was at the highest speed. After several accidents the engineers decided they were wrong.

The streets beneath the elevated lines were dark. As the trains rattled by, they spewed out ashes, hot cinders and live steam onto the sidewalks below and into the second-story windows of the buildings they passed. During the great blizzard of 1888 some 15,000 New Yorkers were trapped in elevated trains on tracks that had become blocked by snowdrifts, and a number of enterprising souls made a tidy business out of raising ladders from the street and helping passengers climb down, at a dollar a head. At least one train that was too high for a ladder to reach was stalled in the air for sixteen hours while the passengers were kept from freezing with whiskey that was hoisted up from the street by ropes.

The avenues along which the elevated lines ran quickly became soot-blackened slums, their buildings divided into tenements of sunless two-room "Dumbbells" (so called because the floor plans were of a ⬜⊣⬜ shape) or "railroad flats." The word "flat," which had been perfectly acceptable in England and Europe, took on a new connotation in New York. Living in a flat, to a New Yorker, denoted misery and poverty of the meanest kind. At the same time, the elevated trains, which ran northward from the Battery, enormously speeded the city's northward expansion. The entire island, all the way to the Harlem River, was now easily accessible. But in terms of building, it was for the most part an expansion of the poor. The rich remained on Fifth Avenue and Murray Hill.

Visitors from Europe, meanwhile, deplored the noisy ugliness of the elevated railroads. A reporter from the *Revue des Deux Mondes* in Paris wrote condescendingly that he had seen "well-dressed, well-bred New Yorkers clinging to straps, jaded, jammed, jostled, panting in the aisle of these hearselike equipages, to reach their goal." Still, for a city that ranked practicality above beauty, it had to be admitted that the transportation system was now both fast and cheap. During rush hours it cost only a nickel to take "the el" from one end of Manhattan to the other. At other times it was a dime. For all the convenience and economy, as New York became a city of straphangers one also had to be wary of the "dip," or pickpocket, a practitioner whose counterpart could be found in medieval paintings and in all crowded cities of the world.

By the 1880's a number of imposing hotels had already been built in the city. There was the Astor House, on Broadway and Barclay Street, which had been built by John Jacob Astor in the 1830's. Further uptown, and even grander, was the St. Nicholas Hotel on Broadway and Broome Street, which had cost one million dollars to build and could accommodate some eight hundred guests; the St. Nicholas boasted the unheard-of luxury of central hot-air heating. The Metropolitan Hotel was equally costly and sumptuous, and contained a hundred suites of "family apartments," which, it implied, could be leased as permanent residences. But the newer Fifth Avenue Hotel was unquestionably the most elegant in town and advertised "more than one hundred suites of apartments, each combining the convenience and luxury of parlor, chamber, dressing and bathing rooms." Private bathrooms were an extraordinary novelty. The Fifth Avenue Hotel also introduced another controversial feature—an elevator, described as a "perpendicular railway intersecting each story." Theretofore, elevators had been installed only in a few of the taller office buildings. In buildings of only six stories, such as the Fifth Avenue, one expected the drudgery of stairs.

The new luxury hotels gave New York a cosmopolitan, sophisticated air, along with a transient population the city had not known a generation earlier. The plush-covered lobbies and opulent bars and restaurants in these hotels lent a European tone to the city. Still, there was something about Victorian New Yorkers that was put off by all the plush. Proper New Yorkers remained, at heart, rather puritanically moralistic. America still looked to England as her model for social decorum, and Americans felt more at home with English austerity and reserve than with French silk and gaudiness. To some critics the hotels seemed more like palaces of license, caravansaries of carnality, or worse. The effect of the hotels on New Yorkers' morality was pondered, and one social commentator of the time asked whether the hotels did not "open an era of upholstery, with a tendency to live in a herd, and the absence of a subdued and harmonious tone of life and manners?" Upholstery, obviously, was somehow synonymous with sin. Another travel writer warned visitors to the city that "Hotel life is agreeable and desirable for masculine celibates; but he is unwise who takes his wife and family there for a permanent home. How many women can trace their first infidelity to the necessarily demoralizing influences of public houses— to loneliness, leisure, need of society, interesting companions, abundance of opportunity and potent temptations!" Still another found hotel living unsuitable even for masculine celibates. "Gentlemen," he noted primly, "will never consent to live on mere shelves under a common roof!"

MEANWHILE, to everyone's amusement, a newly rich millionaire named Edward Clark was building, of all things, a luxury apartment house at a location that wasn't even an address—Seventy-second Street and Eighth Avenue—so far out of the swim of city life that it seemed like the North Pole. Clark was spending a million dollars on this foolishness, and, obviously, it would never work. Still, New York in the 1880's had become a city of mad, entrepreneurial schemes, many of which didn't work. Into this mood of hectic speculation and crazy chance-taking, Mr. Clark's scheme fitted perfectly. It was an era of folly. Building the Dakota could be Edward Clark's.

Chapter 2

"But Not for the Gentry"

BY 1880, NEW YORK had passed beyond the Age of Innocence, of which Edith Wharton wrote, and had entered what James Truslow Adams called the "Age of the Dinosaurs." In it, fortunes were being made on a scale that had never before been imagined and that were difficult even for the men who made them to comprehend. Twenty-five years earlier there had not been more than five men in the United States worth as much as five million dollars, and there were less than twenty who were worth a million. Now, however, the New York *Tribune* would report that there were several hundred men in the city of New York alone who were worth at least a million, and a number who were worth at least twenty million. The money, furthermore, was being made from sources never before heard of—from steel mills, steam engines, oil from the Pennsylvania hills, and all manner of mechanical inventions from machine guns to washing machines.

To the Old Guard of New York, the impact that all the new money was having upon the city was deplorable. George Templeton Strong, a diarist of the period, bemoaned the "oil-rich shoddy-ites" from out of town who had descended like an invasion upon New York* and wrote:

How New York has fallen off during the last forty years! Its intellect and culture have been diluted and swamped by a great flood-tide of material wealth . . . men whose bank accounts are all they rely on for social position and influence. As for their ladies, not a few who were driven in the most sumptuous turnouts, with liveried servants, looked as if they might have been cooks or chambermaids a few years ago.

With money was supposed to come respectability, and all at once there was emphasis on being "in society." New York society was the subject of much attention in the newspapers, which fulsomely covered the banquets, fancy dress balls and quadrilles tossed by the likes of Mr. and Mrs. Walter Lispenard Suydam, Mr. and Mrs. Columbus Iselin, Mrs. Brockholst Cutting, and Mr. and Mrs. Stuyvesant Fish. There were no motion picture or television stars then to capture the imagination of the public, nor were there any stage actresses who were considered really "respectable," and so every new-rich parvenue—and every shopgirl—had her favorite society figure whose doings she followed vicariously, whose life she longed to emulate, and whose perfumed circle she dreamed of entering.

But entering society was not easy. Society in 1880 was firmly delineated by Mrs. William Astor and her chief lieutenant, Ward McAllister, and her list of the "Four Hundred" New Yorkers who, supposedly, were as many as she could conveniently fit into her ballroom. (When Mrs. Astor's list was eventually published, it turned out to contain only three hundred and four names.)

To get into society, it seemed, required more than money and the ability to surround oneself with the luxurious trappings of money. There was a new and important ingredient called *taste*. Good birth, which was so important a standard in English and European society, could not be purchased by newly rich New Yorkers, but good taste could. In 1870, Charles L. Tiffany had opened his splendid new store

---

*Though he failed to mention it, Mr. Strong himself owned 10,000 shares of Kenzula Petroleum.

on Union Square, which had quickly become the bellwether of taste. In fact, as the New York *Post* solemnly advised its readers, Tiffany's was "a school for taste" for those New Yorkers who needed such an education. Tiffany's was an immediate success.

Good taste implied good breeding, which meant good manners, correctness in all things. In a popular play of the era called *Fashion*, a character with social pretensions named Mrs. Tiffany, a former milliner whose husband has struck oil, declared, "Forget what we *have* been, it is enough to remember that we *are* of the *upper ten thousand!*" But more than forgetting the past was involved; the past had to be covered by a new veneer of polish, and a flurry of books and manuals appeared—how-to books on "etiquette" and *"comme il faut"* and "proper social usage." To judge from some of the social "dos" and "don'ts" published in this period, many people needed to be elevated to *comme il faut* from a fairly primitive state.

One etiquette writer, for example, scolded, "What an article is a spittoon as an appendage to a handsomely furnished drawing room!" And another advised guests at a dinner party against "shaking with your feet the chair of a neighbor"—an activity whose purpose is hard to imagine. It was also suggested that "ladies should never dine with their gloves on unless their hands are not fit to be seen." If a lady should make an "unseemly digestive sound" at table or "raise an unmanageable portion to her mouth," the proper reaction was to "cease all conversation with her and look steadfastly into the opposite part of the room." While at table, advised one writer, "all allusions to dyspepsia, indigestion, or any other disorders of the stomach are vulgar and disgusting. The word 'stomach' should never be uttered at table." The same writer cautioned that "the fashion of wearing black silk mittens at breakfast is now obsolete." Decorum while traveling had to be observed, and when traveling alone, ladies should "avoid saying anything to women in showy attire, with painted faces, and white kid gloves . . . you will derive no pleasure from making acquaintance with females who are evidently coarse and vulgar, even if you know that they are rich."

Men of the era were also instructed in the rules of delicacy; one etiquette manual commented that "The rising generation of young elegants in America are particularly requested to observe that, in polished society, it is not quite *comme il faut* for gentlemen to blow their noses with their fingers, especially when in the street." The gentlemen's habit of chewing tobacco also created problems. "A lady on the second seat of a box at the theatre," wrote one social critic, "found, when she went home, the back of her pelisse entirely spoilt, by some man behind not having succeeded in trying to spit past her." And an English visitor had been surprised to see none other than John Jacob Astor remove his chewing tobacco from his mouth and absent-mindedly trace a watery design with it on a windowpane.

When a French critic reported that it was the custom, in crowded New York omnibuses and elevated trains, for gentlemen who were already seated to let ladies perch on their knees, the New York newspapers angrily denounced this report as a piece of fiction. But these papers themselves were often critical of New Yorkers' manners, and the *Herald* took society to task for "loud talking at table, impertinent staring at strangers, brusqueness of manners among the ladies, laughable attempts at courtly ease and self-possession among the men—the secret of all this vulgarity in Society is that wealth, or the reputation of wealth, constitutes the open sesame to its delectable precincts."

Where one lived and how one lived in New York was also a matter of *comme il faut,* and that was what made Edward Clark's plan to build a large luxury apartment house in the far reaches of the upper West Side seem so preposterous. Society would never place its sacred imprimatur on that part of town. No less an authority than Ward McAllister (or Mr. Make-a-Lister, as he was sometimes called) had declared that he could not bother "to run society" north of Fiftieth Street.*

West Seventy-second Street was not only far north of society's imaginary boundary line, it was also far west of it. The perimeters of Central Park had already been laid on the city's maps, but Eighth Avenue (not yet renamed Central Park West), the park's western border, was still a dirt road. Though Mr. Clark's expensive building would face the park, that section of the park had not yet been landscaped or developed. In the park, opposite and all around Mr. Clark's building site, lived squatters in shacks built of roofing paper and flattened tins—shanties without plumbing or heat, whose owners kept pigs, goats, cows and chickens

---

*This was a thinly veiled slur at Mrs. Astor's arch rival, Mrs. William K. Vanderbilt, whose new mansion was under construction at the corner of Fifth Avenue and Fifty-second Street.

that grazed and foraged among the rocky outcroppings. Those deplorable hovels and their unlovely occupants would be Mr. Clark's next-door neighbors.

Society in London, Paris, Rome and Madrid had been living in apartments for years, but New York was not Europe. New York gentlemen would never live "on shelves under a common roof," and apartment houses, like the gaudy hotels, were regarded as architectural inducements to immorality. There was even more to it than that. Apartment living implied a sleazy and suspicious transiency. In those days, as Lloyd Morris pointed out, "Failure to own your own home was a confession of shabby antecedents or disreputable habits."

The fact that the poor of New York were tenanted in the miserable railroad flats merely added to the stigma of apartment living. But more than that, to the sensibilities of Victorian New Yorkers there was something very Parisian, and therefore naughty, about the thought of having bedrooms (euphemistically called "chambers;" the word "bedroom" was considered as vulgar as the word "stomach") on the same floor as the floor where one dined and entertained. Discreet staircases were expected to separate public from private rooms. Edith Wharton, writing of a somewhat earlier era, had described a certain elderly New York lady whose

burden of . . . flesh had long since made it impossible for her to go up and down stairs, and with characteristic independence . . . had . . . established herself (in flagrant violation of all the New York proprieties) on the ground floor of her house; so that, as you sat in her sitting room . . . you caught . . . the unexpected vista of a bedroom . . .

Her visitors were startled and fascinated by the foreignness of this arrangement, which recalled scenes in French fiction . . . such as the simple American had never dreamed of. That was how women with lovers lived in wicked old societies, in apartments with all the rooms on one floor, and all the indecent propinquities that their novels described.

These attitudes toward single-floor living had remained unchanged. But things had been happening in New York that the highest reaches of society may not have noticed. For one thing, with all the new money that was pouring into the city, New York had become easily the most expensive American city in which to live. Most hard-pressed—since they appreciated the niceties—were the city's genteel, well-educated professional people of moderate means. A house in a respectable, if not affluent, neighborhood could not be rented for less than eighteen hundred dollars a year. A woman who considered herself a lady felt it essential to have at least three in staff. The Irish cook cost from eighteen to twenty dollars a month. A chambermaid, usually also Irish, cost from twelve to fifteen dollars monthly and a nurse for the children, usually French or German, cost about the same. The costs of living had escalated alarmingly. Butter was fifty cents a pound, compared with thirty-five cents or less elsewhere in the country. Eggs were fifty cents a dozen, sugar was sixteen cents a pound, chicken was twenty-five cents a pound and beef was thirty-five cents a pound. A family with an income of six thousand dollars a year—well above the median American income of the era—found itself having to watch pennies. The dinner party, meanwhile, had become a fixed New York institution, and well-bred New Yorkers were expected—almost required—to do a certain amount of entertaining, and to do so on a modest income had become something of a hardship.

Adding to the cost of everything was the fact that New York was becoming a very crowded city. As early as 1870, an angry reader wrote to the New York *Times,* demanding to know why the city was keeping empty land in Central Park "while the middle classes are being driven out of the City by excessive rents." Indeed, it was upon the middle class that the squeeze was most extreme. Of the million people in New York, half the population lived in 40,000 houses of between five and fifty rooms. The other half lived in just 20,000 dwellings, mostly consisting of one room. In addition, more than 24,000 immigrants from Europe and Ireland were crammed into 8,500 basement cells without heat, light, ventilation and, of course, plumbing. New York was threatening to become a city of the enormously rich and the desperately poor.

One of the first New Yorkers to realize that "nice" people of slender means might provide a market for a special sort of housing was the aristocratic Mr. Rutherfurd Stuyvesant. His father, Lewis Rutherfurd, had been an astronomer and scholar, but his mother was a descendant of the last Dutch governor, Peter Stuyvesant, and so when the Stuyvesant fortune passed to her son, Stuyvesant Rutherfurd reversed his name to suit his circumstances. Stuyvesant embarked upon a daring experiment. In the late 1860's he hired Richard Morris Hunt, the

architect of the *Tribune* Tower and the first American to graduate from
the École des Beaux Arts in Paris, to convert a row of town houses on
Eighteenth Street, near Irving Place, into "French flats." The resulting
apartment house was called the Stuyvesant, and was a five-story walk-up
with two apartments to a floor. As had long been the case in Europe,
the best apartments were on the ground, or "principal" floor, and there
was even a concierge at the front door. Each apartment in the Stuyvesant contained about seven-and-a-half rooms and, though each boasted
such amenities as high ceilings, a pair of wood-burning fireplaces (one
in the parlor, one in the dining room) and—the ultimate luxury—its
own bathroom, the rooms were rather small and not particularly sunny,
and the manner in which the apartments were laid out was crude and
inconvenient. All the "indecent propinquities" that Mrs. Wharton had
noted were observable—chambers visible from parlors—and all the
rooms were connected by a narrow, twisting, sunless hallway. The lone
bathroom was located closer to the tiny servant's room than to the three
master chambers, and there were other shortcomings. There were
hardly any closets (New Yorkers, after all, were used to armoires), and
kitchens were placed at a considerable distance from dining rooms and
even further from the dumbwaiters and service stairs.

Still, despite all this, and to everyone's surprise, the Stuyvesant was
an immediate success, and all of its apartments were rented before the
renovation was completed. "It seemed incredible," as Lloyd Morris put
it in *Incredible New York,* "that young people of the highest genealogi-
cal merit would consent to dwell in a building which, after all, was only
a superior version of the tenements inhabited by the poor." And another observer was pleasantly surprised to find that the list of the
Stuyvesant's tenants "produced a very old Knickerbocker sort of effect
upon the outside mind." It was noted, however, that residents of the
Stuyvesant were careful to refer to their homes as *apartments,* not
"flats."

Once Mr. Stuyvesant had demonstrated that apartment living could
be made appealing, if not to the rich-rich, at least to the respectably
well-to-do and the middle-class prosperous, other builders cautiously
began to follow his example. In the late 1870's plans for three more
luxury apartment buildings were being drawn up, each of them more
ambitious than the Stuyvesant. The first was 121 Madison Avenue at
the foot of fashionable Murray Hill. Each two floors of this building,

when it was completed, contained five duplexes of seven, eight or nine rooms. Again, each apartment had only one bath, though the servants' rooms were supplied with wash basins and given a toilet to share. Next came the Spanish Flats, so named after its Spaniard builder, Juan de Navarro, on Seventh Avenue between Fifty-eighth and Fifty-ninth streets. The Spanish Flats was an eight-building apartment complex, with thirteen apartments to a building. Entering a Flats apartment, one would find an 18- by 25-foot reception foyer, a 22- by 28-foot drawing room, a dining room of nearly the same size, a slightly smaller library, a large kitchen with a butler's pantry, four bedrooms with fireplaces, roomy closets and, again, a single bath. For servants, there were cells in the basement. The stigma of the term "flats" still remained, however, and the Spanish Flats was soon renamed the Central Park Apartments.

The third important building of the era was the Chelsea, at 222 West Twenty-third Street, then one of the most fashionable addresses in town. But the Chelsea was more an apartment hotel than an apartment house, since most of its suites had no kitchen facilities. Tenants were expected to use the restaurant-dining room on the ground floor.

All these developments were being watched with considerable interest by Edward Clark. There were other matters that he had also been watching closely. When the maps of the lines and the grades of the West Side street system were filed by the Central Park commissioners in 1868, there was a great West Side real estate boom. Eighth Avenue, it was predicted, on the west flank of the park, would become a street of millionaires' mansions outdoing even Fifth Avenue in spectacle and grandeur. West End Avenue, it was asserted, would one day become a magnificent shopping street, and an even grander future was predicted for Riverside Drive, the beautifully winding parkway that had been laid out, addressing the Hudson River and the New Jersey Palisades, between Seventy-second and One Hundred Twenty-fifth streets. Between 1868 and 1873 the price of land north of Fifty-ninth Street and west of Central Park increased by more than 200 percent. But then the speculative boom in West Side land was put to an end by the Great Panic of 1873, and the value of West Side land decreased sharply, though some building activity continued on the East Side.

In 1877 there was renewed interest in the possible future of West Side properties. That was the year the American Museum of Natural

History was completed, after three years of building, on the west side of the park between Seventy-seventh and Eighty-first streets. This was taken as an omen that the upper West Side would one day be a citadel of culture for New York's billowing aristocracy, and that other great museums, monuments and schools would follow. Columbia University was already planning to move uptown and to turn the steep ridge of land called Morningside Heights into a "civic Acropolis." It was in 1877 that Edward Clark made his initial move and, taking advantage of still-depressed real estate prices, purchased two acres of land from August Belmont for $200,000 and began to plan his building.

Clark's building was to be the most opulent and lavish and at the same time tasteful that New York had ever seen, far outdoing any apartment house that then existed anywhere in the world in splendor of detail, size and scale of its apartments, and costliness of its appointments. Its interiors would replicate, and even surpass, the mansions of Goulds, Vanderbilts, Astors and Goelets. When he broke ground in 1880 his budget—an even million dollars—was unprecedented, and he had not gone far before he decided to pour yet another million into the project. From the beginning such extravagance was denounced as foolishness by both his business associates and his fellow clubmen. It would never work. The apartments would never rent. Friends urged him to give up his concept of a residential building and to turn it into a hospital or an asylum. The fact was simply that New Yorkers would never want to live that far uptown—not "nice" New Yorkers, anyway. "You may attract a few purse-proud nabobs from the world of trade," warned one friend. "You are building for them, sir. But not for the gentry!"

Mr. Clark, it would turn out, was hoping to attract a clientele somewhat different from the gentry.

Another friend commented, with some sarcasm, that, in putting up a building so far north and so far west of civilization, Mr. Clark might just as well be building in Dakota, which was then still a territory and not yet a pair of states. Clark, who was not without a sense of humor, rather enjoyed the metaphor. He instructed his architect to make the most of it, and the building's design was embellished with certain Wild West details—arrowheads, ears of corn and sheaves of wheat in bas-relief on the building's interior and exterior façades. Above the building's main portico a carved stone Indian head in bas-relief would be placed, gazing sternly out at West Seventy-second Street, as the building's trademark.

Originally, Edward Clark had planned to call his building the Clark Apartments. But now, as the vast edifice slowly arose in the middle of what did indeed seem a prairie setting of great, untenanted plains, New Yorkers were simply calling it "Clark's Folly." And so, in a gesture of airy defiance to the critics and skeptics and naysayers, he announced that its name would be the Dakota.

Chapter 3

Clark and Singer

EDWARD CLARK had learned a great deal about American tastes and attitudes, and how to shape and change them, from selling, of all things, sewing machines.

Oddly enough, though servants were still relatively cheap in the United States in the nineteenth century, they were becoming increasingly hard to find. In 1882, the *Century* magazine had complained that

The liberty and equality idea has converted a large proportion of our lower classes into would-be ladies and gentlemen, who put up with domestic servitude as a repugnant chrysalis state, preliminary to the winged bliss of perpetual idleness. A servant who is willing to be called a servant, who looks forward to servitude as a life-work, is almost unheard-of nowadays. Any honest effort to correct this assumption so common in our lower classes, to teach them the true dignity of work, and to train them in habits of industry, and cleanliness, and intelligent labor, should meet with the fullest sympathy.

There was, in fact, already an effort underway in New York to train people to think like servants. In 1877 Miss Emily Huntington had established the Kitchen Garden Association; "Kitchen Garden" was Miss Huntington's little play on the word kindergarten, because, in her association's program, small children were taken from "the poorest classes; the little waifs and strays of humanity who crowd the door-steps and alley-ways of the most squalid streets," and were taught not to read and write but how to do housework. Miss Huntington's was a six-month course. First the tots were taught how to use matches and build a fire with charcoal or coal. Next came the learning of "games . . . dear to the heart of every little girl, such as scrubbing, ironing and folding clothes, tending the door, etc., etc." The course progressed with instruction on how to polish silver and china, how to wait on table, how to wash dishes, how to sweep, dust, make beds and polish furniture. At the end of the course, "A good situation is promised to them at twelve years of age if they have learned their lessons well." By 1881 nine hundred and ninety children were enrolled in the Kitchen Garden in New York alone, and Miss Huntington was expanding her operation to other cities.

Meanwhile, faced with the growing servant problem, more and more women were turning to a wealth of new mechanical gadgets and devices to help them with their household chores. But one home appliance that had not at all caught on was Elias Howe's invention, the sewing machine. For one thing, the machines were bulky, expensive and always breaking down. But there was another, more important psychological reason for womens' aversion to sewing by machine. Sewing was women's work, without question. Wealthy women sewed for pleasure and relaxation; they tatted, did embroidery, crochet and crewel work, and needlepoint. Poorer women sewed out of necessity, darning and mending their childrens' and husbands' socks and underthings, sewing buttons on shirts, and turning hems on handkerchiefs and tablecloths. For a poor unmarried woman, being a seamstress was one of the very few available occupations that were respectable and honorable. But the point of a woman and her sewing was that it was done by hand, with her needle and her thread, her thimble on her finger and her work arrayed prettily on her lap. The idea of sewing with a machine, which involved treadles, pulleys, knobs and gears, was actually repugnant to Victorian women, and to men. Sitting at a machine looked—well, mannish. Sewing machines were not *comme il faut* with women of any American social class.

OF THE BACKGROUND of the man whose name today is synonymous with the home sewing machine, Isaac Merritt Singer, very little is known. It is likely that the family was originally Jewish, and that the family name in Germany, from whence Isaac's father emigrated, was Reisinger, a common German-Jewish name. At the age of twelve Isaac Singer ran away from home, and for the next forty years of his life he was an itinerant unskilled laborer, often unemployed. For a while he had dreams of becoming an actor and headed something called the Merritt Players (eschewing the name Singer, perhaps because of its Jewish sound), a traveling acting troupe that made its way around the east with performances of Shakespeare for rural audiences. But the Merritt Players soon disbanded because, it seemed, no one could get along with Isaac Merritt Singer.

He was tall, handsome and muscular, but he had a foul mouth and a violent temper. After his brief acting career he worked at various odd jobs, none of them for very long because he so quickly managed to alienate or offend his employers. Singer also launched what was to be his most impressive career—as a womanizer and polygamist. At one point, he was married to five women, none of whom was aware of the existence of the other four, and was supporting as many as six mistresses on the side. Though he apparently beat, abused and otherwise mistreated his women, they seemed magnetized by him and by what must have been his imposing sexuality. The numbers of offspring from his various unions began to mount. Once, having just married a new wife, Singer decided that it might be prudent to shed himself of the previous one. He visited her with the aim of getting her to agree to a divorce, and only succeeded in getting her pregnant with another child.

There were many patented mechanical sewing devices by 1851 when, by sheerest accident and luck, Isaac Singer happened to become involved with them. Singer had, at this point, spent most of his untidy life more or less as a vagrant, marrying women, giving them babies and supporting himself with odd jobs as an unskilled laborer. Then, one day when he was working in a Boston machine shop, a Lerow & Blodgett sewing machine was brought in for repairs, and the job of fixing it was given to Singer. Suddenly, it was as if some long-buried resource in

Singer's mind burst to the surface and flashed like a comic-strip light bulb above his head. Within twelve hours he had made a sketch of a better machine, and eleven days later he had built one. It produced an even, single-thread chain stitch that no other machine had ever been able to achieve before.

But when Isaac Singer set about to peddle his device, he immediately found himself in legal trouble. It seemed that his invention really amounted to a successful amalgamation of bits and pieces of other, earlier inventions, most of which were protected by patents. Without incorporating the patented property of others, Singer's machine would not work at all. Altogether, some twenty-five different patents were involved. At least three of them belonged to Elias Howe, who threatened to sue for patent infringement. Singer approached Edward Clark, then a lawyer practicing in New York. Singer had come to Clark at least once before to help patent a slicing machine that had turned out to be a complete failure. Just why, after that first unsuccessful venture with Singer, whose reputation as an unsavory character was by then widespread, Clark agreed to take him on again is unclear. But Clark accepted Singer's very complicated case and, in return, asked for a 50 percent share of I. M. Singer & Co.

Edward Clark's background was altogether different from Isaac Singer's. Clark had been born in 1811, in the upstate New York village of Hudson, where the Clarks had been respectable middle-class residents for several generations. Coming to New York in the 1840's, Clark made a fortunate marriage to Caroline Jordan, the daughter of Ambrose Jordan, a prominent attorney who later became Attorney General for the state of New York. Mr. Jordan took his son-in-law into his firm, making him a junior partner, and the firm became known as Jordan, Clark & Company. Thus established, the young Clarks began to make their way into New York society.

It wasn't easy for them, thanks to Edward Clark's somewhat chilly personality. He was already a frustrated capitalist. In an era when one of society's most inviolable rules was, "Never talk about money, and think about it as little as possible," Edward Clark seemed interested in talking and thinking about nothing else. "His eye is always on the dollar," a contemporary had noted. Clark was slope-shouldered with a large nose and a skimpy beard, and wore tiny steel-rimmed spectacles and a thoroughly unconvincing wig. His demeanor was that of a small-town accountant, and he spoke in a flat and nasal upstate voice. Though he was devoutly Protestant—Clark taught a regular Sunday School class—he was at heart a tough-minded huckster with a promoter's instinct and no small talent for making deals. This was what no doubt drew him to the unlikely character who was to become his partner and make him a splendidly rich man.

With Clark's help, the company was able to buy up most of the patents needed to produce the Singer machine. A number of the inventors involved were impractical, unbusinesslike types who, for small sums, were willing to part with their patents. Others had died, and their widows were happy for the tiny windfalls that selling their patents produced. But one holdout was the stubborn Mr. Howe. What ensued was known at the time as "The Great Sewing Machine War." The war was fought first in the press, in acrimonious and insulting newspaper ads in which Singer and Clark called Howe a charlatan, and Howe called Singer and Clark knaves, scoundrels, liars and thieves. This mudslinging led to more threats of lawsuits for libel, and the case eventually went to the courts.

At first, ingeniously, Clark tried to defend Singer's machine on the grounds that, in fact, the sewing machine had been invented centuries earlier by the Chinese—since the Chinese at one point seemed to have invented nearly everything—and that therefore Howe's patents had no validity. This argument failed to persuade the court, however. At the height of the rancor, Howe appeared in Clark's office and demanded $25,000 for his patents. Clark, in a rare, unwise move, threw him out. He should have paid Howe's price because, in the end, in a court-negotiated settlement, Singer and Clark were forced to agree to manufacture their machines under a license from Howe, for which Howe was to be paid a royalty of twenty-five dollars per machine sold. By the time Howe's patent expired, in 1867, Howe had earned over $2,000,000 in Singer royalties.

Though the settlement with Howe marked the end of the company's conflicts with the inventors, it was only the beginning of troubles between Clark and Singer. The two men could not have been more mismatched. Clark tried hard to play the role of a polished, old-family aristocrat. Singer was a bully and a roughneck. Clark was cool and logical, Singer was hotheaded and impulsive. And yet from the outset it was clear that the two men needed each other badly if the Singer

sewing machine was to succeed. Singer needed Clark's business acu-
men and what would turn out to be Clark's extraordinary ability as a
promoter and salesman, and Clark needed Singer's suddenly apparent
mechanical genius. According to Isaac Singer's biographer, Ruth Bran-
don,* "Neither could do without the other, and so for years they were
irretrievably and unwillingly bound together . . . However . . . at the
beginning of their association, each may have asked himself several
times whether he had really got such a good deal as all that."

As a businessman, Isaac Singer was completely without scruples and,
to get what he wanted, thought nothing of resorting to threats and lies.
Once, when one of his shareholders, whom Singer wanted to buy out,
was taken ill, Singer visited the man at his sickbed, drew a long face
and said, "I've just talked to your doctor. He thinks you won't get over
this. Don't you want to give up your interest in the business altogether?" Singer then persuaded the frightened man to sign over his
shares for a mere $6,000. The shares were worth at least ten times that
amount. Later, when the gullible ex-shareholder recovered, he learned
that Singer had never even met his doctor.

It was not long before Clark and Singer had grown to thoroughly
detest each other, and only the mounting success of their sewing-
machine business kept them lock-stitched together. Noticing the expanded life-style that Singer and his New York "wife," Isabella,
were enjoying, Clark was once heard to cry, "Curse them! I am
making them all rich!" Singer, in turn, frequently muttered, "If
anything serious should happen to Clark, by God, I will give the
family a tussle for the property." Once, Singer buttonholed an asso-
ciate and said, "Have you ever seen Clark with his wig off?" The
bemused man replied that he had not, and asked why. "Because he
is the most contemptible-looking object I ever saw with his wig
off!" said Singer.

The situation between the two equal partners was not helped by the
fact that as far as the Clarks were concerned, their association with the
Singer company had become a social anathema. Though Clark and
Singer were becoming equally rich, New York society—which never
would have accepted the unsavory Mr. Singer or any of his various

A Capitalist Romance: Singer and the Sewing Machine (Philadelphia: Lippincott,
1977).

wives and lady friends—now treated the Clarks as if they were tainted with the Singer curse. Socially, Caroline Clark considered Isaac Singer absolutely beyond the pale, and would not permit him inside her house. Once she told a woman visitor that she "wished Mr. Clark would sell out, and leave the low occupation that he was engaged in, and the nasty brute he was associated with." Mrs. Clark clearly felt that her husband had left a respectable practice of law, lowered himself into "trade" and into a partnership with a genuine lowlife.

What Caroline Clark may not have realized was that her husband was becoming the true hero of the Singer Sewing Machine Company, and was creating a market—out of nothing—in which one day every American housewife, of every economic level, would want a sewing machine or, as she would call it, "a Singer."

Clark embarked upon an advertising campaign that was nothing if not innovative. Who, he reasoned, could be considered a more ladylike person than a clergyman's wife? Churches, he also realized, inevitably had sewing circles, and if a minister's wife could be persuaded to try a Singer machine, it was likely that the other ladies of her circle could be similarly persuaded. Writing his advertising copy himself, Clark directed one campaign specifically to churches, offering Singers to ministers' wives at half price, saying with delightful candor, "Whenever one of our machines is put to use, and especially if it be in a prominent place where numbers of persons have an opportunity of seeing its operation, other sales are sure to be made in the same society or neighborhood. For this reason, it is a matter of importance to us to have one of our Singer machines employed within the circle of each religious society in the United States." The campaign was so successful that even the widows of clergymen wrote begging for chances to buy half-price machines.

To potential purchasers who were members of the laity, Clark devised a different advertising tactic. Since the machines were still expensive, he addressed a campaign to husbands—who, after all, would probably be the ones to make the final decisions to buy. He played artfully on masculine guilt over the long hours of drudgery wives spent with their needles and their mending, and how these hours deprived wives of precious time they could otherwise spend with their children, their homes, their husbands and womanly cultural pursuits. "The great importance of the sewing machine," stated a typical Singer brochure, "is in its influence upon the home; in the countless hours it has added to women's leisure for rest and refinement; in the increase of time and opportunity for that early training of children, for lack of which so many pitiful wrecks are strewn along the shores of life . . . in the comforts it has brought within the reach of all, which could formerly be attained only by the wealthy few." If, in other words, a man was unwilling to buy a sewing machine for his wife, he ought to recognize himself as the cad he was.

An advertisement of the period depicts a husband coming home from a day at business and saying to his wife that it is far too long since they have shared an evening together. Come, he says to her, put on your prettiest dress and we will go to dinner in a restaurant and then on to a concert. Ah, the poor soul replies, she cannot; she is far too behind in her sewing; seamstresses are hard to get, and expensive, and even with a seamstress one has to spend so much time explaining to the girl what must be done, and supervising her work. The husband smites his brow and says, "I cannot withstand that appeal! I must go and see these Machines! I must have one! Mary, you shall have your evenings, aye, and your afternoons, too, for relaxation and mental culture! I must have been asleep not to have seen through all this before!" Apparently this appeal shamed a sufficient number of husbands because Singer sales continued to climb upward.

Another of Clark's innovations was to employ women, always of the most genteel sort, to tour American cities and offer demonstrations showing how quick and easy it was to learn to sew by machine, and how much better were the results. (Singer demonstrators still offer free lessons on the machines today.) Even more important, Clark was one of the first to introduce a totally new selling concept—the installment purchase plan. Buying "on time" had rarely been tried before. Clark found that the system worked as successfully then as it works for the thousands of companies that have copied it since. Finally, though most of Edward Clark's sales pitches were male-oriented, he was shrewd enough not to overlook appeals to feminine independence and economic liberation. "The great popularity of the machines may readily be understood when the fact is known that any good female operator can earn with them *one thousand dollars a year,*" said one of Clark's ads.

In the twenty years since their 1851 alliance, the hostile partners, Clark and Singer, had both become very rich men. The Clarks had ensconced themselves in a huge mansion off Washington Square, for which Mrs. Clark may have partially forgiven the "nasty brute" whose tinkering was responsible for it all. Isaac Singer's life continued in its usual disordered style. When Singer died in 1875, all sorts of wives, mistresses and illegitimate children appeared to challenge Singer's will and lay claims to shares of the millionaire's estate. The court battles over Singer's fortune—and the scandalous carryings-on that were revealed during them—made headlines for months, as more and more details emerged about what the New York *Herald* solemnly called "A Very Ghastly Domestic Story."

In his will Isaac Singer acknowledged twenty-five children, only eight of whom were legitimate. And since he had trouble remembering all his childrens' names—egregiously misspelling them in the will—it is likely that he fathered a great many more.*

To his credit Edward Clark put his personal feelings about Singer aside and came gallantly to the support of Isabella Boyer Singer, the wife with whom Singer had spent most of his final years, in her claim to be the legal widow. Isabella eventually won her case and went on to live a glamorous life in Paris, where she married a duke and became Bartholdi's model for the Statue of Liberty.

With Singer's death Clark became president of the Singer Company

---

*The most famous of Isaac Singer's illegitimate sons was the dandified Paris Singer, who for many years was the dancer Isadora Duncan's principal lover. Paris Singer, with his friend Addison Mizner, was also responsible for transforming Palm Beach from a sleepy Florida sandpit into a dazzling resort for the very rich. There are various versions of how this happened and how the huge, fanciful Mizner houses got to be built. According to one, Mizner, who had never designed anything before and was also hard of hearing, was grumbling about having nothing to do. "Why don't you take up archeology?" said Singer. Mizner clapped his hands and said, "Architecture! I'd love to try that!" According to another story, both men were in Palm Beach and complaining of boredom. Singer said to Mizner, "What would you like to do most?" Mizner looked around at the small frame houses that comprised the settlement and said, "I'd like to build something big, that wasn't made of wood, and paint it yellow." A third version blames Palm Beach indirectly on Isadora who, it is said, was having a fling with a handsome young gym instructor. Disconsolate, Paris Singer brooded until he hit upon the idea of creating a new Palm Beach as a substitute for the attentions of his faithless mistress. Paris Singer, meanwhile, had an illegitimate child of his own by Miss Duncan.

and, freed from the burden of his unpleasant partner, found himself with time to devote to other money-making projects. One of these was his unprecedented apartment house, whose design he had entrusted to one of the most exciting young architects in New York.

"Clark's Folly," however, despite all the ridicule and head-shaking it evoked, was not undertaken as a flight of fancy, nor was Edward Clark endeavoring to build a monument to himself, as some people assumed. He saw the Dakota, purely and simply, as a business investment. Life at the Dakota, he was convinced, could be sold to the New York public through the same selling techniques that had sold Singer sewing machines all over the world. Like a sewing machine, the Dakota would offer convenience, a short-cut route to opulent living with none of the problems of upkeep, and at a fraction of the expense that went with owning a private house. Like a sewing machine, the Dakota would offer "leisure for rest and refinement" and "comforts . . . which could formerly be attained only by the wealthy few."

Clark was now approaching seventy and had grown more than a little cynical about the public and what it wanted. The public could be made to want anything, if it were sold to them the right way. But one thing the public did seem to want in 1880 was to emulate high society and the way high society lived. Very well. The Dakota would provide such emulation. The Dakota was designed to convey the impression that, though one might be living in an apartment house, one was really living in a mansion. The Dakota would be an imitation of the rich-rich New York life—not the real thing, but a mirror image, an illusion. There were plenty of New Yorkers, Edward Clark figured, who would pay for that. For that, they would even sacrifice a good address.

One other thing that Clark had noticed selling sewing machines was that the class system in America had changed drastically since the Civil War. There were no longer just two classes in America—the miserable poor and the wealthy few. There was now a huge middle class, and even that was divided into a number of different economic strata. There were rich and successful New Yorkers, like the Clarks themselves, who had never been invited to one of Mrs. William Astor's balls. There were many New Yorkers, like the Clarks, who lived on Fifth Avenue near the Belmonts and who had never been asked to one of August Belmont's famous dinners. There were many men and women who could afford sable lap robes in their landaus who were not part of the Four

Hundred, and who, like Clark (though not, of course, his wife), had stopped caring.

Furthermore, if despite the efforts of Miss Huntington and her Kitchen Garden classes, the servant class was indeed disappearing from America, the Dakota was designed as a hedge against that very possibility. As the mansions and town houses grew too costly to maintain and too difficult to staff, there would be the Dakota, with its own maintenance and housekeeping staff and private dining room. Edward Clark, in other words, seemed to have sensed that New York had already entered its era of upholstery. He had learned to work around class and the power structure, and had discovered that New York's power source was somewhere other than in the ritualized world of Mrs. Astor. He was designing a building for a new class of New Yorkers of means much like his own.

Edward Clark had not needed to be very shrewd to also notice something else. By the 1880's New York was on its way to becoming the largest and most important city in America. In less than ten years the city's population had doubled, climbing to one and a half million. Men who, a generation earlier, had headed for the California gold fields in search of riches were now streaming back into Manhattan as the island of golden opportunity. At the same time, 150,000 immigrants from Europe were arriving in America each year, and most of these were settling in New York City. Within another ten years it seemed likely that the population would double again. Already the city's water supply had become inadequate, though an engineer named Benjamin Church was at work on plans for an aqueduct that when completed would pour an additional 300,000,000 gallons of water daily into the city from upstate reservoirs. As the city grew it had nowhere to grow but northward, uptown. Seventy-second Street and Eighth Avenue might have seemed inconveniently remote in 1880, but within ten years, as Clark correctly guessed, it would not.

Today, when New York has become a city bristling with luxury apartment buildings, when it no longer matters, socially, whether or not one lives in an apartment house—and when Manhattan has become an island of apartment dwellers with only a handful of families remaining in private residences—Edward Clark seems to have been blessed with remarkable foresight. At the time, asked by a reporter from the *Tribune* whether he was a little "nervous" about the risks involved in his costly and seemingly experimental venture, Mr. Clark's reply was characteristically brusque: "I am not."

When asked why a man sixty-nine years old, who had spent most of his life manufacturing and selling small household appliances, should suddenly at the end of his career fling himself into the construction of a major building, Mr. Clark replied, "To make money."

Chapter 4

The Architect

THE STYLE of the Dakota's architecture has been officially labeled German Renaissance. But it has also been called other things, such as Victorian Château, Victorian Kremlin, Brewery Brick, Pseudo-European and Middle European Post Office. In other words, to use a term much favored by architects, it is "eclectic."

The architect whom Edward Clark chose to design his building, Henry Hardenbergh, went on to achieve a national reputation as a designer of elaborate hotels—among them the old Waldorf-Astoria and the Plaza in New York, the Willard in Washington and the Copley Plaza in Boston. In later years he would come to take himself with great seriousness. Described by a contemporary as "Napoleonic in stature," he was diminutive, and to overcome this he took to placing his office desk and chair on a platform so that visitors would have to look up at him. He was also quite voluble, and in a 1906 interview with Sadakichi Hartmann in *The Architectural Record,* Mr. Hartmann noted with some satisfaction that for every twenty words of questions, Mr. Hardenbergh would respond with two hundred words of answers. Mr. Hartmann commented on Hardenbergh's "wiry" physique and his "shrewd eyes," and also noted, "This man knows what he is about . . . I thought to myself, I am sure he deserves the reputation he has of *having a roof on every house he builds,*" meaning, perhaps, that Hardenbergh was known for completing every task he undertook. When Clark selected him in 1879, however, Hardenbergh was still relatively unknown, and quite young—only thirty-two. To an earlier interviewer, in 1883, when the Dakota was still unfinished, Hardenbergh confessed that he was "still trying to find himself."

Despite his youth, Henry Hardenbergh was most definitely a gentleman of the Old School and was descended from a New York family which had been among the city's earliest settlers. The first Hardenbergh arrived in what was then the Dutch colony of Nieu Amsterdam in 1644, some three years before the arrival of Governor Peter Stuyvesant. Henry Hardenbergh's great-great-grandfather, the Reverend Jacob Rutsen Hardenbergh, had been a founder of Rutgers College. After studying under the architect Detlef Lienau, considered one of the nineteenth-century masters of the German Renaissance and Beaux Arts styles, young Hardenbergh designed and supervised the construction of a library and chapel for his great-great-grandfather's college. One of his first New York assignments was to design the Vancorlear Hotel, which used to stand at the corner of Seventh Avenue and Fifty-fifth Street. Though they were of different generations, and though Edward Clark and Henry Hardenbergh did not move in quite the same New York social circles, it was Hardenbergh's grandiose execution of the Vancorlear that first drew him to Clark's attention as an architect. The Vancorlear was a transient hotel that consisted only of suites. What Clark had in mind was an apartment house that would be run like a hotel. He hired Hardenbergh and told him, in effect, that the sky was the limit. Hardenbergh, sensing that this was to be his first important building—one that could make his reputation—decided to take a no-holds-barred approach.

What emerged from his drawing board was nothing if not ambitious. What Hardenbergh designed was essentially a huge, hollow cube, roughly as tall as it was long and wide. To this basic structure were added elaborate embellishments—ledges, balconies, decorative iron railings and tall columns of bay windows climbing eight stories high. A tall, iron-gated archway, flanked by iron planter urns provided the main carriage entrance from the Seventy-second Street side of the building and led into an H-shaped interior courtyard, designed as a carriage turnaround. In the center of the courtyard Hardenbergh placed two stone fountains, each spouting a dozen iron calla lilies. The courtyard led to a more modest arched entrance on the building's Seventy-third Street side, which was planned as a servants' entrance. (The building had not been open long, however, before servants complained that the Seventy-third Street entrance was not convenient. It was then decreed that this gate be kept permanently locked, to be opened only for funerals. Over the decades the "undertaker's gate," as it came to be known, has been opened about once a year.)

The capstone of the building, however—the climax, the icing on the fantastic birthday cake—was the two-story-high roof, or, more accurately, succession of roofs. The Dakota's roofs did indeed resemble a miniature European town of gables, turrets, pyramids, towers, peaks, wrought-iron fences, chimneys, finials and flagpoles. The roof was shingled in slate and trimmed with copper, and it was peppered with windows of every imaginable shape and size—dormer and flush, square, round and rectangular, big and small, wide and narrow. Nestled among all this, Hardenbergh designed a railed rooftop promenade with gazebos and pergolas and canopied sunshades. The courtyard below would also be circled with an awninged promenade.

The original specifications of the building called for "Suits [sic] of Apartments for fourty [sic] two families besides Janitors." Hardenbergh had originally designed the interior space so that each of the seven main floors would contain six apartments, described in the building records as "French flats," roughly the same in size and layout. But Edward Clark had begun renting apartments in his building-to-be to friends, acquaintances and other interested tenants long before the building was completed, thus giving future tenants the opportunity to select the size, variety and the number of rooms they needed. This meant that Harbenbergh's floor plans for the building changed almost daily, as apartments were enlarged and divided to suit tenants' wishes. Walls came down and doorways were created as the architect tried to fit individual apartments together like pieces of a jigsaw puzzle. In the beginning he had planned to place the largest apartments on the lower two floors. This was because elevators were still something of a novelty and not entirely trusted (in contrast to today, when the higher the apartment is, the more desirable it is considered to be). Also, Hardenbergh reasoned that lower-floor living would seem more familiar to New Yorkers who were accustomed to living in town houses. The eighth and ninth floors were to be used exclusively as laundry rooms, service and storage rooms, and servants' rooms. Then Hardenbergh hit upon the idea of turning the second floor into hotel-style guest rooms that could be rented to tenants to put up out-of-town friends. And in each of the four corners of the eighth floor he designed four smaller apartments. When Hardenbergh finally finished juggling rooms and spaces, there were sixty-five apartments in the Dakota, ranging in size from four to twenty rooms.

Scale and massiveness were stressed throughout the building. Many apartments had drawing rooms that measured 20 by 40 feet and bedrooms that were 20 by 20. In the sixth-floor apartment Hardenbergh designed for the owner (Clark thought he could popularize upper-floor living by putting himself near the top), was the building's largest room —a ballroom-sized drawing room 24 feet wide and 49 feet long, with a fireplace at either end and ceilings graced by a pair of Baccarat crystal chandeliers. The Clark apartment also contained seventeen other "chambers." Because Clark wanted floor-to-ceiling windows, these were given to all the other sixth-floor apartments to provide exterior symmetry. In all the apartments wood-burning fireplaces abounded (the Clark apartment had seventeen), and in the beginning the fireplaces plus coal-burning stoves in the kitchens provided the building's only heat. Wood and coal were delivered to the apartments daily, and the ashes from the fires of the day before were daily swept out. Gas was used only to light the chandeliers. Still under construction when the building opened was the subterranean boiler room beneath the lot next door, which would eventually provide steam heat and would also contain dynamos for generating "electric illumination." Because he foresaw further development in the neighborhood, Clark specified that the Dakota's boilers be big enough to supply heat to all the blocks from the north side of Seventieth Street to the south side of Seventy-fourth Street between Eighth and Columbus avenues. For his new neighborhood, Hardenbergh designed what amounted to a miniature Consolidated Edison, and for a number of years it served as just that.

Hardenbergh's plans specified that the foundation was to be laid on "solid rock," and foundation walls were to be from three to four feet thick. The thickness of the exterior walls of the first floor was 24 to 28 inches, the second through fourth floor, 20 to 24 inches, the fifth and sixth floors, 16 to 20 inches, and above the sixth floor, 12 to 16 inches. The walls were tapered in this fashion to give them added strength. The floors themselves were three feet thick, arched and beamed and braced with brick and concrete. Between each layer of brick flooring, like a thick sandwich spread, was placed a layer of Central Park mud, which had been dug up in the park's landscaping process—for sound-proofing as well as fireproofing. Fireproofing was an obsession with Hardenbergh because, for aesthetic reasons, he wished to eschew fire escapes. All partitions within the building were of brick and fireproof blocks. The ceilings on the ground floor were fifteen and a half feet high. With each successive floor, ceilings were lowered imperceptibly until, on the eighth and ninth floors, where the help were to live, they were a mere twelve feet high.

Over two hundred miles of plumbing were cemented into the thick walls of the Dakota to service the cast-iron wash basins, sinks and laundry tubs in the Dakotan kitchens. Bathroom fixtures were all of porcelain, including seven-foot-long bathtubs that crouched on claw-and-ball feet. In the beginning, however, bathrooms were in somewhat scant supply in Dakota apartments—again because Victorian sensibilities were involved. (Called water closets, they were considered unmentionable necessities.)

Though individual needs and whims of the Dakota's first tenants played havoc with Mr. Hardenbergh's original floor plans, some elements of his interior design remained that were innovative at the time and have since become almost standard in the layouts of luxury apartment houses. There was his "stem" system of elevators, for example. Each of the four passenger elevators—placed just inside the four corners of the courtyard—was designed to service two, or no more than three, apartments to a floor. Elevator lobbies were therefore small and intimate, creating a sense of privacy, eliminating the feeling of being in a building that housed more than two hundred other people—and also eliminating long, echoing corridors through which children would be fond of running. Apartment kitchens, meanwhile, opened out onto a similar system of four service elevators—a novelty in themselves in the 1880's.

But for all the practicality of some of his ideas, it was in the area of

purely frivolous and expensive ornamentation that Henry Hardenbergh's heart clearly lay. By temperament he was more an interior and
exterior decorator than an architect. He covered the Dakota with
carved stone friezes and mullions, surrounded the outside dry moat
with an elaborate iron fence adorned with the fierce, bearded heads of
sea gods entwined with sea urchins with human faces. Inside were the
carved marble mantels, no two of them alike, the carved plaster ceilings, the walls paneled with oak and mahogany, the heavy doors and
over-doors and mortices with hardware of the heaviest solid brass. (In
the Clark apartment doorknobs and plates and hinges were overlaid
with sterling silver.) There were inlaid marble floors, wrought-iron
staircases, walls wainscoted in rare marbles and choice hardwoods,
bronze lamp fixtures and railings in the elevator lobbies. The elevators
themselves were extraordinary examples of the millworker's art—deli-
cate, open cages of carved, spindled wood set in fanlike patterns.

Then there was the private dining room, designed to resemble an
English baronial hall. The floors were of inlaid marble and the bases
of the walls were of hand-carved English quartered oak. The upper
portions of the walls were finished with bronze bas-relief work—designs
of Indian heads, arrowheads and ears of corn—and the ceiling was also
of hand-carved English oak. Dominating the room was a huge fireplace,
big enough in which to hold a small party, made of Scotch brownstone
and engraved with more Western symbols. In other words, the Dakota
was built not only to last forever but to astound. A persistent rumor
in the Dakota has it that one of the first tenants buried $30,000 in cash
in the floor of his seventh-floor apartment. If true, the money reposes
beneath the parquet of what is now John Lennon's and Yoko Ono's
bedroom. It would cost at least $30,000 to dig up the bedroom floor,
and besides, the Lennons don't really need the money.

The thick walls and floors were designed not only to insulate the
Dakota in winter and to keep it cool in summers when air conditioning
was unheard of, but also to block out the city's noises, dust and stench.
Though the upper reaches of Eighth Avenue were still relatively quiet
and soot-free, the Eighth Avenue streetcar rattled by, and it was assumed that the West Side would soon be as noisy and smelly as the
rest of town. The Dakota was designed to protect its residents from all
of that.

But one aspect of Henry Hardenbergh's design—in a building that over the years has posed a number of riddles—remains a mystery. Though he covered the Dakota's exterior with elaborate ornamentation on the north, east and south sides, he left the west face of the building absolutely blank and unadorned, as though when he got around to that side of the building, he had lost interest or run out of imagination. To be sure, the west side of the building could be regarded as the "back" of the Dakota. And yet this back side overlooked one of the building's most gracious attractions—the private park with its clay tennis and grass croquet courts, an area of Dakota land roughly equal in size to the acre upon which the building stood. In the building of New York brownstones it had become something of a tradition to leave the backs of buildings blank, and these were called "party" or alley walls because they usually faced an alley or an air shaft. But the Dakota's back did not face an alley; it faced a garden. Is it possible that Hardenbergh anticipated the day when the Dakota's back would indeed face an alley? That would not happen for eighty-five years, until, as we shall see, Louis Glickman entered the picture. Until then, the Dakota'a west-facing façade wore an embarrassed and unfinished look. From its own pretty garden, the Dakota looked truncated, as though Mr. Hardenbergh's great château had been neatly and cleanly sawed in half.

Two events occurred in 1882, meanwhile, when the building was only half completed, which affected its history profoundly. The first was the official renaming of Eighth Avenue as Central Park West. This was an indication that the city, too, had faith in the expansion of the West Side, and it gave Mr. Clark's building a somewhat prettier address. The second was the sudden death, of a heart attack, of Edward Clark at the age of seventy-one. When he heard this news, Henry Hardenbergh was dumbstruck. What would become of the project now? For several anxious weeks Hardenbergh worriedly waited to hear whether or not Clark's heirs would call the costly effort off. He spent his time characteristically—designing Corinthian columns to embellish the old Third Avenue trolley-car barns. He was, however, eventually reassured that the building was to continue as planned.

When the Dakota was at last completed, on October 27, 1884, four years, almost to the day, from the date when ground had been broken, it was greeted with an article in the New York *Daily Graphic* headlined:

A DESCRIPTION OF ONE OF THE MOST
PERFECT APARTMENT HOUSES IN THE WORLD

The article led off almost breathlessly to say

Probably not one stranger out of fifty who ride over the elevated roads or on either of the rivers does not ask the name of the stately building which stands west of Central Park, between Seventy-second and Seventy-third streets. If there is such a person the chances are that he is blind or nearsighted. The name of the building is the Dakota Apartment House, and it is the largest, most substantial, and most conveniently arranged apartment house of the sort in this country . . .

A 2,500-word paean of praise to the building followed, and the article was reprinted in the New York *Times*. Throngs of people journeyed uptown to look at the new wonder of the city, and hundreds of requests for apartments in the Dakota poured in. But it was too late. The Dakota was already fully rented. It had not even had to advertise.

NOT ONLY WAS THE COMPLETED BUILDING a commanding presence on the city skyline, but it also afforded its tenants extraordinary views. Bizarre though it seemed, the location Edward Clark had chosen for his folly had rare advantages. It was on one of the highest points of land in Manhattan. From the Dakota's upper windows one could see the entire island and much of the surrounding countryside as well. To the east, across Central Park with its picturesque castle and lake, was the museum and the Mall, and beyond all that it was possible to see the blue waters of Long Island Sound and the hills of Brooklyn. From the west the view was equally panoramic and took in the Hudson River, the Palisades and the distant Orange Mountains of New Jersey. When the famous Hudson-Fulton Ship Parade was held from New York Harbor up to Albany, Dakotans could watch much of its course from their roof. To the north lay the hills of Tarrytown, and to the south one could admire the steeples and church spires of lower Manhattan in an era when God had not yet been replaced by Mammon in the city's order of priorities. One could also see the tall towers of the Brooklyn Bridge, Governor's Island, the green tip of Staten Island and the waters of Lower New York Bay. As the *Daily Graphic* remarked with wonder at the time, "Every prominent landmark in the landscape can be discerned from this location, and the great buildings of the lower city are as prominently marked as if the sightseer were floating over the island in a balloon." In those days it was not difficult for New Yorkers to remember that they lived in a seaport. Today, of course, nearly all these stirring views have become obscured by New York progress.

The article in the *Graphic* went on to comment that the Dakota "guaranteed to the tenants comforts which would require unlimited wealth in a private residence." This, of course, was the key to the building's immediate popularity. One could live like a king at the Dakota without paying a king's ransom to do so.

The rents, which Edward Clark had set before his death, seemed more than reasonable for the period. A ten-room apartment could be leased for three thousand dollars a year, and tenants wrote out their monthly rent checks to one "Edward S. Clark." At first, some people were not sure who, exactly, Edward S. Clark was, since the original Edward Clark had used no middle initial. The terms of Edward Clark's will were complicated, and since the estate was vast there were many individual bequests. In terms of the Dakota, however, the will was quite specific. Clark had not left the building to his son, Alfred Corning Clark, whose interests were art and music, and did not include real estate. Edward Clark had skipped a generation and left the building to his grandson and namesake, Edward Severin Clark.

The news that he had become the proprietor of the Dakota and the possessor of an enormous apartment with a ballroom-sized drawing room—as well as the boss of one of New York's most flamboyant architects—must have bewildered Edward Severin Clark. When he fell heir to the Dakota he was only twelve years old.

Chapter 5

East Side, West Side

IN A WAY, the fact that the stewardship of the Dakota had passed to a little boy may have amounted to one of the very first in a long series of reprieves that would be granted to the building over the years. Young Edward Severin Clark and his family were already comfortably rich from Singer Sewing Machine Company stock. Their financial affairs were in the hands of bank trustees and lawyers, and they had moved into a social world—denied to the founder of the fortune and his wife —in which the making of mere money was considered a tasteless, unsuitable concern. One of the delights of the Dakota from the beginning was that it appeared to be run more as a charitable, luxurious rest home than as a business. When something went wrong, one simply rang downstairs and someone immediately appeared to fix it. If one got a bit behind in one's rent, no angry landlord appeared at the door; it was simply assumed that, in time, the arrearage would be paid. No one seemed to remember that the senior Mr. Clark had put up the building to make money or to care that, despite its popularity, it didn't really show much of a profit. Had the elder Mr. Clark lived, he certainly wouldn't have tolerated such a situation. He would either have raised the rents, dispensed with some of the building's costly little extra services or disposed of the property altogether.

In its earliest days, meanwhile, the clientele of the Dakota was pretty much of the sort the senior Mr. Clark had expected—prosperous New York businessmen and their wives, solid folk who cared more about their pleasant, busy lives than about striving to be in society. They tended also to be older people, either childless or couples whose children had grown and moved away, and this gave the building a reputation it didn't deserve—that children were unwelcome at the Dakota. The fact was that the Dakota, at first, was not convenient to the city's better schools, though a number of excellent ones—Ethical Culture, Collegiate and Trinity among them—would soon come to the West Side.

From the beginning, the Dakota's clientele conveyed a vaguely intellectual and artistic tone. Socially, this set the early Dakotans immediately apart from the members of Mrs. Astor's inner circle, where anything that smacked of intelligence and wit was actually frowned upon. In Mrs. Astor's world, conversation was almost studiedly irrelevant, and its topics were restricted, as Lloyd Morris puts it, to "thoughtful discussions of food, wines, horses, yachts, cotillions, marriages, villas at Newport and the solecisms of ineligibles." Anything that might remotely be considered an idea was eschewed at the Astor dinner table. During the day Mrs. Astor's set had the dinners of the previous evenings to discuss. Actors, opera singers, composers and people connected with the theater in any way were considered socially disreputable. Writers, painters and sculptors were not deemed worth discussing—or buying—until they had been suitably dead for a number of years. Politicians were vulgar, nor were educators or even clergymen regarded as fit for inclusion in fashionable society. The only "working" people to whom the Four Hundred gave the nod were high-ranking members of the military, and the Astor–McAllister list included at least five generals and two colonels and their respective ladies. Needless to say, an imported titled Britisher, such as Sir Roderick Cameron, went sailing onto the sacred list. Mrs. Astor and her friends' one concession to the arts was to attend the opera at the Academy of Music on Monday and Friday nights during the winter season, but the dictates of fashion precluded any real appreciation of music. *Comme il faut* required that one not enter one's box until the end of the first act. Then, during the second interval, one socialized with one's friends in the neighboring boxes. Then, before the third-act curtain lifted, one went home.

At Mrs. Astor's Fifth Avenue house, entertainments were equally ritualized. Dinner was at seven, and an invitation to dine with the Astors meant arriving at *seven*, not a moment later. If too early, one waited in one's carriage outside the door and alit to ring the bell at clockstroke. The gentlemen wore white tie and tails, and the ladies long gowns and their best jewels. The ladies took their wraps to a downstairs cloakroom, and the gentlemen took theirs upstairs. In the gentlemen's cloakroom, white envelopes were arranged on a silver tray, with a gentleman's name on each envelope. Inside was a card with a lady's name on it—the lady he was to escort in to dinner. The ladies and gentlemen gathered again downstairs, and there their hostess received them in her black wig and nearly always wearing black, the better to show off her jewels, which included "the costliest necklace of emeralds and diamonds in America," or "the finest sapphire"—all, of course, from Tiffany's.

A butler appeared with a tray, and cocktails were served. There was never a choice of drinks. Mrs. Astor preferred something called a Jack Rose, and a Jack Rose was therefore what was offered, one to a guest, and in rather small glasses. A maid then entered with a tray of canapés —one apiece. Nobody would have dreamed of asking for a second canapé, much less a second drink. In exactly fifteen minutes dinner was announced. At the table were printed place cards and menus, each embossed with the Astor crest, outlining the courses through the appetizer, soup, fish, meat or game, salad, cheese and fruit, dessert and coffee, with perhaps a sherbet course somewhere in the middle.

Dinner lasted at least two hours, and through it all one had to keep an attentive eye on the hostess to catch the exact moment when she "changed the conversation." When Mrs. Astor shifted the focus of her attention from one dinner partner to the other, the entire table shifted with her. At approximately half-past nine, Mrs. Astor rose, and the table did likewise. The ladies and gentlemen separated—the men to the library for brandy and cigars, the ladies to the adjacent drawing room for mirabelle and gossip. In exactly half an hour a butler opened the doors between the two rooms, and the gentlemen joined the ladies for another thirty minutes. At half-past ten, Mrs. Astor rose again, the signal that it was time for everyone to go home.

But the new residents of the Dakota were a rather different sort of folk, with different notions of what civilized New York life might consist of—notions which Mrs. Astor would have found dangerously radical. There were the Steinways, for example (ironically, Theodor Steinway, perhaps because of his sensitive musical ears, frequently complained about the sound of pianos being played in nearby apartments). As piano merchants, the Steinways would never have been eligible to join the Astor set; even worse, they were immigrants, having arrived in New York from Germany as recently as 1850, and they spoke with accents. Then there was John Browning, an educator, and the founder of the Browning School on the West Side, which later on would educate a whole generation of Rockefeller brothers. (Mr. Browning's two daughters, Miss Edna and Miss Adele, were both born in the Dakota in the early 1890's and continue to live there to this day.) Then there was Mr. Gustav Schirmer, the great music publisher.

The Schirmers were the building's leading host and hostess of the day, and their guest lists indicated that New York social life might have a bit more to offer than the Four Hundred. The Schirmers had the odd notion that there were actually *interesting* people in New York, and that interesting people also passed through from out of town. Herman Melville, by then well into his seventies, often walked with his little granddaughter in Central Park. He had been living quietly in New York for years, convinced that his literary career was over, working as a customs inspector on the Hudson River piers. The Schirmers "discovered" the almost-forgotten author of *Moby Dick,* and gave a dinner for Melville and his wife. The Schirmers apparently found Melville charming but a little sad. He was working again on a final novel, to be called *Billy Budd.* But, he said, he was sure his book would never be published unless he had it privately printed, because his popularity of more than thirty years earlier had all but vanished. (In fact, *Billy Budd* was not published until many years after Melville's death.)

Another celebrated guest of the Schirmers was William Dean Howells, the poet, belletrist and raconteur who, it turned out, could not be invited to the same dinner parties as Mark Twain; the two authors vied so vociferously to upstage each other in terms of story-telling and producing *bon mots* that they threatened to resort to fisticuffs.

Through Howells, the Schirmers were introduced to a thin, intense young novelist named Stephen Crane, whose first novel, *Maggie: A Girl of the Streets,* had still been unable to find a publisher because its contents were deemed too sordid for the tastes of the times. He was now working on a second book with a Civil War setting, to be called *The Red Badge of Courage.*

The Schirmers also found stimulating company in some of the prominent political figures of the day, and one of their great friends was Senator Carl Schurz, a former major general in the Union Army, and later Secretary of the Interior under President Rutherford B. Hayes. The Schirmers and the Steinways were good friends, since both families were in the music business and in no way competitors. In fact, both families had emigrated from Germany at about the same time—as a result of the Revolution of 1848—had settled near each other in the West Fifties in New York, and had moved together into the Dakota. Many Schirmer parties overflowed into the Steinway apartment, and vice versa. A number of these entertainments were musical in nature, and every important composer or performer who passed through New York was entertained at dinner by the Schirmers, and visiting artists were always eager to step next door to try out one of Mr. Steinway's new pianos.

Once the Schirmers gave a dinner for the composer Peter Ilyich Tchaikovsky, who was passing through on an American concert tour. After dinner, thinking that Tchaikovsky might be pleased with the view, Mr. Schirmer took him up to the roof of the Dakota and pointed out the park below and the city lights beyond. Tchaikovsky, whose English was limited, misunderstood the whole experience and came away with the impression that the entire Dakota was Mr. Schirmer's house. "No wonder we composers are so poor," he wrote in his diary. "The American publisher, Mr. Schirmer, is rich beyond dreams. He lives in a palace bigger than the Czar's! In front of it is his own private park!" In *The Life & Letters of Peter Ilyich Tchaikovsky,* by Modeste Tchaikovsky, a letter is quoted in which the composer also speaks of the Schirmers' "house":

Schirmer took us on the roof of his house. This huge, nine-storied house has a roof so arranged that one can take quite a delightful walk on it and enjoy a splendid view from all sides. The sunset was incredibly beautiful . . . We sat down to supper at nine o'clock . . . and . . . were presented with the most splendid roses, conveyed downstairs in the lift and sent home in the Schirmers' carriage. One must do justice to American hospitality; there is nothing like it—except, perhaps, in our own country.

Still, a number of Mr. Schirmer's relatives thought that the Schirmers had chosen a very peculiar address. Mrs. W. Rodman Fay, for example, who is Gustav Schirmer's granddaughter, recalls that she was "bundled up in scarves, sweaters, coats, mittens, long woolen underwear and heavy boots" for the carriage ride uptown to see her grandparents for the required ritual of Sunday dinner. "My mother was always sure I'd catch cold going way up there," she says. "To her, it wasn't a trip. It was a *journey.*"

Others of the building's early tenants, meanwhile, were ordinary, successful, unartistic businessmen and their families. There was Alexander Kinnan, for example, who was president of the Union Dime Savings Bank, and Adolph Olrig, another banker, and Samuel Hamilton Kissan, a member of the Board of Governors of the New York Stock Exchange. William Pipsey was a woolen merchant, Alfred J. Cammeyer made shoes, Tarant Tatum was a lawyer and commodore of the New York Yacht Club. Calvin H. Allen was president of the Union Copper Mining Company and of the Western New York and Pennsylvania Railroad, and William Arbuckle Jamison was a sugar refiner and a director of the Chase National Bank. Two spinster sisters named Adams were also early Dakotans, but they were no kin to the redoubtable Adams clan of Boston. Their money came from Adams Chewing Gum. Then there was Mr. C. F. Bates, who was a sportsman of the era and also something of an eccentric. Early Dakotans chuckled at the odd way Mr. Bates drove himself home in his tandem dogcart (a horse-drawn vehicle, not dog-powered). Bates always handled the reins himself, while his two coachmen sat stiffly facing the rear and his driver sat idle at Mr. Bates's side in front.

The new style of New York society that families such as the Schirmers began to represent was catching on—particularly on the West Side. The Dakota, fully rented before it even opened its doors, seemed to be a big success, though no one but the Clark family knew that the building had not yet managed to turn a profit. Ground was being broken for other luxury apartment houses, or "family hotels." In the

Dakota's wake came the Osborne on West Fifty-seventh Street, which, because of its proximity to Carnegie Hall, quickly became a truly "artistic" building, much favored by musicians and composers. Then came the New Century Apartments on West End Avenue, the Graham Court on Seventh Avenue, the famously gingerbread Dorilton on West Seventy-first Street, the wedding-cake Ansonia on Broadway, and the Majestic and the Beresford on Central Park West. Taking their cues from the Dakota, all these buildings offered huge rooms, high ceilings, plentiful fireplaces.

The West Side, it suddenly seemed, was becoming a Mecca for those who preferred apartment living, and were choosing a social life independent of the rules and rituals of the Four Hundred. In fact, the whole mood of the West Side had become one of airy independence—by no means an attempt to answer or defy Mrs. Astor's version of "society," but simply to be free of it and to create a social milieu, and neighborhood, that would be unrestrained by the rest of New York. West Side apartment living might not be really fashionable, but it was becoming, to use a term that was then coming into use, "smart." (That term, in fact, describes the character of the Dakota as it was to evolve over the years.) To be smart implied a who-cares? attitude, and a bit of daring. The Dakota's private tennis and croquet courts were daring and innovative in themselves. Tennis was by no means the universally popular game that it would become, and croquet was downright *avant-garde*— even, to Victorian New Yorkers, a bit *risqué*. ("Croquet," a social critic of the times had ominously warned, "can lead to things.") The narrow streets in the western portion of Greenwich Village might be becoming the "Bohemian" quarter. But the Upper West Side was becoming Bohemian with, as an addition, more than just a touch of class.

The Dakota had also started a vogue for naming West Side apartment houses after Western states and territories. Soon there would be luxury buildings called the Nevada, the Montana, the Yosemite and the Wyoming.

Much West Side land was being set aside for new schools, churches, hospitals, and other public and cultural institutions. By 1897 Shearith Israel synagogue, the worshiping place of America's oldest and proudest Jewish congregation, had established itself in elegant new headquarters on Central Park West at Seventieth Street. A year later the Fourth Universalist Society—now the Church of the Divine Paternity—had come to the southwest corner of Seventy-sixth Street and Central Park West. Among the church's more prominent worshipers was Andrew Carnegie, who regularly attended Sunday services there. Within a few years the New-York Historical Society was building its splendid new headquarters on the opposite corner. The Society for Ethical Culture, with its church and adjoining school, occupied the western flank of the park between Sixty-third and Sixty-fourth Streets, and further uptown on Eighty-eighth Street, the Walden School, considered a pioneer in progressive education, was built. The Dutch Reformed Collegiate Church and its adjacent, and more traditional, Collegiate School had come to West End Avenue and Seventy-seventh Street in 1892. The latter had been in continuous operation since 1638, when Manhattan was still a Dutch colony, and both the school and church remain notable examples of the gabled Dutch architectural style. All these institutions were designed to serve the growing numbers of what the New York *World* called "the Neo-Cliff Dwellers of the Northwest," whom Mrs. Astor would have simply dismissed as *nouveaux riches.*

By 1890 the Dakota's grand façade still faced the shacks and shanties, chicken coops and pigsties of squatters in the park. Opposite the Dakota's entrance on Seventy-second Street stood a vacant lot enclosed by a ramshackle picket fence, a half-hearted attempt to keep out more squatters and their livestock. (Squatters would remain a problem until as late as 1894 when the Hotel Majestic—now replaced by the Majestic Apartments—was built across the street from the Dakota.) To the west of the Dakota lay a heap of rubble where horse-drawn carts delivered bricks and mortar for the construction of the Olcott Apartments, which would become the Dakota's first real neighbor. A number of nearby West Side streets still conveyed something of the air of a shantytown, with open cesspools, blacksmith shops and cheap saloons. All this the Dakota managed somehow grandly to ignore, for New York was already becoming a city unique for the fact that, even in the finest neighborhoods, the wealthy and the poor lived cheek by jowl.

At the same time, north of Seventy-second Street, and particularly along West End Avenue, a number of expensive private houses were being built. Edward Clark and Henry Hardenbergh had helped lead the way when Clark had commissioned the architect to design a row of town houses on the north side of Seventy-third Street, to create an instant neighborhood for the Dakota. Several of these houses are still there. Architecturally, these new buildings seemed to have a special exuberance and flair. On the older, stolider and more conservative and conventional East Side, builders had lined the streets with uniform, traditional high-stooped houses, all of the same stone, and in the process the East Side had acquired a certain brownstone monotony. But as the Elegant Eighties gave way to the Gay Nineties, the new West Side houses began to display an originality and spontaneity of style. Most were built on the so-called "American basement plan." The high, old-fashioned front stoop was abandoned, and a visitor entered on street level into a large, formal reception hall. A staircase led up to the sitting room, music room and dining room on the floor above. On the upper two floors—usually these houses were four stories tall—were "boudoir bathrooms." Kitchens were placed in the basement, and the second-floor dining rooms were served by dumbwaiters. Often these town houses had gardens in the rear, but these spaces were frequently used for extensions to provide other rooms—smoking rooms, libraries and additional bedrooms.

The most obvious difference about these new West Side houses lay in their façades. The East Side brownstone traditionally had a flattened roofline and symmetrical rectangular windows. The new West Side houses had gabled, dormered, peaked or pyramid roofs, bay windows often of stained glass, arched doorways. Instead of displaying a dreary brownstone sameness, the new houses were faced with a variety of materials, with everything from whitest marble to blue-gray sandstone, with brick that ranged in color from gray to the Dakota's own pale yellow, from the softest rose to the deepest red. The new architectural individuality gave the West Side a sense of variety and fun that the East Side lacked. Going up to the West Side in 1890 felt like entering an entirely different city, one with its own special mores, customs, usages and social tone.

MORE THAN THREE quarters of a century have passed, and the West Side still remains "different." Different—but not fashionable. For all the dreams of the early builders and developers (the grandeur that was planned for Central Park West, for West End Avenue, for Riverside Drive), the West Side never caught on nor achieved the social acceptability of the East Side. Though there is little logic to it, many of the sober East Side town houses have survived as elegant private residences, while the more fanciful West Side houses have for the most part been divided into apartments or rooming houses. The huge mansion that Mrs. Alfred Corning Clark (daughter-in-law of the original Edward Clark) built in 1900 of white marble and red brick on Riverside Drive —it had a colonnaded private bowling alley—is gone. So is the Schwab mansion which was just down the street from Mrs. Clark. The East Side palaces of Andrew Carnegie, Otto Kahn, Henry Frick and J. P. Morgan still stand, though they have been put to other uses.

Just how the mystique that the East Side offered better addresses than the West evolved is not all that hard to fathom. In the late nineteenth century, it had a lot to do with the West Side's physical distance from society's traditional epicenter on Fifth Avenue, where New York ladies saw each other daily on their rounds of shopping. To New Yorkers, "The Avenue" was only Fifth Avenue. Then too, there was the elaborate and time-consuming ritual of visiting and calling-card-leaving, a rite so complicated that only the most dedicated could master its intricacies: which card should be left by a lady, which by a husband and wife, which should be left by children, how many cards should be left for each member of the family being called upon, which corners should be turned down, and when the letters P.P.C. should be inked in the lower left-hand corner of a card (*pour prendre congé*—to take leave, indicating that one was going out of town). A great deal of a woman's day was spent depositing the little cards at the houses of her friends and, since a lady with a sable lap robe would not use the elevated trains to deliver her calling cards, and traveled instead in her coach-and-four, the West Side simply seemed too far away.

Later, when America entered the era of the automobile, there was a noticeable tendency for the affluent of American cities to build their homes on the east side of town rather than the west. This occurred when it was noticed that with this arrangement, the motorist had the sun behind him and not blazing in his eyes when he drove to work in the morning, and behind him again when he drove home at night. But why this notion should have persisted in Manhattan to the present day —when hardly any New Yorkers drive themselves to and from work— is unclear. Compared with the airy views available to those who live on unfashionable Central Park West, those who live on the East Side's fashionable Park Avenue live along a boring, airless tunnel of granite and glass, where apartment buildings merely look at one another. Beneath the surface of much of Park Avenue run the tracks of the Penn Central Railroad's New Haven division, which causes Park Avenue buildings to tremble and china to rattle whenever a commuter train hurtles through the subterranean tunnel. Aesthetically, Park Avenue has almost nothing to recommend it. It is like Chicago's Lake Shore Drive without the Lake, Boston's Beacon Hill without the Common, San Francisco's Russian Hill without the Bay, and Rittenhouse Square in Philadelphia without the Square.

On fashionable upper Fifth Avenue, meanwhile, where apartments have an identically graceful view of the park as can be had from Central Park West, park-facing apartment dwellers must close off the view with heavy draperies on most clear afternoons because of the descending sun's punishing glare. Fifth Avenue is further handicapped by being the traditional course for New York's periodic noisy parades, which not only stop all traffic on the street but leave it strewn with garbage, refuse, half-eaten hot dogs, discarded noisemakers and paper hats. Then, too, there is the fact that for a long stretch of upper Fifth Avenue the pungent animal stench from the Central Park Zoo permeates the living rooms of some of New York's wealthiest people. Despite all this, the east side of Fifth Avenue between Sixty-first and Ninety-sixth Streets remains one of New York's most desirable addresses.

South of the park, New York's most elegant stores—Saks, Tiffany's, Gucci, Elizabeth Arden and so on—have been established on the east side of Fifth Avenue, mysteriously bolstering the East Side mystique. (An exception is Bergdorf-Goodman, which is on the Avenue's west side; when the late Edwin Goodman opened his emporium there, he was warned that he was putting his store on the wrong side of the street where "no one wants to shop.") Two almost identically appointed hotels face each other on opposite sides of Fifth Avenue—the Gotham on the west side and the St. Regis on the east. The St. Regis is fashionable, the Gotham is not. Even the New York Telephone Company, in the days before it began its relentless switch to an all-digit system, seemed to endow East Side telephone exchanges with grander-sounding, old-family names—TEmpleton 8, BUtterfield 8, REgent 7, ELdorodo 5, RHinelander 4, BEekman 4, and so on. To West Side exchanges went less flossy, more prosaic prefixes such as CIrcle, LEhigh, UNiversity and SUsquehanna.

The most subtly pervasive differentiation, however, between the

East Side and the West has been the fact that the West Side has long been considered "very Jewish." In a sense—and in the sense that New York itself is very Jewish—it is. In the nineteenth century, New York society (with the exception of August Belmont, who "passed") was markedly non-Semitic. By the early twentieth century, with hundreds of thousands of Russian and Polish Jews pouring into the city as a result of czarist pogroms, society became quite anti-Semitic. Even the older established German-Jewish banking families, a number of whom had built mansions on Fifth Avenue, looked askance at their "unwashed" co-religionists from Eastern Europe. And so, faced with the snobbishness of the East Side, where they were unwelcome, upwardly mobile East European Jews tended, as other immigrants had done before them, to settle on the West Side, bringing with them their traditional emphasis on education, culture and the arts.

The West Side was rapidly becoming New York's cultural center, but this fact in itself was a drawback to the area in the minds of some New Yorkers. To some people a close proximity to culture was offensive. New Yorkers have long placed a high priority on privacy—the quest for privacy amounts almost to an urban paranoia—and culture inevitably involved the coming and going of the public, as visitors streamed in and out of theaters, museums, schools and churches. Culture attracted out-of-towners, tourists, strangers, children, crowds.

Not to everyone's taste was the idea of living next door to public places, along with the people who ran and supplied them. Today, the stamp of culture on the West Side, with Lincoln Center as its focal point, is more pronounced than ever. The difference between the two sides of town is apparent at a glance. Along Columbus Avenue on an average balmy evening, throngs of people stroll on their way to and from theaters, concerts, lectures, restaurants. Across town, along the quiet stretches of Fifth and Park Avenues, and on the streets between, people come and go in limousines and taxis; there is virtually no pedestrian traffic after dark. Behind their closed shutters and drawn curtains, East Side residents have sealed themselves within lives that are sheltered from the street—locked-up, private.

In the twenty-five years between 1885 and 1910 the West Side had become a neighborhood bristling with luxury apartment houses. Dozens followed the Dakota's lead—the Graham Court, the Chatsworth, the Langham, the Manhasset, the Hendrik Hudson, the Prasada, the

Kenilworth, the Apthorp, the Alwyn Court, the Turin and the Lucania to name just a few—while wealthy East Siders continued to live in private town houses. But the phrase "luxury apartment house" remained, in a social sense, something of a contradiction in terms. Luxury was not the equivalent of fashionability, and the proud and snobbish East Side was not going to be tricked into thinking that it was. The West Side had become a land where people lived in layers. It was a land of prosperous immigrants. It was a place where people rented, rather than owned, their homes—a world of public housing versus private. The men who lived at the Dakota might be presidents of banks and manufacturing companies, but they were still, to society's way of thinking, "in trade," and therefore associated with the working class.

Finally, in addition to the social, there was the inescapable economic factor. Fashionability in New York *did* have a lot to do with cost, and everyone knew that West Side land had always been less expensive than East Side land. (The effect was circular: lower cost of land meant decreased fashionability, and vice versa; in the end, every New York story is a story of the price of real estate.) Everyone knew that one of the attractions of West Side apartment living was that for much less money, one could inhabit much more space. The corollaries to this were obvious: One lived on the East Side if one could afford the expensiveness of it, on the West Side if one couldn't quite; one lived on the East Side by choice, on the West Side out of necessity.

It was not until after 1910 that expensive apartment houses began to be built in any number on the East Side. That was the year that the noisy, smoke-belching locomotive lines running into Grand Central Terminal were electrified, and the forty acres of unsightly railroad yards and track that ran along Fourth Avenue were covered over and paved. The result was Park Avenue—a wide, straight street that stretched northward to the horizon and had a parklike mall running down its center. With the trains gone, builders immediately began developing Park Avenue as a prime East Side residential address. Two blocks over, upper Fifth Avenue also benefited from the disappearance of the trains, and grand apartment houses began going up along the east flank of Central Park as well. These years prior to World War I accounted for 563 Park Avenue (1910), 635 Park Avenue (1912), 960 Park Avenue (1912), 410 Park Avenue (1914), 820 Fifth Avenue (1916) and 907 Fifth Avenue (1916), many of which remain among New York's most fashionable addresses today. By then the population of Manhattan Island had grown so staggeringly, along with the cost of land, that tiered living was the only practical answer. And the new East Side apartment houses were elevated to instant fashionability because, after all, they were on the East Side.

The new East Side buildings were noticeably different from the older West Side buildings, however, in at least two ways. Architecturally, they were much more restrained, their exteriors almost austere, less gaudily ebullient than West Side buildings, more in keeping with the East Side's brownstone primness and propriety and aversion to show. Also, the new East Side buildings were not christened with exotic names. The practice had not gone out of fashion, exactly; it was just that it seemed "too West Side."

Chapter 6

Snobs in Reverse

THE DAKOTA's First Families—the F.F.D.'s, as they sometimes referred to themselves—were a predictable mix of an aspiring few (who might one day decide to elevate their status by moving to an East Side address) and a comfortable majority who were perfectly content with who they were and where they lived, and who simply ignored East Side snobbery. Gustav Schirmer's son, for example—a grown man when his family moved into the Dakota—would marry and settle his family on the East Side, first on Gramercy Park and later on Murray Hill. Other families like the Steinways would refuse to be swayed by fashion and would remain loyal to the Dakota for two generations.

Very quickly the Dakotans managed to develop a reciprocal snobbishness and sense of exclusivity about their particular principality on the Park and the acre of real estate upon which the Dakota rested. Dakotans often congratulated themselves for having the soft morning sunlight with which the building was blessed, and for escaping the fierce afternoon sunlight with which Fifth Avenue was cursed. A frequent comment heard in those days was, "It's so *windy* on Fifth

Avenue!" (Though why Fifth Avenue should be windier than Central Park West is anyone's guess.) Though squatters' shacks—at least in the beginning—were scattered on all sides about the hems of the Dakota's lacy skirts, their presence was explained away with the comment that they gave the neighborhood "a pleasant rural air." Another pronouncement that became popular at the Dakota was, "Fifth Avenue takes a turn at Seventy-second Street, crosses the Park to the Dakota, and then goes back East again." But of course Fifth Avenue didn't do that, and it was all an attempt at an illusion. Central Park West was not Fifth Avenue, nor would it ever be. In their hearts of hearts Dakotans knew that the Dakota had been built as an imitation of the rich New York life, not the real thing. The Dakota was designed to convey the impression that, though one was in an apartment house, one was really in a mansion. But it fooled no one (no New Yorkers, anyway), and this the Dakotans knew.

Dakotans today continue to be more than a little defensive about their address and the ambiguous status of the neighborhood. The evening crowds on the sidewalks of Columbus Avenue are brought forth as a plus—there is a sense of safety, they say, in numbers, whereas one would feel frightened walking alone at night on a deserted East Side street. "At night," they say, "the muggers and the burglars are all working on the East Side. No one would want to hurt us over here, because this is where the muggers *live.*" The neighboring side streets may be a little dingy but, loyal Dakotans insist that in this very fact they find a certain cozy charm.

Paul Goldberger, for example, who is the architectural critic for the New York *Times* and, though a recent tenant, a thoroughly converted Dakotan, speaks of the "pleasant sleaziness" of the neighborhood. "I like to walk west to Columbus Avenue and then down to Lincoln Center," he says. "All sorts of funny and interesting shops and boutiques are springing up like the ones along First and Second Avenues."

There are also in the neighborhood a great many small, family-run businesses—drug stores, meat markets, bakeries, food stores, fruit and vegetable shops and delicatessens, not to mention a wide variety of ethnic restaurants. "There's no sense of neighborhood on the East Side," Goldberger says. "Here, there is. The shopkeepers get to know you, and everyone smiles and waves at one another. It sounds silly to say that the West Side is friendlier than the East Side, but it's true."

Paul Goldberger has Jo Mielziner's former bachelor digs. "When I bought my apartment in 1976 it was really in terrible shape, which was odd. You'd think that a famous set designer wouldn't have let his own place get so run-down. The kitchen was really primitive. To me, the thing that's special about the building is that it's the only exclusive, expensive and social building that has everything from big twenty-room spreads down to small studios and little rooms that have to share a bath. Still, the building and the address are not quite socially acceptable. It exists in a kind of social limbo. It's a cross between a SoHo loft and a Fifth Avenue apartment house. If you're a basic, boring WASP, you wouldn't live here. And anyone who wouldn't want to live in this building because it's on the West Side, we just wouldn't want living here."

George Davison-Ackley, a wealthy lawyer who has flung together two large Dakota apartments for his own bachelor quarters, says, "When I first moved here, and invited people to parties, I'd put One West Seventy-second Street on the invitations. East Side friends used to phone with regrets, just because they didn't want to come to the West Side. So I started putting 'The Dakota' on my invitations. People never regret now. They come to see my apartment and the building, just because it's the *Dakota.* Do you know that I have friends who actually *keep score* of how many Dakota apartments they've been inside?" In other words, Dakotans feel about the Dakota much the way, as it has been said, Bostonians feel about Boston: They believe in the Fatherhood of God, the brotherhood of man, and the neighborhood of the Dakota.

Still, to East Siders there will probably always be something a little comic about the West Side. Like New Jersey, which is also funny to New Yorkers, the West Side is the butt of all the jokes. Even when the Dakota was informally christened the Dakota, it was done in a sense of fun-poking. But because any neighborhood, whatever its shortcomings or inconveniences, becomes a section of similarly moneyed and similar-minded people who prefer to live with their own kind, the West Side has survived all the ridicule. Where a person lives becomes a habit, usually a pleasant one, and whether an address is considered fashionable or not is simply a matter of taste. In New York, the West Side has attracted those who were willing to gamble, to take chances, to risk being considered offbeat. To live on the West Side took, and takes, a creative, pioneering view of life—qualities one often associates with the peculiarly Jewish *élan.*

Today, easily half the people who live in the Dakota are Jewish. This was by no means always so. In the early days the building did not welcome Jews at all. The Majestic, across the street, became known as "the Jewish building." The Dakota's anti-Semitic policy probably stemmed directly from Edward Clark himself, and may have had something to do with Clark's loathing of Isaac Singer and his allegedly Jewish heritage. During the 1920's and 1930's, when social anti-Semitism was particularly rampant in New York and elsewhere, it was said that there were no Jews in the Dakota. Then one slipped in, a Mrs. Erich, a member of the distinguished Lehman banking family. She got by the screeners, it is assumed, because no one guessed that Erich could be a Jewish name. When it was discovered that, indeed, a Jew lived in the building, people said, "We *do* have Jews in the building—a perfectly *lovely* Jewish person."

Those days, happily, have more or less passed, though they did not pass all that long ago. Henry Blanchard has been active on the Dakota's board since 1961. He says, "I never wanted to have anything to do with admissions policy. I remember once there was a board meeting up in the Jacksons' apartment, and I was getting a little bored with all the talk about elevators. Suddenly, C. D. Jackson turned to me and said, 'How do you feel about Jews in the building? How do we know who's Jewish and who isn't?' I said I certainly didn't care. I said, 'Why ask me?' I thought it was very odd, because C. D. Jackson was Jewish himself, though he never made a point of it. The name was originally Jacobson—his family had the Jacobson Marble Company. But, I suppose, working for Henry Luce, whose father was a Protestant missionary, it was better not to be Jewish. . . ."

"Today, we've got a perfect New York melting pot—Jews, WASPS, and now with Roberta Flack we've got our black." says Paul Goldberger. Miss Flack, of course, did not come into the building without a certain amount of huffing and puffing on the parts of some people. And some people have noticed that over the years the building has never had any black employees. Today, there is even an Arab in the Dakota—Princess Mona Faisal, who, when asked to give her occupation on a Dakota questionnaire, put down "Saudi Arabia."

Pauline Pinto is a strikingly beautiful redhead—Alabama-born, a former actress now working as a psychiatric social worker, divorced from a Spanish businessman, living alone in the Dakota with her three young sons, two by Mr. Pinto, the third by a previous marriage. The walls of her apartment are all covered with sleek vinyls in beiges and dark browns. Mirrors shimmer everywhere. At Pauline Pinto's dining table one sits on long, low sofas covered with oyster-colored velvet. The apartment has, among other luxuries, a sauna. Sitting in a long, green Moroccan caftan, sipping a Scotch Mist, Mrs. Pinto seems the epitome of New York chic and glamour as she talks of what it is like to be beautiful, rich, single, and living in Manhattan.

"My husband and I got this apartment in 1967 or 1968 because we were thinking of separating. This looked like our apartment in Madrid, it reminded us of Europe. The building lends itself to the Edwardian style. I still keep an apartment in Madrid. I don't know why. I'm attached to it, and I don't know what to do with it.

"The East Side is a cliché. I used to live on the East Side, on Seventy-first between Fifth and Madison. I went to all the right places —P.J. Clarke's and Michael's Pub. But here, I see people who look like me every day. It's healthy. If you've ever been in the art world, you want to be a star. My cousin directed *Saturday Night Fever*—it was his first success. Now I'm trying to catch up with my cousin. I feel the New York pressure *terribly*. I do more in ten days than most of my friends will do in a year. My friends are writers, book people, people who come through, friends from California—a terrific variety of friends. Right now I'm going out with a psychiatrist. I go to Nan Kempner's parties. I like to be with people who are doing things.

"I'm interested in a theater group called the Performing Garage— I think it's beautiful. I'm interested in the Organic Theatre from Chicago. I'm interested in the Theater of Cruelty—neorealism takes energy, you know. As a single woman I don't feel bad going out alone. In Spain they would call you a *puta* if you went out alone. I said to a woman the other day that I lived on the West Side. Her eyebrows went up. I said, 'I won't be a cliché.' "

It has always been assumed that the people who lived at the Dakota were somewhat different from other fashionable New Yorkers. "My family nearly died when I said I was moving to the West Side," says Mrs. Davenport West, a doctor's widow in her eighties, who moved into the Dakota in the 1920's—she no longer remembers the exact year. Mrs. West is something of an anomaly in a building of anomalies. She is not a bit Bohemian but is a proper *Social Register* type who says, modestly, that her father "thought there was a future in New York real estate and that it might grow," and thereupon acquired quite a lot of it. Actually, though like many Dakotans her late husband was of the high-income, professional working class, and though Mrs. West is not the sort of woman who would say so, she is one of the wealthiest people in the building. She was a Phelps, an heiress to the Phelps Dodge Industries fortune, grew up on a huge estate in New Jersey and still maintains a summer place in Harwich Port, on Cape Cod, called "Malabarra," which rivals the Kennedy compound in Hyannis Port in terms of size and luxury. Mrs. West's father was a noted yachtsman, the first man to circumnavigate the globe in a private sailing vessel. In her Dakota apartment Mrs. West keeps a small collection of precious antique clocks. A man from Tiffany's comes once a week to wind them.

In the 1920's, Mrs. West recalls, there was a shortage of good apartments on the East Side. "My husband said, 'Why don't we try the West Side?' and I said, 'Well, why not?' Of course it was our second choice." The Wests looked at the Dakota, liked what they saw, and took the apartment in which Mrs. West still lives. "People said, 'How can you stand it?' " Mrs. West says. "My friends told me we'd hate it, moving over *there*, with all those bourgeois, *nouveau* people. They told me that they were sure they'd never see me again. But the building was so nice. Before we moved in, my friends came over, one by one, to see what kind of Hell's Kitchen we were living in. They said, 'Well, the apartment *is* nice,' as though they hated to admit that it could be, but then they'd always add, 'But Dorothy—it's the *West Side!* How could you?' Of course they meant the neighborhood, and of course the neighborhood *was* a little crummy."

For all the crumminess, Mrs. Davenport West has no intention of ever leaving her large apartment, which she "thinks" has seven rooms and knows has three bathrooms and four working fireplaces.

AND YET IF the building today is a "melting pot" it is one in which the contents have not quite melted. The Dakota pot seethes and boils with ingredients that have not quite come together, and feuds and rivalries and jealousies and factions abound. Some people, for example, feel that, among other things, the Dakota itself has been divided along an East

Side–West Side axis. "The people who live on the sunny side [the east] are entirely different from those who live on the shady side [the west, which is now permanently in the shadow of the Mayfair Tower Apartments]," says Sheila Herbert, a young advertising woman who grew up in the Dakota and, like a number of "Dakota babies," ended up with her own apartment there. Sunny-siders, Miss Herbert feels, are more sunny-dispositioned, more outgoing and gregarious, give more and better parties, have done splashier things in terms of decorating their apartments. The John Lennons, Roberta Flack and the flamboyant restaurateur-entrepreneur, Warner LeRoy, are all examples of sunny-siders. Shady-siders are more quiet and reserved, more conservative and staid, less given to party-going and party-tossing, and socializing with their neighbors. Mrs. West is a shady-sider.

Miss Herbert may have a point. But there is more to it than that.

Chapter 7

Class vs. Cult

AT EVERY POINT in New York's history, it sometimes seems, there have been social observers willing to offer the opinion that the city "just isn't what it used to be." This not very profound observation has also been made about the Dakota. The building has always managed to engender an intense self-pride among its residents, and part of this is based on the Dakota's long struggle to change as little as possible in an ever-changing city. This struggle has set the Dakota apart, psychologically, from the rest of New York and, particularly, from the Dakota's growing number of new neighbors on the West Side.

The Dakota was not only different and special, it was better—"The only *really* good address on the West End," as Mrs. M. A. Crate used to remind her friends. Mrs. Crate was the building's first housekeeper and served in that capacity until her death in 1931. With its feelings of superiority the building tended to turn inward upon itself, to isolate itself, to become a bit inbred. For years everyone in the building felt it necessary to own a Steinway piano, if not two, in a demonstration of loyalty to the Dakota Steinways. The building bought its dairy products from Edward S. Clark's farm. The Dakota quickly became not only smug but self-centered, and if the burgeoning West Side was becoming a separate city within a city, the Dakota became a private village within the separate city. As far as the rest of the city was concerned, the Dakota's apartness from the general scheme of things made it the object of some curiosity. When the building opened, sightseers had flocked up to Seventy-second Street on the Ninth Avenue el to gape at it, to wonder about who lived there and what they were really like. Over the years tourists and passers-by continued to wonder. Aloofly, the Dakota did not offer a ready answer.

When the first edition of the New York *Social Register* appeared in 1887, no residents of the Dakota were listed in it, which was hardly surprising since the *Register's* list was loosely based on Ward McAllister's tally of those New Yorkers whom he and Caroline Astor considered socially acceptable, plus the list of those who attended the opening night of the National Horse Show, which annually launched New York's winter social season (the two lists overlapped more than a little.) The *Social Register* made it official that the Dakota was socially below the salt, but in some ways the Dakotans may have been grateful for the snub. Journalists and newspaper editors had taken over the role, formerly assigned to clergymen, of watching over the city's morals. And now that Who Was Who had been officially codified and published, it was easier for editors to see who the city's alleged leaders were and to scold them when they misbehaved. One editor who turned misbehavior to profit was Colonel William D'Alton Mann, whose gossipy and widely read *Town Topics* was actually an instrument of blackmail. When an Astor or Gould or Vanderbilt was suspected of committing an indiscretion, he was contacted by one of Colonel Mann's minions who would warn that unless a certain sum were paid, *Town Topics* would print the story it had heard. Away from the mainstream of New York social life, the Dakotans were spared this sort of thing.

After Mrs. Astor's death in 1908 no real New York social leader came forth to fill her place. In fact, New York had no real arbiter of *comme il faut* until 1922, when Emily Post's *Etiquette* was published.[*] Though *Etiquette* became a national bible of manners, the setting of

---

[*]Mrs. Post had helped bring about the downfall of Colonel Mann. Her husband had been guilty of an indiscretion, had been approached by the Colonel and confessed to his wife that a large sum was required to keep it out of print. True to her code, Emily

the book is very much New York. The famous Post characters—the aristocratic Wellborns, Oldnames, Titheringtons and Kindharts—are all New Yorkers. So are the ostentatious Miss Millions, the penny-wise Miss Smallpurse, the haughty Mrs. Toplofty and the somewhat raffish Mr. and Mrs. Worldly and Bobo Gilding. Some were even identifiable. (Bobo Gilding reminded many people of fun-loving Willie K. Vanderbilt.) No Gildings, Oldnames or Smallpurses lived at the Dakota, though Mrs. Post made at least one condescending allusion to West-Siders in her book, calling them "the new Spendeasy Westerns." This was a good general description of the Dakota's tenants. Though not as rich as the Belmonts, Vanderbilts or Goulds, the early Dakotans were families of men who had made money—first-generation money.

The first actor did not move into the building until the late 1930's. He was a gentle, soft-spoken man named William Henry Pratt, whose professional name was Boris Karloff. At the time there was a feeling in some quarters of "There goes the neighborhood." ("The building's going theatrical, but it doesn't know it yet," said Miss Adele Browning.) Boris Karloff's good friend Basil Rathbone lived just down the street, and the two sinister-looking men made an awesome pair when they strolled together in the park—it was Sherlock Holmes and Frankenstein. Mr. Karloff liked to tell a sad tale. Every Halloween, he used to say, he set out a bowl of candy for the building's trick-or-treaters. But no children ever rang his bell. They were too frightened of the heavy-lidded, wired-jaw monster he played in the movies.

Long before the arrival of Boris Karloff, however, there were members of the first Dakota families who felt that the building had hit upon sorry times, and that the Dakota—and New York in general—just weren't what they used to be. By 1932, for example, Miss Cordelia V. Deal had lived at the Dakota for nearly fifty years. She had moved into the building with her parents when it opened and now, a spinster in her eighties, she lived alone with an attendant. "Everything now is in the *moderne* style," she complained to an interviewer at the time. Miss Deal pointed out William Eichhammer, the Dakota's head painter,

---

refused to be blackmailed and notified the police, who arrested Mann's lieutenant as the money was being passed to him. Later, the Posts were quietly divorced.

who had been with the building as long as she. Mr. Eichhammer had painted the walls for the original tenants in beautiful frescoes, friezes and French tints. "Now he's painting everything over, in plain white, because everybody wants *moderne.*"

Miss Deal was obviously a voluble woman as she recalled the old days. "During the summers the building was empty," she reminisced. "Everybody went away, to Long Island, or Westchester, or the Adirondacks, or the Jersey Shore. If you went to Long Island, the husbands didn't stay behind. The whole city would be empty in the summers. Now if people go away, it's just a weekend. Goodness me, what kind of a summer is that? When I was a girl, I never *knew* what it was like to perspire, because in hot weather we were always at some cool shore place. People went to Europe for the summers, too, and each family had its favorite boat. In the country there were dress-up parties for the children. The country was very formal then. Women wore long dresses and pearls for picnics. People with children went to Atlantic City, too, at any time of the year, even in January, because Atlantic City was good for your health. Goodness me, every time I had a sniffle I was whisked off to Atlantic City to get the ocean breezes and the good sea air. The place to stay was the Marlborough-Blenheim.

"I remember there was something called 'The Ladies' Mile,' which ran down Broadway from Twenty-third Street to Eighth. That was where the ladies shopped, in their long 'walking dresses' every afternoon. The ladies had to pick up their skirts to cross the street, and gentlemen stood on the street corners to catch peeks of ladies' ankles. A. T. Stewart and Company was there, and Arnold Constable, and Lord and Taylor. But for quality, Altman's was the best. Later came Siegel-Cooper, on Sixth Avenue and Nineteenth Street. In the center of the store was a huge fountain with a statue at the center like the Statue of Liberty, all lit with colored lights. All around were little tables and chairs where they served ice-cream sodas that were the talk of the town. It was the place where everyone met. Everyone said, 'Meet me at the Fountain,' and it meant Siegel-Cooper's.

"People were politer then, it seems to me. Mothers went for tea at Sherry's, and the children had hot chocolate. Young men sent young ladies candy from Sherry's. It came in lovely lavender tin boxes, and you saved the boxes to keep your toiletries and love letters and other treasures in. There was so much more service then. The manicurist came to the house. The hairdresser came once a week to wash my mother's hair. If she were going to a ball, she came to *dress* her hair. The chiropodist came to the house. The dressmaker came to the house. People have taken to using colored people for servants now, but in those days they were always white. The maids were Irish or German, and the coachmen were usually Scotch, for some reason. Goodness me, we had a cook, a laundress, a chambermaid, a governess and a coachman, and we were not all that rich. For a while, Father had a valet. I remember when automobiles were a big issue. Some people refused to give up their horses. Father's first car was a 1905 Winton that opened from the back. There were no school buses. Fathers would drop the children at school on their way to the office. The Benjamin School was for girls, and Robert Louis Stevenson was for boys. Collegiate, Horace Mann and Ethical Culture were for intellectuals, which wasn't a very fashionable thing to be.

"When Mother and Father moved to the Dakota, it was brand new, and some people said they thought it was too 'flashy.' But we loved it because of the Park. Every Sunday, we went riding in the Park, and the ladies rode sidesaddle. We went for picnics in the Park, and in the winter there was a pond for skating with a little house where you changed into your skates, and a boy who put your skates on for you. When you came in from the cold, they served hot chocolate in the little house. It cost a penny. Goodness me, looking back it seems to me as though I grew up on hot chocolate. In the summer the whole family would take the night boat to Albany. You left in the evening and arrived in the morning. It wasn't considered 'fitting' to take your chauffeur on the boat with you, so the chauffeur drove up and met you in Albany with the car. Then we drove on to Lake Placid. That was just for August. In July we went to the Jersey Shore. There was a song I remember—

> Why do they all take the night boat to Albany?
> That's what's been puzzling me.
> They say they go there just for the ride,
> But all the same they travel at night . . .

"Nobody talked about crime. Nobody talked about security. Here at the Dakota no one bothered to lock apartment doors. There was some talk I remember about bribery and corruption in the city government, particularly during the Boss Tweed period. I remember that Mother and her friends would have tea and talk about men and their mistresses. It seemed every man had a mistress. This was considered perfectly acceptable, as long as the mistress wasn't a member of one's own 'set.' I remember hearing Mother say that one man at the Dakota had his mistress right here in the building. *That* was considered shocking. We were told never to speak to that woman, to that man, or to that man's wife."

OF COURSE Miss Deal was talking about changes in the city's style. In substance, the Dakota had changed not all that much. "Moderne" might have become the vogue, and people might be painting over frescoes, but Miss Deal was still one of the oldest living Dakota loyalists and would only depart, unwillingly, a few years later through the Seventy-third Street door.

For people like Miss Deal—in addition to the service and extraordinary cubic footage which the Dakota offered—the most attractive aspect of the Dakota's changelessness was the fact that, while the cost of everything else in the city of New York was going up, the cost of living at the Dakota had stayed just about the same. No one had given much thought to the dollars-and-cents reason for this, but it had a lot to do with the adoption, in 1913, of the Sixteenth Amendment to the United States Constitution authorizing taxes on the net incomes of individuals, and the progression principle, which was introduced five years later. By 1933 the Dakota was losing some $300,000 a year, and to the accountants who managed Edward S. Clark's huge estate the Dakota had become an interesting tax write-off.

The Dakota, however, in its dreamy way, had begun to believe that the low rents were maintained out of sentiment, out of some sort of humanitarian feelings that flowed from Mr. Clark in far-off Cooperstown. This seemed the easiest explanation for such gentle treatment. After all, the building had begun to accumulate a number of elderly people, such as Miss Deal, who lived on fixed incomes, and who could raise the rent on tenants like that? Rents were often arbitrarily arrived at and could be subject to negotiation. Once, when a long-time tenant, a Mr. Hartenstein, was undergoing financial reverses, the building's management came to him and said, "Please don't move out—we'll lower your rent."

In 1931 the building's manager was Mr. George P. Douglass, and when Mrs. Charles J. Quinlan was looking at an apartment that year, Mr. Douglass told her that the rent would be $4,000 a year. Mrs. Quinlan remarked that her husband might find that a trifle high. Mr. Douglass smoothly replied, "Why don't your husband and I have lunch, and we'll discuss it." This, it might be remembered, was in one of the worst years of the Great Depression. While foreclosures and evictions were taking place all over the country—in farm communities in Nebraska and in luxury lakefront properties in Chicago—the Dakota complacently continued to take care of its own.

Mr. Douglass was succeeded by Mrs. Elise Vesley as the Dakota's "lady managerette," and to her fell the task of screening prospective tenants. Her methods were whimsical, to say the least. When Ward Bennett, now a successful designer, was a struggling young sculptor looking for a place to live in the late 1940's, he learned that single rooms, which had formerly been servants' rooms, were occasionally available under the slanting eaves of the Dakota's eighth and ninth floors. He approached Mrs. Vesley for an interview. At the time, Bennett had become involved with Vedantism, the Eastern religious cult that was being promoted in the United States by Christopher Isherwood and Swami Prabhavananda, and for his interview he happened to be carrying an Isherwood-Prabhavananda volume that he had just borrowed from the library. Mrs. Vesley, who, if she chose, could be quite frosty, was exceptionally cordial to Mr. Bennett. She showed him a room that she offered to let him have for forty dollars a month, including breakfast and maid service. Mr. Bennett then asked Mrs. Vesley if she would like him to supply references. "No references necessary," said Mrs. Vesley, and tapped the Isherwood book. Mrs. Vesley, it turned out, was one of the leaders of the Vedantist movement in New York.

Mrs. Vesley had undergone a deep personal tragedy. Her handsome young son, the apple of her eye, one day had been struck down by a truck on Seventy-second Street, just in front of the Dakota, and killed. She never quite got over that and, as a result, was a bit peculiar and was always partial to the handful of children who were then in the building. One of her projects was trying to maintain the Dakota's roof garden in its battle against the elements, and she also considered herself an authority when it came to matters of decorating. When a tenant decorated an apartment in a manner she disapproved of, she let the fact be known, which did not make her universally popular in the building. In addition to Vedantism, Mrs. Vesley believed in psychokinesis, and claimed that with the power of her mind she could move large objects. Once a tenant returned home from a holiday to find his living-room furniture completely rearranged. When he complained to Mrs. Vesley, who naturally had access to all apartments, she insisted that she had not been in. She had, however, been thinking about the poor arrangement of the furniture, and she admitted that the furniture might have been rearranged psychokinetically from her office.

With World War II came rent control, which fixed the Dakota's pleasantly low rates. But rent control, which made it difficult to raise rents, did not eliminate—at the Dakota, at least—the possibility that rents could be negotiated downward. When an antiques dealer, Frederick Victoria, and his wife were expecting their first baby, they went to the Dakota and Mrs. Vesley, looking for a larger apartment. Though they admired the apartment Mrs. Vesley showed them, the Victorias confessed that they could not afford the rent. Something about the Victorias had clearly struck Mrs. Vesley's fancy because she immediately said, "Then you can have it for whatever rent you're paying now."

Though the Dakota had never offered anything longer than a one-year lease, the matter of leases was another that was treated somewhat casually. When the Henry Blanchards moved into their large fifth-floor apartment in 1954, the building's management cheerfully went about repainting and decorating to the Blanchards' specifications. Some time later, when all this was done, the management said to the Blanchards, "By the way, we haven't given you a lease yet. Do you intend to stay?"

Considering the pleasant coziness of the management-tenant relationship, it was not surprising that, from the beginning, the Dakota gained an astonishing record of tenant loyalty. Ninety percent of the building's original tenants remained there until they died, and in 1934, on the building's fiftieth birthday, two of the original tenants were still in residence—Miss Deal, in four rooms, and Mr. Maxwell D. Howell, in nine.

Between 1884 and 1929 there was not a single vacancy at the

Dakota. Then the stock market misbehaved badly, and this had its effect on the Dakota as it did on other buildings in New York. At the time of the Crash the towering Majestic Apartments was under construction across the street, on the site of the old Majestic Hotel. Earlier, a careful survey of New York tastes in apartments had indicated that suites ranging in size from eleven to twenty-four rooms were what New Yorkers wanted most, and the Majestic's floor plans had been drawn up to suit this preference. Now the plans were hastily redrawn to provide apartments of two to fourteen rooms. At the Dakota the Great Depression did not cause many tenants to move out. It did, however, cause a number of tenants to pull in their horns, and quite a few of the larger apartments were divided into smaller units during this period. But the vacancies these divisions created had a way of being filled immediately, and there was nearly always a waiting list for them. Through it all, the building never advertised and never hung out a sign.

And how the building's owners, the Clarks, pampered the Dakota and its tenants! Once, while a Dakota tenant was away for the summer, a pipe burst in his ceiling and water destroyed an entire panel of antique wallpaper. The wallpaper was irreplaceable, but the Dakota's private painting crew was brought in. Painstakingly, they reproduced the wallpaper's intricate pattern by hand in paint—so perfectly that when the tenant returned he was unable to notice any difference.

TENANT LOYALTY was also based on more powerful, almost mystical, forces. The building seemed to inspire among its residents a kind of wild, irrational passion that approached religious fervor. Those who worshiped at the Dakota's altar were not just tenants but followers, members of a sect. The Dakota, while it might never be a symbol of New York class, became a symbol of a New York cult. From the beginning the building seemed to take on a human personality—and a quirky, almost demented one at that. One did not live at the Dakota long before it could be sensed that here was not an ordinary apartment house but a living, breathing Presence, a wild lover whose behavior could neither be explained nor predicted but whose embrace one craved regardless. Things were always going wrong. Ceilings leaked, pipes burst, plaster fell. Tiles perpetually slithered from mansard roofs, and in the nooks and crannies of the building's eaves, dormers, gables, finials and balconies, a larger-than-usual proportion of New York's pigeon population found convenient addresses. The wood-burning fire-places worked, but they often, mysteriously, spewed their smoke into someone else's apartment, even though no known connections existed between individual flues. From the earliest days, putting the Dakota back together was a continuous, daily operation and yet—because it was the Dakota, a Presence, not a thing—the Dakota was mended, patched, coddled and cared for with the kind of desperate, distracted emotion that a parent reserves for a permanently sickly or retarded child. It would not be possible, a psychiatrist might say, for a group of otherwise sensible people to have a love-hate relationship with a giant piece of not-very-good Victorian architecture. With the Dakota, it was possible.

The building never did make a great deal of sense. It cost a fortune to heat. A modern efficiency expert would have found the Dakota a model of total inefficiency. Much of the interior, from the gabled attics to the enormous basement, was simply wasted space. The interior courtyard was wasted, valuable real estate. The layouts of the apartments themselves were not at all clever. Space was squandered in long, snaking corridors and hallways. Some rooms had huge windows, while others had no windows at all. Doorways opened upon other doorways. Kitchens were placed half a block away from dining rooms. And yet the random, senseless quality of the building was what the Dakota's residents loved most about it. In the end, though there was no building in New York remotely like it, the Dakota, to its worshipers, seemed a particular symbol of the city. The Dakota could have happened no-where else.

Chapter 8

Spooks

As THE CULT of the Dakota grew and flourished, as the building aged, and as more and more of the first families made their quiet way out the Undertaker's Gate, it is perhaps not surprising that the building should have acquired its share of ghosts. Long before Roman Polanski used the Dakota's exterior for his film *Rosemary's Baby*, there were rumors to the effect that the building was the scene of all sorts of strange, eerie, supernatural goings-on.

In Ira Levin's novel, the apartment house in which most of the action takes place was not called the Dakota, but was made to sound very much like it. When the movie crew arrived the Dakota again became quite a tourist attraction. And while one of the film's goriest scenes—a suicide—was being shot, the carriage entrance and courtyard were used. For several days a mangled and bloodied "corpse" lay in the courtyard, in full view of startled passers-by, many of whom thought the mannequin was a real person.

Some wags have nicknamed the Dakota "the Dracula" because of its ominous and forbidding appearance, and a number of the building's employees insist that the building is haunted. Chatting with a doorman one rainy night while waiting for a cab, Rex Reed confided that one of the Dakota's former residents he would most like to have known was the late Boris Karloff. (Mr. Reed *thinks* that he has Boris Karloff's old apartment, but he is wrong.) The doorman lowered his voice and said, "He'll be back—wait and see."

Aside from this sort of thing, there have been other odd happenings within the building that are harder to explain. Jo Mielziner, for example, was one man who was particularly devoted to the Dakota, and he kept scrapbooks of bits and pieces of Dakota history. He often said he suspected there were "spirits" in the place. He died in 1976 outside the Dakota's door, in a taxi, on his way home from a visit with his doctor. For several weeks after his death, queer things went on in the building's cavernous basement. Tenant Wilbur Ross, a banker, was summoned suddenly to the basement by a frightened porter who reported that a heavy snow shovel, which had been hanging properly against a wall, had all at once flung itself twenty feet across the room and landed in the middle of the floor. Later, neatly stacked plastic bags of garbage that had been waiting to go out by the service door similarly flew into the center of the room. Mr. Ross himself, an American representative of the House of Rothschild and a man one would not expect to be impressed by spiritualist phenomena, insists he saw a heavy metal bar make the same uncanny journey through the air and land a short distance from his feet. When he tried to lift the bar it was too heavy for him. During this same period one of the four ancient service elevators, manually operated affairs requiring cables and pulleys, suddenly began to rise from the basement level of its own accord. It took four strong men, wrestling at the cables, to bring it down again. In time these manifestations ceased, but it was widely assumed that they had something to do with Jo Mielziner's impatience with his new whereabouts.

Then, just as New York has had its Mad Bomber and its Son of Sam, the Dakota for a period had its Mad Slasher or, as he was sometimes called, the Phantom of the Dakota. The Mad Slasher seemed primarily intent upon vandalizing the cages of the new automatic passenger elevators that had been recently installed. He gouged deep, violently angry slashes into the paneled elevator walls. He could not have had anything to do with the ghost of Jo Mielziner because Mielziner himself had designed the new elevators and had been very proud of them. The slashes appeared high up on the elevator walls, so they could not have been inflicted by a child, and the cuts were so deep that a person of some strength seemed indicated. New slashings appeared week after week; the perpetrator had to be someone within the building. Rumors flew as to who it might be, and neighbors looked at neighbors with heightened suspicion. At the same time, strange piles of shredded paper were found in the ninth-floor corridors, as though someone were trying to start a fire. Then, one afternoon, a full gallon can of paint fell —or was hurled—from the rooftop into the courtyard below, narrowly missing a tenant who was walking through. The can exploded on the pavement. No painting had been going on on the roof at the time. Now the suspicion turned to fear. Was there a murderer in their midst? Volunteers posted themselves, hidden with field glasses, to try to catch the Phantom at his work. Though they managed to observe various private diversions in their neighbors' apartments, they noted nothing untoward. Then, as suddenly as the Slasher's activities had begun, they stopped. No clue as to who the Slasher might have been has ever been uncovered, though there remain, not surprisingly, a number of theories.

Writer Rex Reed had his own unsettling experience. Shortly after moving into his eighth-floor five-room apartment, he and his decorator, Richard Ridge, began extensive renovations. The work was nearly completed. None of the workmen who had been in the apartment smoked, Reed himself was out for the evening and his apartment was presumably empty. And yet, somehow, a pile of shavings and scraps just inside his front door caught fire. The fire was discovered, but by the time it was put out smoke and water damage required the apartment to be redone from scratch. "It was horrible," he says. "When I came home, I thought, 'Welcome to the Dakota!' My God, this place really is haunted." The cause of the fire was never determined.

The Dakota's elevators have always occupied a special place in the building's history. When first installed they were original Otis hydraulics and they were the first elevators in New York to be placed in a residential building. For years they were operated by a team of Mary Petty-type, white-haired Irish ladies who wore dresses of black bombazine—a fabric unheard-of since the turn of the century—relieved with touches of white lace at the wrists and collars. Even after the elevators were automated in the early 1960's, they made their journeys between floors with agonizing slowness and had a persistent habit of stopping at the wrong floors.

An odd report once came from a group of men who were doing some interior painting in the building. A beautiful little blond child had suddenly appeared in the corridor, wearing high white stockings, patent-leather shoes with silver buckles and a dress of yellow taffeta that seemed to come from another century. She was bouncing a red ball. "It's my birthday," she said and, still bouncing her ball she disappeared down the corridor. The description of the little girl in the yellow dress matched no child then in the building, and she has never been identified. Not long after that, one of the painters slipped from a scaffold and fell through a stairwell to his death, and the little ghost girl was regarded as a messenger of ill omen.

For years Mrs. Henry Blanchard was convinced that the Blanchards' fifth-floor apartment was haunted. All sorts of strange rumblings, creaks and mutterings seemed to emerge from the vicinity of her pantry. Finally, however, a plumber convinced her that these noises were caused by air bubbling in the water pipes behind the plaster. "I'm a little disappointed," says Mrs. Blanchard, "to find out that my ghost was air." On the other hand, Frederic Weinstein, a writer, and his wife Suzanne are not at all certain that the noises they hear in their third-floor apartment have a natural explanation. In their dining room they often hear footsteps, restless pacings back and forth. Weinstein, furthermore, has noticed that, though he is usually not clumsy, an unusual number of accidents have befallen him in the dining room. He has tripped and fallen, skidded on floors and rugs, slipped from stepladders, had chairs slide out from underneath him. The accidents keep happening, just as the sound of footsteps continues to be heard. Not long ago Frederic Weinstein had a most curious experience. He was walking home to the Dakota and, before crossing the street, paused to look up, as apartment dwellers often do, at the windows of his apartment, which faces both Seventy-second Street and the Park. He was startled to see, through the windows of his living room, an enormous crystal chandelier suspended from the ceiling, ablaze with light. He checked the windows again, counted the floors. It was obviously his apartment; no other apartment occupies that particular third-floor corner. And yet he knew that his apartment contained no crystal chandelier, nor had it as long as he had lived there. Of course when he got upstairs the crystal chandelier had gone. But there was, as there had been from the time the Weinsteins had taken the apartment, a round nipple protruding from the center of the living-room ceiling from which, once upon a time, a chandelier of some sort had clearly hung.

If it had not been for these weird events, Frederic Weinstein would have paid little heed to another odd thing that happened in his apartment not long ago. He had been playing a Ouija-board-type game with his children—one that involved lettered tiles that spelled out the board's answers. During the course of the session the spirit-messages appeared to be coming from a little girl. When he and the children had finished with the game, Weinstein stacked the lettered tiles neatly and put them on a bookshelf. Several days later, however, he discovered that two of the tiles had made their way into pockets of one of his suits. A third turned up in his eyeglass case. As he withdrew them, one by one, the letters were "I," "C" and "U." This, he feels, was intended to convey to him that someone in the apartment was saying, "I see you." It is, he assumes, the same party that is causing him to stumble in his dining room.

One of the most bizarre supernatural experiences at the Dakota involves the John Lennons. The Lennons have become the Dakota's Mystery Couple, though when they first expressed an interest in the building, there was no small amount of resistance to them. They were assumed to have an unconventional life-style. It was feared that they would have large, noisy parties with music and amplifiers. As a result of some drug-related charges in England, there had been a period when the United States State Department had wanted John Lennon out of the country, and there were those at the Dakota who felt the same way about him. But after moving into the Dakota the Lennons kept to themselves, gave few if any entertainments and expressed a wish for absolute privacy. At the same time, when they emerge from the building in their unusual costumes (Lennon in blue jeans, a long black cape, a Mexican sombrero, often sucking a baby's pacifier; his stocky little wife, also in jeans, in one of a variety of fright-wig hairdos) and step into their His and Hers chauffeur-driven silver limousines, they are a bit conspicuous. In their disguises, however, the Lennons are seldom recognized on the street and are usually dismissed as run-of-the mill New York eccentrics.

Still, the Lennons continue to amaze. In the elevators, in front of other tenants, John and Yoko Lennon openly discuss their finances, reportedly saying such things as, "Well, we fooled them, didn't we? It wasn't thirteen million dollars they were offering—it was only three." The Lennons' immediate neighbors on the seventh floor were not too pleased when John Lennon crisscrossed the staircase balustrade in the elevator entrance with twine, ostensibly to keep the Lennons' young son Sean from falling through the railing. Lennon also keeps a studio on the ground floor, where he plays his guitar, and neighbors were put off to see that he had scrawled HELTER-SKELTER in large letters across one wall (forgetting that "Helter-Skelter" had been the title of a Beatles record long before it became associated with the Charles Manson family.) Later, HELTER-SKELTER was removed, and the walls were painted to simulate blue sky and clouds. John Lennon, when he encounters his neighbors, is usually pleasant and friendly; his wife seems less so. As a result of the Lennons' presence in the building, the Dakota switchboard has had to handle as many as thirty calls a day from fans trying to be put through to one or the other of the Lennons. At times, small groups of fans gather outside the building, hoping to catch a glimpse of the Lennons as they come or go. The fans may not always recognize the Lennons, but they know their cars, and each time a silver limousine appears there is a small, collective gasp. Occasionally photographers lurk as well, in which case—alerted by José, the doorman—the Lennons trick them by using the basement service door. Unsolicited gift packages are always arriving for the Lennons, either through the mail or delivered by hand, and when one of these was found to contain a chalky substance that did not quite look like talcum powder, John Lennon ordered that all such gifts be placed immediately in the garbage can.

At times, too, Lennon fans have succeeded in slipping past the security guards and gates, and getting into the building. There they become nuisances, ringing doorbells trying to find the Lennons. A number of people in the Dakota were rather amused when, at the inaugural reception for President Carter, John Lennon stepped forward and introduced himself to the President. The President looked blank. "I used to be a Beatle," Lennon explained, a trifle lamely. The President continued to look blank.

When the Lennons moved to the Dakota, they took the apartment that had formerly belonged to the actor Robert Ryan. Robert Ryan's wife Jessie, to whom he was devoted, died of cancer at the Dakota, and because of the unhappy memories and associations the apartment held for him, Ryan moved out soon afterward—to 88 Central Park South, which has become sort of a haven for ex-Dakotans who, by reason of divorce, widowhood or other change of circumstance, have felt it necessary to depart from their beloved building. There, Ryan himself later died.

Before settling in the Ryans' old apartment, the Lennons decided that it would be wise to hold a séance to see what spirits might be inhabiting their new home. A medium was summoned, and she very quickly made contact with Jessie Ryan. Mrs. Ryan informed the Lennons that she considered their apartment her home too, and that she intended to stay there. She would not, however, disturb them in any way. They could lead their lives as they wished. Jessie Ryan was apparently as gracious and charming from the Beyond as she had been in life.

Yoko Ono Lennon then telephoned the Ryans' daughter Lisa to tell her that her late mother was still happily at home in the Dakota. Lisa Ryan was not particularly pleased or amused at this news. "If my mother's ghost belongs anywhere, it's here with me—not with *them*," she said.

Perhaps the most interesting ghost, however, was the "man with a wig" who appeared in the late 1930's to an electrician named John Paynter, who was working in the building at the time. Paynter had become fascinated with the building's wiring, and some of the pieces of circuitry were so antique and unfamiliar to him that he frequently had to take them home with him to take them apart and study them to see how they worked. Late one evening he returned to the Dakota and descended to the basement to continue tinkering with wires and fuses. All at once, out of the shadows, appeared a small man in a frock coat and winged collar. He had a short beard, a large nose and wore tiny, steel-rimmed glasses. The man glared fiercely at Mr. Paynter for several moments, then reached up, snatched off the wig he was wearing and shook it angrily in Paynter's face. Then, just as swiftly, he disappeared. The "man with a wig" appeared to Mr. Paynter on four subsequent occasions, each time pulling off the wig and making the same angry gesture.

Mr. Paynter had never heard of the first Mr. Edward Clark. But

Clark had a short beard, a large nose, wore small, steel-rimmed spectacles and a wig. If the apparition was indeed Mr. Clark, the angry gesture might have been Mr. Clark's way of expressing his feelings about the fact that the building was losing money.

Part Two

THE CHRISTMAS CRISIS

Oh, blessings on this lordly pile
That saves us from the city
And makes us, in asylum, smile
On those outside—with pity! . . .

FROM "Ballad of the Dakota"

Chapter 9

The Panic of 1960

NEW YORKERS, New Yorkers like to say, pull together in times of crisis. They are magnificent at rising to difficult occasions. In a blizzard they reach out to help the aged lady cross the street. In a transit strike New Yorkers with automobiles offer lifts to strangers. In a blackout they emerge to help direct traffic and open up their houses to the hapless and the stranded. New Yorkers have learned to cope with life's worst vicissitudes, and this *nil admirari* attitude, they say, is one reason why New York considers itself a city of survivors. Only the fittest make it here. The unfit, having tried and failed, go home to Peoria, where they do just fine. The notion that New York is a community of success is perhaps the greatest source of the New Yorker's immense self-pride.

We are not talking here of Harlem, or of the Bronx, or Queens, or Brooklyn or Staten Island. These remain, Rand-McNally notwithstanding, foreign places. New York—the New York that counts—consists only of the lower two thirds of Manhattan Island, and some might limit the New York territory to an even smaller strip of real estate than that —to the blocks immediately east, south and west of Central Park.

By 1960 the Dakota had become a survivor in itself—New York's oldest standing luxury apartment dwelling, a city showplace for nearly eighty years. Its very appearance—that block-long crenelated façade of weather-stained yellow brick and chocolate-colored stone, surrounded by a dry moat—was no longer technically beautiful but was imposing, not to say daunting. If New York had become a city of expanded egos, the Dakota had become a building designed to swell the ego even more. Its very scale seemed to boost and bolster a sense of self-importance among those privileged to call the Dakota home. From within its apartments, vast by contemporary standards, with their lofty ceilings, their floor-to-ceiling windows, one could feel in command of the city. New Yorkers had long been known for their ability to retreat, tortoise-fashion, within the protective shells of their homes, but the carapace of the Dakota was now the thickest one in town. The Dakota had become a fortress within a fortress, and this lent its residents a feeling of instant superiority. There was, after all, nothing left in New York quite like it, nor was there anywhere else in the country. It had become a little like an exclusive suburb. It had the pomp and circumstance of Shaker Heights and Grosse Pointe, the glamour of Beverly Hills, the self-satisfaction of the Main Line, but though there were similarities to all these "good addresses," the Dakota was more so.

Living at the Dakota has also been described as like living in a small European village; at least one tenant says he half expects to see the women of the building gathered at the courtyard fountains to do their wash. For years, however, it was more like living in a small, private kingdom, each apartment a separate duchy with its ruling lord and lady.

Though there was no real precedent for the Dakota, it seemed to fill, from the moment it opened its doors, a particular New York need. New Yorkers, to a greater degree than residents of most large cities, are obsessed with privacy, and the Dakota was designed for this—to insulate and protect privacy, as well as nourish the egos it sheltered. In New York, neighbors are neighbors only in a rather special sense, and there is the distinct feeling that too much urban familiarity breeds discontent and that proximity breeds distrust. The massiveness of the Dakota's construction and design was such that those who lived there would never have to endure the discomfitures so commonly associated with apartment living today—the sounds of children's footsteps running on the floor above, the noise of a domestic argument next door, the smell of someone's cooking permeating the elevator shafts. Each tenant was provided with a place of splendid isolation from all the others. In this hothouse atmosphere, egos increased in size to championship proportions, developed idiosyncrasies, whims, quirks, fetishes, peculiarities, temperaments and tempers.

There were almost daily indications and reminders that those who lived at the Dakota were people of particular importance. For one thing, in addition to other blessings, for years Dakotans seemed to be given special consideration in terms of what it cost. Nowhere in New York could so much cubic footage be had for so little rent—ten rooms for $500 a month, for example, and seventeen rooms with six bathrooms and eight working fireplaces for $650. In 1884 these Dakota rents had seemed substantial. But the astonishing thing was that by 1960 they had risen hardly at all.

Then there was the caliber of the people who, at one time or another, all lived inside the principality—seemingly a cross-section of New York City leadership. At least three foreign ambassadors—the Dutch, the Portuguese and the Finnish—lived at the Dakota along with the French Minister of Cultural Affairs. There had been the distinguished Schirmers and Steinways. Other celebrated tenants have included the likes of Boris Karloff, Eric Portman, Judy Holliday, Jose Ferrer and his wife Rosemary Clooney, Zachary Scott and his wife Ruth Ford, Jo Mielziner, Sidney Kingsley, Marya Mannes, Theresa Wright, Gwen Verdon, Arthur Cantor, Robert Ryan, Fannie Hurst, Paul Gallico, Marian Mercer, Carter and Amanda Burden, Judy Garland, Susan Stein Shiva, opera singer John Brownlee, Kent Smith, Betty Friedan, fashion columnist Eugenia Sheppard and her husband Walter Millis, William Inge, Syrie Maugham, John Frankenheimer, Ted Ashley, Jack Palance, Gregory Ratoff. Admiral Alan G. Kirk represented the military at the highest level, and C. D. Jackson, the publisher of *Time*, represented publishing. Later were to come Lauren Bacall, Rex Reed, photographers Peter Fink and Hiro Wakabayashi, ex-Mrs. Paul Simon, Dotson Rader, restaurateurs Larry Ellman and Warner LeRoy, the Leonard Bernsteins, filmmaker Albert Maysles, Roberta Flack, John Lennon and Yoko Ono. If, in other words, New York were considered to be the capital of American art, culture and fashion, the Dakota seemed to be the Capital of the capital. As such, it seemed almost sacred—inviolable, impregnable, invulnerable.

Therefore, considering the amount of *hubris* the building had generated among its tenants over the years, it was with considerable shock that on the afternoon of Friday, December 17, 1960—while the rest of New York was going about its business of pre-Christmas shopping—the residents of the Dakota learned that their special status was about to come to an abrupt end and that they might have to face a life as ordinary mortals. That was when Mr. Ernest A. Gross, then one of the building's most distinguished residents, an international lawyer and three-time delegate to the United Nations General Assembly, was sitting in his Wall Street office and a call came through from William J. Zeckendorf who, though he later fell from grace, was then the unquestioned czar of New York real estate and who, in the years since World War II, had been busily reshaping the Manhattan skyline. "I want to introduce myself," said Zeckendorf to Gross. "I'm your new landlord." Ernest Gross froze. Though Mr. Zeckendorf's telephone call was by way of a greeting, it also conveyed in no uncertain terms a warning to Gross and his fellow Dakotans. Whenever William Zeckendorf acquired an old, unprofitable building like the Dakota on a choice piece of land, he razed it and erected in its place a shiny tower of steel and glass which was a modern model of efficiency and economy. "Buildings like the Dakota don't make sense in New York anymore," said Mr. Zeckendorf. Immediately, Ernest Gross called his friend and Dakota neighbor, C. D. Jackson, and apprised him of the situation. Zeckendorf had the Dakota, and he was preparing to tear it down. Some ninety families would lose their treasured homes.

THAT SOMETHING of this sort might one day happen was not entirely unexpected. Tenants of the Dakota had been watching, with some apprehension, as the building's owner, Stephen C. Clark, passed his seventy-fifth birthday and moved toward his eighties without committing himself as to what his plans for the building's future might be. The Dakota had now belonged to the Clark family for three generations. Everything the Dakotans had they owed to the benevolence— and extravagance (or perhaps nonchalance)—of the Clarks. There had been the building's famous services, for example. When the Dakota first opened its doors to rental tenants in 1884, it had a full-time operating staff of 150 people. In addition to the customary elevator men and women, doormen, janitors and porters and watchmen, there was a resident housekeeper who supervised a staff of resident maids. There was a resident laundress with her own laundry staff, and laundry was picked up at individual apartments in special wicker baskets and returned washed, ironed, darned and mended and with buttons sewn on, each piece separated with a sheet of pink tissue paper. There was a gentlemen's tailor in the basement. There was a house carpenter, two house painters, a house cabinetmaker, a house electrician, plumber and glazier. Before the days of the automobile, there had been Dakota stable boys to handle visiting carriages and a separate Dakota stables two blocks away for tenants' horses, landaus and coupés.

On the ground floor of the Dakota proper there was a full office staff operating under a "lady managerette" and a paging system whereby individual tenants could notify the front desk of their needs and wishes. The Dakota even had a baronial private dining room, with its own captains and white-gloved waiters, just for tenants and their guests. Each afternoon a printed menu was discreetly slipped beneath each apartment door so that tenants, if they desired, could phone down to Miss Kay, the dining-room managerette, and specify their orders for dinner in advance. Here, for $1.50, one could select, to quote from a 1907 bill of fare:

Caviar   Oysters

Celery   Salted Almonds   Olives

Cream of Asparagus

Broiled Spanish Mackerel

Pommes Parisienne   Cucumbers

Partridge, Fantaisie

Potatoes soufflées   Peas

Champagne

Lettuce and tomato en surprise

Neopolitan ices   Gâteaux assortis

Café

Napkins and tablecloths were of the heaviest linen. Silver was of such heavy plate that even today such pieces of the original set as have been salvaged show no sign of wear. Goblets and finger bowls were of stained glass. In each of the four passenger elevators, a silver tray was placed for messages, mail and calling cards.

As the twentieth century progressed, of course, more and more of these lovely little services began to disappear. The laundry and tailoring and housekeeper and maid service went first. Not long after World War II, the dining room—which had never been a profitable or really practical operation—closed for good. The front-office staff was reduced to four, and by 1960 the building's entire staff was down to only forty-five. Still, for New York this was a high staff-to-tenant ratio, and that the building had been kept up as well as it had was, in large part, thanks to the Clark family.

As Stephen C. Clark entered his twilight years the Dakota became very solicitous of the family. Stephen and Susan Clark, who lived across the Park in East Seventieth Street, were frequently invited to dinners by various of the Dakota's distinguished tenants, all of whom were eager for some hint of what would happen to their building when the inevitable happened to him. It was perhaps not exactly a coincidence that, in March 1959, *Architectural Forum,* a Luce publication, published a lengthy photographic essay extolling the architectural splendors of the Dakota. Lest the Clark family fail to be impressed by the article, C. D. Jackson had the photographs put together in a twenty-two-page album inscribed "To Stephen Clark with the compliments of C. D. Jackson and the editors of *Architectural Forum.*" Marya Mannes, already a well-known author, lecturer and critic, showered Mr. Clark with a series of charming little verses, each calculated to convey to him how much his tenants loved him, and his building, and how certain the tenants were that he, or someone just like him, would always care for them.

She need not have wasted her ink, nor should the others have wasted their dinner invitations, their birthday cards or their thoughtful little Christmas gifts. When Stephen Clark died, in September 1960, there was an anxious wait for news of his will. Then it was learned that Clark had not left the Dakota, which he had owned outright, to his children or grandchildren. He had left it instead to the Clark family's foundation. At first this seemed well and good, though there was a certain nervousness in the building since dealing with the caprices of a foundation, or committee, is not the same as dealing with an individual. What the tenants of the Dakota did not realize, however, was that under New York State law a foundation cannot operate or own an unprofitable property. And, by 1960, the Dakota was not operating at a profit if, indeed, it ever had.

AS FAR AS Ernest Gross was able to ascertain that Friday evening, Mr. Zeckendorf had not become the Dakota's landlord—yet. What Zeckendorf had done, it seemed, had been to make the Clark Foundation an offer of $4,500,000 to buy the building. He had made his offer at five o'clock on Friday and had given the Foundation until noon the following Monday to accept or reject it. The Foundation had indicated its willingness to accept, or so Mr. Gross was told, and Zeckendorf had already advanced a certain sum in what, in real estate parlance, is called "earnest money." In his hastily arranged meeting with C. D. Jackson, Gross pointed out that the Dakota only had two and a half days—over a weekend, at that—to come up with a matching or perhaps better offer.

A hasty meeting of Dakota tenants was called, in which Gross and Jackson attempted to explain the nature of the catastrophe, the disaster, that was at hand. All sorts of people whom nobody had seen before came out of the woodwork. Lauren Bacall, newly widowed and who had come into the Dakota only recently, sat on a table and shouted unprintable curses at all involved; she had just finished decorating her apartment at some expense. Beside her sat Judy Holliday, in tears; she had already been pronounced ill of incurable cancer and wanted to die in the building she considered home. Even old Miss E. Bruce Leo, who had not set foot outside her eighteen-room apartment in years, appeared in a picture hat and a long, trailing gown. Some said Miss Leo was already a hundred and two, and she had become the Dakota's Madwoman of Chaillot. (Among other oddities, she kept a stuffed horse in her parlor.) "I will not be put out of my house! I will not be put out!" Miss Leo kept shouting. Almost everyone shouted, cursed, stamped, sobbed and pounded their chairs on the old dining room's inlaid marble floor. The meeting had started in confusion, and quickly it became chaotic. Order was impossible, and when the meeting broke up it was not so much adjourned as dispersed as an angry, violent mob.

Ernest Gross and C. D. Jackson returned to the Jackson's apartment for drinks and to ponder how, if at all, the Dakota might be saved.

WHAT GROSS AND JACKSON had discovered that night was that New Yorkers, in times of crisis, do not *necessarily* pull together. At that December meeting, everyone in the Dakota was pulling for himself, for his or her own precious place of residence. Sometimes, in times of crisis, people need a leader or captain, and co-captains were what Gross and Jackson decided that night to be. The sizes of the egos involved in the Dakota were such that they had to be brought under some firm command if anything at all were to be accomplished. The Dakota had often been called New York's answer to Grand Hotel. It might, more aptly, have been compared with Ship of Fools or the Orient Express. Though there had never been, as far as is known, any actual murders at the Dakota Apartments, there had been a number of odd, untidy doings. All had had to do with the capricious and unruly egos of the Dakota's passengers. Like a great ship, the Dakota had developed creaks and sighs and moans. Nevertheless, there had been compartments in which many people passed their days; there were stewards and porters—whose palms needed periodically to be greased—to care for their needs, and there had been someone continuously passing through to collect the fare. On board the Dakota some had been traveling *grande luxe*, in First Class accommodations, others had settled for Cabin Class, and still others had been in steerage. But now that it had been abandoned by the Clark family, the Dakota was a ship without a pilot, and, like the great luxury liners of the past, it seemed doomed.

And yet, there were special problems. The Dakota was, after all, a part of New York City. All around it the restless seas of New York had seethed and surged and battered the Dakota's tarnished sides. Those who called the Dakota home should have been more anxious about those seas because, for years, everything that had happened to the city of New York (and was to happen in large cities throughout the country) happened, in microcosm, to the Dakota. The building had come to represent everything that was pleasant and rewarding about life in New York, but it also reflected everything about New York life that was threatening, frightening and uncertain. Every battle or crusade that the city had undergone had also been confronted, on a smaller scale, at the Dakota. But no one had noticed much of this. The Dakota had been regarded by its residents as a charming anachronism, one that would never change. Now the Dakotans were discovering the truth of the ancient axiom that nothing is more certain than change—and they cared for this discovery not at all.

As in any old structure, there had been strange, recurrent scuttlings —"mice in the walls." The Dakota's mice were both real and figurative —tiny creatures that had been nibbling and gnawing at the Dakota's famous underpinnings of respectability, security, pride and doughty longevity. Behind the Dakota's stern, implacable façade—the buff-colored brick, the carved Nova Scotia freestone trimmings, the niches, balconies and balustrades with spandrels and panels and cornices of terra cotta, the friezes and finials and gargoyles and oriel windows— changes had been taking place. Now Dakotans would have to face up to their existence, and swallow a bit of pride.

One of the traditions at the Dakota had long been the annual gathering of tenants, at Christmas time, to sing carols in the building's spacious inner courtyard. The singing was traditionally followed by hot buttered rum, cookies and sandwiches in the large fifth-floor apartment of Mr. and Mrs. Henry Blanchard, who were among the building's long-time residents. It was a time, once a year, when neighbors made at least a show of being neighborly, but for this sort of thing to happen once a year was considered quite sufficient. Celebrity tenants such as Miss Bacall, whom one scarcely saw during the balance of the year, made brief, gracious appearances, and the mood of these gatherings was generally polite and friendly. But the band of carolers that gathered in the chilly court on Christmas Eve of 1960 was edgy, nervous, frightened, confused by agitated rumors and speculation. But, for the first time, the distinct and disparate personalities who shared a roof at 1 West Seventy-second Street had something in common: uncertainty and fear of what was about to happen.

Chapter 10

The Rescue Team

IN 1907 OLD Mrs. Frederic Steinway had her usual list of complaints, which she passed along to the Clarks: "Porter service very bad. Dan drunk. Wet trunks, etc. . . . Elevator boys dirty; smell bad; dirty shoes; not shaven; dirty linen, etc. Complaint of Jim at the gate. Improper service in the way of opening carriage doors, holding umbrella on rainy days, carriages neglected for automobiles; general inattention. Table and dining room not up to the mark; maids' table poor, not enough to eat." Mrs. Steinway's memorandum was only one of dozens with which the Clarks, as landlords, daily had to cope.

In 1960, Messrs. Ernest Gross and C. D. Jackson, having taken the helm, found themselves battered with a similar series of proposals, criticisms and suggestions from the Dakota's tenants. Some were realistic. It was suggested that the tenants go, en masse, down to the Clark Foundation in the old Singer Building and appeal for mercy "on our knees." Someone suggested that Stephen Clark's widow might be appealed to and persuaded to intercede on the building's behalf. Other proposals were more wild-eyed. It was suggested that all the tenants arm themselves with pistols and, when the wreckers came, shoot it out with them, Western-style. Appeals to the Mayor, the Governor of New York, the President of the United States were suggested. At least one faction favored bringing in the Mafia to deal with Mr. Zeckendorf directly, and in no short order. During another, only slightly less disorganized meeting with the angry tenants, Ernest Gross said firmly, "We are here to decide two things: One, do we want to save the Dakota? Two, are we willing to admit that big rooms, high ceilings and low rents can no longer go hand in hand?" In other words, the Dakota might be saved, but it would cost money.

From the outset both Gross and Jackson—one a lawyer, the other a magazine publisher—realized that what they both lacked was any sort of expertise in the field of real estate. At Gross's suggestion a man named Peter Grimm of the firm of William A. White & Sons was brought in for consultation. Grimm was a suave, debonair and immensely likable man, well versed not only in real estate but in the intricate and competitive ways of New York society. Realtors did not customarily swim in the perfumed upper waters of society, but Peter Grimm did, and he had an interesting suggestion. Mr. Louis Glickman, he pointed out, was a real estate man who had often engaged in deals with Zeckendorf. More important, Mr. and Mrs. Glickman had social ambitions—particularly in the art and music worlds—but they had recently suffered from perfectly dreadful press. It had involved Carnegie Hall, which the Glickman Corporation had acquired and announced plans to raze. This had created a terrible fuss throughout New York's artistic community. Under the leadership of Isaac Stern and Mrs. Franklin Roosevelt, a Save Carnegie Hall Committee had been formed and the entire cultural community of New York had come forth to stand valiantly behind it. In the end the committee was successful, but in the process Louis Glickman had been virtually hanged in effigy. Realizing his sudden unpopularity, Glickman had done his best. At the suggestion of his press agent, Tex McCrary, Glickman had personally offered to pledge $100,000 to save Carnegie Hall, but in the stormy goings-on few people were impressed by this, and the name Glickman had become anathema in the world to which he aspired. Now, said Peter Grimm, if Mr. Glickman could be persuaded to save the Dakota —an address so dear to artists and musicians—some of the status that Glickman had lost over Carnegie Hall might be restored to him.

On Sunday of the crucial weekend, four men—Gross, Jackson, Grimm and Glickman—sat down to lunch at the then all-male Oak Room of the Plaza Hotel, and quickly got down to business. Yes, Louis Glickman was interested. He knew the Dakota well. He had a number of friends who lived there. He agreed that the Dakota was a landmark, unique to New York, and should be saved. He was also particularly interested in the Dakota's parking lot which adjoined the building's west side, and which occupied nearly as much acreage as the building itself.

The parking lot had originally contained the building's private tennis and croquet courts. It had also been the site of a rose garden, and the roses had done particularly well, apparently because the garden was planted above the Dakota's steam boiler room, sunk in the soil beneath. There had also been a grassed play area, suitably fenced, for tenants' children, and a private grassed run for tenants' dogs. During World War I, Dakotans had turned a plot of this land under and had planted peas, potatoes, asparagus, carrots, cauliflower and lettuce in their own patriotic little victory garden, "to help our country in its time of need."

In the early days of the Dakota, west-facing apartments—even though the west side of the building contained the basement service entrance—were in great demand not only for the garden view but because turn-of-the century women liked to sit in their windows overlooking the tennis courts to observe, for example, which ladies wore short skirts and which gentlemen removed their shirts.

By 1960, however, the rose garden and the tennis courts were just a romantic memory shared by a few old-timers. During the Depression, in order to supply the building with more revenue, this entire area had been converted to the more mundane use of parking cars. At the time, Mr. Stephen Clark, accompanied by his uniformed chauffeur carrying a lap robe, had personally visited his tenants to convey the sad news, saying, "In New York, all good things must go." During the 1960 Christmas Crisis his words echoed ominously.

Mr. Glickman wanted to be sure that if the building were sold, the parking lot would go with it. He was assured that it would. He then came up with a proposition. Glickman proposed to offer the Clark Foundation $4,600,000 for the property, slightly more than the $4,-500,000 that had been purportedly offered by Zeckendorf. Glickman, who was then in a position to do so, would offer the Foundation cash.

He would then arrange for mortgage financing and set up a procedure whereby the Dakota's residents could buy individual apartments back from the Glickman Corporation for a total price of $4,800,000—a profit to Glickman of a mere $200,000—thus turning the building into a co-operative, owned by tenant shareholders. To Messrs. Gross and Jackson, $200,000 seemed a modest price to pay. There seemed to be very little time in which to find another savior, and here was Louis Glickman, with cash, offering immediate salvation. The details of making the building a co-operative could be worked out over the long months ahead, but Louis Glickman was the bird in the hand.

Louis Glickman also wanted the parking lot, but to Gross and Jackson, in their agitated state, this seemed the easiest of things to give up. They agreed that if the deal went through, the parking lot would be Glickman's. The two men returned to another anxious gathering of tenants and announced that a man had come forth to help them save the building, and that his name was Louis J. Glickman.

CONSIDERING THE number of strange occurrences that have punctuated the Dakota's long history, it is not surprising that the story of the Christmas Crisis of 1960 should contain a puzzling mystery of its own. The mystery revolves around two questions. The first: Was the Dakota, despite the certainty of its tenants during those anxiety-ridden days, ever really threatened with demolition? And the second: What were the precise roles of the two New York real estate men, William J. Zeckendorf and Louis J. Glickman?

What is certain is that on Monday morning following the Plaza lunch Mr. Glickman offered the Clark Foundation $4,600,000 cash for the Dakota and the parking lot. The Foundation accepted Glickman's offer, and Glickman, as he had promised to do, embarked upon the long process—it would take the better part of the following year—of selling the building back to the tenants as a co-operative, keeping the parking lot for himself. This he was soon able to sell for $2,000,000 to the Mayfair Corporation, which quickly drew up plans to erect a twenty-seven-story apartment tower where the rose gardens had been and where ladies and gentlemen of another era had played tennis and croquet. The Mayfair Tower, of course, would throw the entire west flank of the Dakota into permanent shadow, to the dismay of all Dakotans with west-facing apartments.

Though there were still misgivings in the building—some tenants felt that they could not afford to buy their apartments, while others knew that maintaining their apartments as co-operatives would cost them far more in monthly charges than they had paid in rents—there was still the undeniable relief that Glickman had saved the Dakota from the grasp of Mr. Zeckendorf and his wreckers' ball.

Time plays tricks on memories to be sure, but at least one Dakota resident has an entirely different recollection of what happened. According to Mrs. Henry Blanchard it was not Mr. Zeckendorf who announced he was buying the building and going to tear it down but *Mrs.* Zeckendorf. Winifred Cecil Blanchard and her husband are well-respected, if not commanding, figures at the Dakota. He has been called the building's unofficial nursemaid and she, a former operatic soprano of some note (and before her marriage to Blanchard, the Baroness Mazzonis di Pralafera) is still, despite a lingering illness, an ample, cheerful woman of easily elicited opinions. "I remember it perfectly," she says. "Mrs. Zeckendorf came up to me and said, 'My husband has just bought your building, and he's going to tear it down.' That was when we all panicked."

Mrs. Zeckendorf denies that she ever made such a remark.

Mr. William Zeckendorf has since died, but Mr. Louis Glickman is still alive and very much in the real estate business. Today Mr. Glickman says, "Bill Zeckendorf was never involved *at all.* Not in any way. He was never in the picture, not even for a minute. People may think he was because he and I had put together a couple of deals before that, and people associated my name with his, and vice versa. What's more, there was *never* a question of tearing the building down. It just wouldn't have been feasible. The building is built like the Rock of Gibraltar. It would have cost more to tear it down than the property was worth. The people at the Dakota came to me because the Clark Foundation wanted to sell it and they needed my know-how to help them turn it into a co-op. They were babes in the woods. I helped them pull it off."

But if there was "never a question" of tearing the building down, and if William Zeckendorf was "never involved," then who made that Friday telephone call to Ernest Gross, saying he was Zeckendorf, the "new landlord," with the thinly veiled threat of demolition? One cannot question the honesty nor the memory of Ernest Gross. Perhaps the Christmas Crisis, the whole panic, was engineered by someone else as part of a deception, a hoax on someone's part to get the building disposed of in a hurry.

To confuse matters even more, Grace Jackson, C. D. Jackson's widow, today has yet another set of recollections about the crucial events of December 1960. According to Mrs. Jackson, Mr. Zeckendorf called Mr. Jackson, not Mr. Gross, to say, "I'm your new landlord." Furthermore, Grace Jackson blames the whole crisis on the shilly-shallying tactics of Matthew S. Ely & Company, the real estate firm that had been handling the building. "We'd asked the Ely people to make an offer to the Clark Foundation long before Zeckendorf called C. D., told him he'd paid his earnest money, and was going to close the deal the following Monday morning. Later, Ely explained that he'd never submitted our bid because he knew he couldn't match Zeckendorf. After that we got rid of Ely." In a story that now has more versions than *Rashomon*, it is possible that the actual truth will never be known.

Experts in the field of New York real estate, meanwhile, point out that William Zeckendorf would not have had the $4,500,000 he allegedly offered to buy the Dakota in 1960. By that year the affairs of Zeckendorf and his company, Webb & Knapp, were already becoming hopelessly tangled. Zeckendorf had by then vastly overextended himself, and had begun his long toboggan ride to eventual disgrace and the bankruptcy courts.

But if Zeckendorf was indeed involved, it might have been as a "front" for someone else. By 1969 he had taken to doing a bit of this —pretending to be interested in a property in order to soften the market for another buyer, or to inflate the price for a seller. But in the Dakota's case, if he was fronting for someone, whom was he fronting for? The Clark Foundation? Certainly the Clark Foundation wanted to divest itself of the Dakota promptly, if necessary to the first bidder, and the Foundation had never shown much interest in what would happen to the building. Louis Glickman? Glickman and Zeckendorf had indeed worked together on deals in the past, and both were known for putting together deals of Byzantine complexity.

As for the Dakotans themselves, human beings, in times of crisis, often tend to create their own myths, monsters, demons and ghosts out of their collective fears. At the same time, people usually prefer to believe that they are their own heroes, that they are in control even as they are being controlled by circumstances. Twenty years later William Zeckendorf is still the one most often cited as the villain who forced the Dakota to decide whether or not to become a co-operative on such short notice. To others the villain was Glickman, and even those who view him as a savior are quick to add that he was a savior who had his price. In the minds of a few people the shades of Zeckendorf and Glickman have become blurred and are indistinct from one another.

A few things are certain. In the jungle of New York real estate, lambs often unwittingly lie down with lions. If the Dakotans, the lambs, had possessed the shrewdness and technical ability to co-op the building themselves, they would have saved themselves a lot of money. If the Clark Foundation, a charitable institution, had been charitable enough to help the Dakotans in their time of need and to assist them in turning their building into a co-op, the Dakotans would have saved money and the Foundation would still have made money—on the parking lot, if nothing else. Louis Glickman, in the process of turning the Dakota into a co-operative, made $2,200,000.*

New York, in other words, has long been a city of deals, trades and traders—a city constantly and often chaotically changing itself, tearing itself down and rebuilding itself on a gamble or a dare, never satisfied or certain that it is finished or, more often, that the ultimate financial risk and chance for gain has been achieved. In New York very little happens without someone—not necessarily the good guys—making money. It is a city, as a result, of reprieves and commutations of sentences, through each of which there is money to be made. In keeping with New York's special personality, Louis Glickman gave one special building another in a long series of reprieves, as well as made for himself—as he puts it with no small amount of pleasure—"one sweetheart of a deal."

He had also, in his own eyes at least, redeemed himself in the eyes of New York's artistic community. But that seems to have been secondary. What counted was the deal.

*Edward Clark had paid $200,000 for the land in 1877. When Louis Glickman was able to sell roughly half this land in 1961 for $2,000,000, it was clear that the value of West Side real estate had increased by 1,000 percent in a little more than eighty years.

Part Three

CO-OPERATIVE: "WITH OTHERS IN A COMMON EFFORT"

So long as people in the Park
  Can point to the Dakota,
Blessed be the name of Stephen Clark
  By his devoted quota—
Blessed be the name of Stephen Clark
  By his devoted quota!

FROM "Ballad of the Dakota"

Chapter 11

After the Crisis

AT THE DAKOTA no one paid too much attention to what had been the fate of the earlier luxury apartment houses that had preceded it on the New York scene. The Stuyvesant had been successful for a while, but as the Irving Place neighborhood deteriorated the Stuyvesant lost favor and was converted into a rooming house. In 1957 it was razed. The more ambitious building at 121 Madison Avenue was gutted and stripped of its balconied façade in 1940, and its sumptuous duplexes were divided into two- and three-bedroom apartments. Though the building still stands, it offers no clue to its former social pretensions. The Spanish Flats, though the apartments were luxurious, was not an economic success. It was torn down in 1927, and the only reminder of it is the Navarro Hotel, not far from where the Flats once stood, named after the Flats' architect. By 1905 West Twenty-third Street was no longer fashionable, and the Chelsea Apartments was converted into a full-scale commercial hotel. Oddly, though the neighborhood is somewhat seedy, the Chelsea is still a popular stopping-place, particularly for visitors from Europe who find its Old World, Edwardian charm comfortingly familiar.

At the Dakota, meanwhile, there had been occasional shivers of alarm about the building's future prior to the Christmas Crisis of 1960. Most of these anxious moments involved what a new Clark landlord might, or might not, want to do with the building. In the hierarchy of Clarkdom, Stephen C. Clark had been preceded as owner of the Dakota by his older brother, Edward Severin Clark, the very young man who had inherited the half-completed Dakota in 1882. Edward Severin Clark had been a shy, withdrawn child, and he grew to be a shy, withdrawn and gentle man. As an infant, he had been dropped by his nurse on a stone floor, and the damage to his legs had never properly been corrected. He walked with a pronounced limp. He preferred country to city life, and spent most of his time at Fenimore Farm, his estate in upstate Otsego County, where his friends affectionately referred to him as "Severino," and where his employees respectfully addressed him as "the Squire." He rarely visited the Dakota; when he did he usually stayed in one of the second-floor guest rooms. His huge sixth-floor apartment remained empty, its furniture under sheets and its Baccarat chandeliers in bags. His stays in the city were so brief that he did not feel it worth the trouble to take the big apartment out of its wraps. Nor did he ever seriously consider renting it. The fact that one of the largest spaces in the building produced no income seemed of no concern to him.

Perhaps because of his physical affliction, Severino Clark never married, and he devoted himself to philanthropies, among them a gymnasium and a hospital that he gave to Cooperstown. And since his apartment building never operated in the black, perhaps the Dakota could be added to his list of charities as well. He was proudest of his prize herd of Guernsey cattle, part of what was considered a model dairy farm. Most Dakotans had never met Severino Clark. After writing out their monthly rent checks to him, Edward S. Clark was forgotten.

Reassuringly, the rents were hardly ever raised. From time to time, from far off Cooperstown, polite suggestions came down from Severino Clark to the Dakota's manager:

Regarding the management of the dining room and kitchen for the coming season I would say, that while I do not wish to criticize Justin, or those who were under him, I do feel that it will be for the best interest of all concerned to have an entire new force in that department, also the same as to the dining room, with the exception of Jean, who I would like to install in the second position and also to act as my waiter. However, if you find that this does not work satisfactorily it can easily be remedied later. I would also like to retain the baker, unless you have some good reason for making a change, for his work has always been most satisfactory; the rolls he makes have always been especially liked by my mother . . . it is not my wish to hamper you in any way with the management, as the responsibility rests with you.

In 1907 Clark commented on "the trouble we have experienced with noise from the dining-room pantry in washing the china," and suggested that "perhaps a vestibule on the pantry side might prove sufficient." The manager, Mr. Knott, replied that the passage between the dining room would be fixed, and added, "I may decide that it will be better to use that pantry for simply silver and glass and do all the dishwashing downstairs." Dealing with help in those pre-union days was never a problem, as Mr. Knott informed Mr. Clark: "Whatever we do with the kitchen will be with the distinct understanding that the slightest dissatisfaction ends the time of the individual and possibly means a clean sweep." Mr. Knott added that a laundry girl had fallen while stepping out of one of the elevators, but that the accident had been "by what seems to have been her own carelessness . . . Nothing broken except possibly a rib." As for the young man who had been operating the elevator, "We discharged the boy."

In other words, the stewardship of Edward Severin Clark remained kindly, paternalistic and distant, and few people who lived at the Dakota during those years had ever laid eyes on him. Then, in 1933, Severino Clark died, and left the building to his younger brother Stephen. Rumors immediately spread that the new owner had plans to sell it or tear it down. These fears, however, quickly turned out to be unfounded, and Mr. Douglass, then the building's manager, was able to reassure the tenants that Stephen Clark had "not the remotest intention" of razing the Dakota, remodeling it in any way, or selling off the protective rectangle of land containing the gardens and croquet and tennis courts (though it would not be long before he would decide to turn this acreage into a parking lot.) "Mister Stephen," Mr. Douglass announced, "will entertain none of the offers which have caused us consternation in past weeks. He has so informed me in person."

The building, which was about to celebrate its fiftieth birthday, would stand for at least another fifty years, said Douglass. With this good news a celebratory luncheon was given in the Dakota's dining room, with speeches and solemn toasts of felicitation and congratulation to the apartment building and its continued good health. Responding to a special toast that was raised to him, Mr. Douglass was almost moved to tears. "I wish," he said, "that I could express—that I could say a little more—about how deeply I feel about all this."

The situation in 1960 and 1961 was considerably more complex. The practice of turning rental buildings into co-operatives was still a relatively new one, and one which many of the tenants did not understand at all. In any building it is a complicated process, and in the Dakota's case—with so much nostalgia and emotionalism involved on the part of so many high-powered and temperamental people—it was even more complicated. To begin with, 35 percent of the tenants had to approve of the co-operative plan for it to go through. For another thing, money had to be raised, if the plan went through, by which individuals could purchase their apartments from the Glickman Corporation. Louis Glickman, meanwhile, was having money problems of his own.

"I'd closed the deal with the Clark Foundation with my own cash, you see, because of the time factor," Mr. Glickman says. "The Foundation wanted cash, and they wanted it right away—otherwise, no deal. I'd had no time to get any mortgage financing." Getting a mortgage, Glickman had supposed, would be easy. He had counted on obtaining financing from one of the many New York banks or insurance companies, but when he went forth to get it he encountered a chilly atmosphere. The Dakota, the banks felt, was just "too old." It was an idea whose time had passed. The services of an outside appraiser were called upon and the appraisal, when it was completed, contained the most discouraging news imaginable: The land on which the Dakota stood, plus the parking lot, was valued at $3,800,000. But the building itself was assigned to have "no value." This, said the appraiser, was because the Dakota was "basically outmoded both in exterior appearance and interior design . . . and because the building operates at a loss, and would do so even without rent control." To give their precious building "no value" was, to the Dakotans, to inflict it with the most heartless insult imaginable.

The team of Messrs. Gross, Jackson and Glickman even tried to approach the Clark Foundation again for a loan—even one as small as $500,000 would be appreciated. The Foundation replied, somewhat frostily, that it preferred to keep its capital "in liquid condition." At the time Louis Glickman, out of pocket some $4,600,000, was, as he remembers it, "not a very happy man."

Nor were the Dakotans happy. Without some sort of mortgage financing, which at the conclusion of the process would have been passed along to the co-operative, the tenants could not possibly afford to buy the building back from Glickman. And without financing Mr. Glickman would find himself the landlord-tenant of a seventy-five-year-old building that was losing money at an alarming rate. Finally, the Glickman Corporation had been turned down by every major New York bank and insurance company. Indeed, it looked as though the whole co-operative idea was about to fall through. At one emotional tenants' meeting during that uncertain period, both Ernest Gross and C. D. Jackson announced that if the plan failed, they would "leave the country" and "forever."

Mr. Glickman then consulted another New York real estate firm, Charles F. Noyes & Company, which suggested that he might do better shopping for a mortgage out of town, where the Dakota and its special problems were not as well known. Glickman turned to Chicago where, to his great relief, he found a mortgagor in the First National Bank of Chicago, which was acting as trustee for the General Motors Salaried Employees Pension Fund.* With this loan Glickman got his cash back, as well as a viable mortgage that he could pass along to the Dakota at the conclusion of the negotiations.

Next began the lengthy process of assessing and pricing individual apartments and selling them to their tenants. Now the New York banks were in a more helpful mood. In April 1961 the Chase Manhattan Bank offered to help tenants with one half of their purchase costs, and at an interest rate of just 3 1/2 percent for two years. This was good

---

*Curiously, considering the difficulties Mr. Glickman had obtaining a mortgage, he mistakenly remembers an entirely different mortgagor. "I got it from two Catholic fraternal orders in Chicago," he says. "One was the Knights of Columbus. The other, I think, was the Knights of Pythias."

news. A polling of tenants was started to determine which tenants wanted to buy and which did not. But suddenly there were unexpected difficulties in what was called "the musical chairs problem."

It was, indeed, a case of musical apartments. A number of Dakotans, understandably, had decided that they did not want or could not afford to buy their apartments, and they began making plans to move elsewhere. Others wanted to buy apartments, but not necessarily the ones they were living in at the time. Some wanted more space, some wanted less. Plans were conceived whereby walls would be cut through in order to annex adjoining rooms from other apartments, while still others wanted to divide certain larger apartments and turn them into several smaller ones. No one, it suddenly seemed, was entirely happy with the space he or she was being offered, and throughout the early summer of 1961 there was a great deal of bickering among the Dakotans, as well as a certain amount of wheeling and dealmaking as tenants haggled among themselves over concessions and trade-offs of apartments and pieces of apartments. Over this confused situation Ernest Gross, C. D. Jackson and Louis Glickman did their best to maintain some sort of order. Mr. Glickman worked on an apartment-pricing formula based on cubic footage, view, number of bathrooms, general condition and other matters. When prices were quoted there was more unhappiness. "A lot of people squawked," Glickman recalls, "but believe me I got them very reasonable prices." Indeed, by today's New York prices the Dakota's prices do seem reasonable. For seven rooms with two baths and three fireplaces, a typical price was $45,000. Lauren Bacall's fourth-floor spread facing the Park was priced at $53,340. The smallest flats —one-bedroom, one-bath, nonhousekeeping units that had been guest rooms on the second floor—were priced at $4,410.

But there was sudden consternation in the building when the New York *Times* published an article about the new Mayfair Tower that was to be erected next door, above what had been the parking lot. The *Times* described the project as a "middle-income development." This, to the Dakotans' way of thinking, sounded as though the immediate neighborhood would be drastically downgraded. Their proposed investments in the building would be damaged if the block slithered down to "middle income." Hastily, Mr. Glickman assured a tenants' meeting that the *Times* had its facts all wrong, as in fact it had.

Still, despite these setbacks, the building moved steadily toward its goal of becoming a co-operative and toward the necessary approval by 35 percent of the tenants. Thirty percent had approved, then 31. In June, however, a loud dissonant voice was suddenly heard. It belonged to one William J. Quinlan, a young lawyer who had been a resident of the building for thirty-one years, "since age one." In a fourteen-page, single-spaced typewritten memorandum, Mr. Quinlan objected to the way almost everything was being handled. He seemed to feel that there was an alternate way by which the tenants could keep their apartments without turning the building into a co-operative. Mr. Quinlan's notion seemed to be that the tenants could hold onto the building by exercising squatters' rights.

At the meeting that was quickly called to discuss the Quinlan uprising, Ernest Gross announced that he found the Quinlan memo "a confused document," and suggested that it be ignored. But it was not to be that simple. Mr. Quinlan had already gathered powerful supporters in the building, including Mr. Joseph J. Noble, another lawyer, and Jo Mielziner who, among other things, was one man in the Dakota whom nearly everyone liked. Presently Mr. Quinlan was calling tenants' meetings of his own, conspicuously not inviting Gross, Jackson or Glickman to attend them. All through June the Quinlan momentum gathered while the Dakota's original rescue team struggled to hang on to the reins. The new co-operative, technically a venture "with others in a common effort," was beginning to seem more like a rout.

William Quinlan, a tall, ruggedly built bachelor, lived with his widowed mother in a third-floor apartment. He had grown up in the Dakota in an era when he and his brother and sister were virtually the only resident children; they had amused themselves with hide-and-seek in the building's basement, and with a game involving lobbing ice cubes from their apartment window into the courtyard fountains. Bill Quinlan had no small amount of sentimental attachment to the building, but he and his mother were not a part of the building's unofficial power structure, as Gross and Jackson were. Gross and Jackson, Quinlan felt, were reacting to the building's situation too emotionally, almost hysterically, and were being high-handed and even haughty in assuming their roles as leaders. "They took the stance that the Dakota had to go co-operative, *or else,*" Quinlan recalls today. "They resented anyone who questioned their authority, or who suggested that there might be some sort of solution other than the one they wanted. They presented it as a take it or leave it situation. I've lived long enough to know that nothing in life is take it or leave it."

At the time, however, Quinlan was not long out of law school. He realized that he himself knew little about real estate law. But he also suggested that Jackson, a magazine publisher, knew even less and that Ernest Gross, whose field was international law, might also be out of his depth in real estate. What Quinlan proposed was reasonable enough. He suggested that a disinterested outside counsel be brought in—someone who was an expert in the field of real estate and, in particular, co-operatives—to answer three general questions: Did the Dakota *have* to become a co-operative, or was there another solution? If becoming a co-operative was the only answer, what rights did the tenants who did not want to join the co-operative have? And if it became a co-operative, what were the best terms that could be arranged? Quinlan suggested a real estate lawyer named Lewis M. Isaacs, a former chairman of the New York City Bar Association, and considered an authority on co-operative apartments.

C. D. Jackson's response to this suggestion was to summon Quinlan to his apartment, "rather in the fashion he'd use to summon a copy boy up to his office," says Quinlan. "He sat me down, and said, 'Now just what are you trying to do? What are your real motives in this? What do you expect to get out of this?' I felt insulted, and I told him so." Mrs. Jackson employed a somewhat different tactic. Encountering Quinlan's mother in a hallway, Grace Jackson said to Grace Quinlan, "Your son is such an *interesting* young boy." The two Graces smiled thinly at one another and parted.

By June 29 a considerable head of steam had been built up and a full meeting of the building was called. For this, Bill Quinlan appeared with Lewis Isaacs, whom he had hired on his own. From a psychological standpoint this may have been a mistake, because it was the first time that an unknown outsider had been brought into the proceedings, and to the highly charged Dakotans any outsider seemed to be coming from the enemy camp. Suddenly the arguments from Quinlan and those who backed him began to seem not only harebrained but arrogant and hostile. The meeting began stormily.

Then C. D. Jackson asked for the floor. Jackson was a man well versed in the uses of politics and oratory. He had made his way upward through the corporate jungle of Time, Inc., and was one of Henry R.

Luce's right-hand men. (He had done so, furthermore, against no small handicap because, as it was mentioned earlier, C. D. Jackson was Jewish, and few Jews had been able to achieve positions of importance in Mr. Luce's empire.) Mr. Luce particularly admired Jackson's ability as a public speaker, for Luce himself often became inarticulate and ill-at-ease behind a lectern.

In a voice heavy with emotion, Jackson began with a recital of the parlous events the building had endured during the preceding months —how, late one Friday afternoon on December 16, 1960, Mr. William J. Zeckendorf (Jackson pronounced the name with loathing) had made an offer to the Clark Foundation, had given the Foundation until Monday noon to accept it, and had planned to tear their precious building down; how, moving quickly, he and Gross had met with Louis Glickman, who had agreed to make the Foundation a better offer— out of his own pocket—and had been able to get the Dakota's death sentence postponed. Now Glickman was in the final stages of turning the building into a co-operative, and all his noble work was being undermined and undone by William Quinlan. Tears welled in his eyes as he spoke, and Louis Glickman quietly dabbed at his cheeks with a white handkerchief. It was Jackson's finest moment, and when he finished, the meeting rose to its collective feet and cheered.

An angry-faced Mr. Quinlan then asked to speak. He was greeted by jeers, boos, hisses and catcalls, along with cries to "Make it short!" He sat down without a further word. Then Ernest Gross stood up to make his own stirring speech, in which he concluded, "Each of you—each and every soul in this room—must make up his or her own mind whether or not to cross the Rubicon!" This was greeted with more cheers, and in a frenzied scene of shouting, yelling, jeering, stamping, chair-banging, with motions being made, seconded and withdrawn, the June 29 meeting broke up.

By July 10 more than the required 35 percent of the tenants had agreed in favor of the co-operative plan. But as late as mid-September Bill Quinlan was still articulating his objections, refusing to buy his apartment, refusing to move out, still talking about squatters' rights— as he would go on doing until, in the end, he faced the fact that squatters' rights did not apply. On October 12 a "gala party" was announced, held in the Dakota's courtyard, and all the tenants and new stockholders in the building were invited. In a gracious gesture the builders of the Mayfair Tower next door were also invited. For the occasion all the staircases and window ledges of the building were decorated with lighted candles. The party was black tie. Cocktails were served at the Henry Blanchards', and dinner was at Mrs. Davenport West's. Zachary Scott, arriving late, rushed upstairs to get into his dinner jacket. People sat on floors and on the stairs, and at the end of the evening—since it was nearly a year since the Christmas Crisis had occurred—a huge birthday cake to the Dakota was brought out, sprouting a single candle.

A month later, on November 15, 1961, the Dakota made its formal transfer from the Glickman Corporation into the hands of the stockholders of the Dakota, Inc. And the Quinlans began making preparations to move out.

There would be other empty apartments now besides the Quinlans.' The Dakota, which had been so proud that it had never had to advertize or hang out an "Apartments Available" shingle, now found it practical to do so. The new board of directors ruled against a shingle, but it did agree to advertise. The Dakota's first ad, in December 1961, did its best to be both persuasive and dignified. It read:

THE DAKOTA

NUMBER ONE WEST 72ND STREET

FACING CENTRAL PARK

THE NEW YORK TRADITION THAT IS

NOW A CO-OPERATIVE

Because it is The Dakota, it is a residence of established worth. Because it is The Dakota, it is the original rather than an attempt at a revival. Because it is The Dakota, it is a tradition in elegance that remains unique in New York's social history. At long last, the great iron gates are open again to apartment seekers. Apartments of impressive size, each with its own master-pieces of decoration. You are invited to inspect the few apartments still available, by appointment with the agent.

Though the Dakota was now indeed officially a co-operative, there were a few loose ends. There was the question, for example, of what to do with the empty, cavernous dining room on the ground floor. Now that every penny counted, the old dining room seemed a particularly flagrant example of wasted space. There was interest on the part of the Explorers' Club to acquire the dining room as a meeting place, but the tenants were reluctant to accept the in-and-out traffic of strangers and outsiders that a club house in the building would involve.

Designer Ward Bennett, meanwhile, had a novel idea for creating an apartment where none had existed before. In the pyramid-shaped central gable that rose above the roof, which had previously been a storage area, Bennett proposed to insert a north-facing skylight and to design a novel living space. The result was a dramatic rooftop aerie with views in all directions. Within the pyramid he built a four-room duplex, the two levels connected by a spiral staircase. The base of the Dakota's massive central flagpole now extends upward through the center of Bennett's dining-room table up through his ceiling. On windy days his dining room creaks like a ship at sea.

But other problems were less easily solved. Most Dakotans had never ventured above the seventh floor. After all, there was no need to. Floors eight and nine, in the original plan, had been designed to contain a great many tiny servants' rooms, laundry rooms, storage rooms and attics, but the eighth and ninth floors were not at all alike. The eighth floor had become a kind of social buffer zone between the luxuries of the seven floors below and the austerities of the ninth floor. Several attractive apartments had been created on the eighth floor, including those of Rex Reed, Sheila Herbert, Edward Downes and David Marlowe, but much of this floor consists of single rooms, without kitchen or housekeeping facilities, connected by a maze of hallways. The ninth floor, on the other hand, is nothing but cells, many of them without windows, and is almost relentlessly dreary. On the ninth floor one felt as though one had left the Dakota and New York completely, and had stepped into the passageways of some strange, gone-to-seed hotel in the British Midlands. Bare light bulbs dangled from broken sockets. Plaster sagged from long-ago leaks. The bare pine floors were embedded with decades of dirt. And yet for all this, it seemed that quite a number of people were living in some of the unappetizing spaces on both eight and nine.

Over the years the cubicles on the Dakota's top two floors had accumulated what could only be described as leftover people. Some were former retainers of families who had died or, in a manner reminiscent of *The Cherry Orchard*, had moved away and forgotten to take their servants with them. Ambassadors, particularly from politically volatile Portugal, had had a way of being assigned to New York and then being called home. When they arrived they brought their servants with them, and when they were recalled—usually in haste—the servants were often left behind, or chose to remain in the land of golden opportunity. In the upper garrets of the building, a sizable Portuguese-speaking population had managed to collect. The top two floors were sometimes redolent with the pungent smells of Portuguese peasant cuisine, as olive-skinned women in kerchiefs and aprons carried steaming dishes through the narrow corridors between their rooms and several primitive communal kitchens where they cooked. Some of those people lived rent-free.

The eighth and ninth floors had also attracted a number of young unmarried gentlemen who, for very little rent, had taken single rooms. Many of these young men had theatrical ambitions—as actors, dancers, chorus boys—and had been drawn to the Dakota by the fact that it was known as an address of stars. Often these young men had roommates who changed with some frequency. Others were former roommates whose sponsors had moved out and who had been left to fend for themselves.

Moreover, over the years the Dakota had gained a certain reputation for inducing longevity among its tenants, and a number of the residents of floors eight and nine were far from the full bloom of youth. There was old Jimmy Martin, for example, who had once sung and danced for Flo Ziegfeld; after an accident in which his eye had been injured by a piece of flying scenery, he had worked as a window washer and later had become a valet for Mr. Frances La Farge when the La Farges lived at the Dakota. But the La Farges had long ago left the Dakota and had moved to a retirement community in Arizona. Jimmy Martin, no longer needed, stayed on in his attic room, surviving on occasional checks from Mr. La Farge.

Then there was Mrs. Fenton Maclay, also elderly and unwell (for many years the housekeeper-companion for old Miss Leo, the building's most notable eccentric), who shared garret space with her son Robert. In similarly cramped quarters—a former laundry room with a small unventilated closet for a kitchen—lived the ill and aging Brown-

ing sisters, Miss Edna and Miss Adele, spinster daughters of the founder of the Browning School, which had educated the Rockefeller
brothers. The Brownings had been born in the Dakota in the early
1890's.

All these were people who, if evicted, would have absolutely no place
to go and who, it began to seem, had indeed acquired some kind of
squatters' rights. The building, in what appeared to be its infinite
kindness and tolerance, had found it simpler to let these strays and
leftovers remain where they were. In fact, at the time the "tradition
in elegance" became a co-operative in 1961, no one had the slightest
idea of who—or how many—inhabited the cubbyholes on eight and
nine. Furthermore, considering the confusing nature of the relation-
ships that existed up there, and the mind-boggling labyrinth of corridors and passageways that connected them all, there was no easy way
to find out. Just as New York had its congested Lower East Side, the
Dakota had its floors eight and nine.

THE OCCUPANTS of the lower seven floors were too busy congratulating
themselves on saving the building to give too much heed to the status
of the attic dwellers. But even for the more affluent First Class passengers on the S.S. Dakota there were problems. Inevitably, in the musical-
chairs process, there had been slip-ups. For example, one tenant, Mrs.
Alice Bloeme, had never been served with the proper legal papers to
purchase her apartment, and it had accidentally been sold to Frederick
Victoria, the antiquary, who had planned to move into Mrs. Bloeme's
place and then sell his own. Alas, he discovered that Mrs. Bloeme was
still the statutory tenant of her apartment, fully protected under the
old rent-control laws, and that there was no way she could be legally
evicted. Nor would Mrs. Bloeme volunteer to move out. She saw no
reason to. For the next ten years Mr. Victoria would be in the unhappy
position of having to pay the large—and steadily growing larger—
monthly maintenance charges on Mrs. Bloeme's apartment while she,
as his legal tenant, continued to pay her modest controlled monthly
rent to him. It was not until 1976 that Mr. Victoria was able to sell
Mrs. Bloeme's apartment to her—and at the 1961 price, a discouraging
$5000. She, then, was able to sell her apartment for $68,288.

On one of several visits to his unwanted tenant, in a futile attempt
to get Mrs. Bloeme to change her mind, Freddie Victoria noticed that

one wall of her apartment was covered with a collection of gold discs, rather like the gold and platinum records that musical performers receive when their albums have sold a certain number of copies. But Mrs. Bloeme's discs were smaller than record discs. When Mr. Victoria asked about them, Mrs. Bloeme explained that the discs were trophies won by her son, who was United States National Frisbee Champion.

"I think that's rather appropriate to the Dakota," says Mr. Victoria a little grimly, "that, in addition to everything else we have had the National Frisbee Champion in the building. It could only happen here."

Chapter 12

The Old-Timers

EVERYONE AGREED that something had to be done about old Miss Leo. There was great speculation about her actual age. In 1966 she said she was ninety-four, but some said she was really a hundred and three. Probably at that point even Miss Leo did not know for sure. No one knew much else about Miss Leo, for that matter. Where had she come from? What had brought her to the Dakota? What did she live on? All anyone knew was that she lived in one of the largest apartments in the building, seventeen rooms on the ground floor, and had lived there longer than most Dakotans could remember.

One seldom saw Miss Leo. She hardly ever went out, and never had anyone in to her apartment. But when she did appear, her appearance was memorable—a tiny, shriveled woman with dyed red hair, more rouge and paint and eyeshadow than it seemed her little face could hold, wearing picture hats, turn-of-the-century chiffon dresses whose hems trailed on the floor, bedecked with rings, bracelets, necklaces and brooches; she caught the eye.

Freddie Victoria spotted Miss Leo one blizzardy night. She was huddled in the archway outside the Dakota's gate, waiting in the drifting snow for a taxi that was clearly never going to come. Freddie asked her if he could be of assistance. "My poor brother is trapped in his office because of the storm," she explained. "I'm trying to get a taxi to go and collect him and bring him home." Freddie Victoria's car was parked nearby, and he offered to drive her to her brother's office. "That would be very kind," Miss Leo said. She gave him an obscure address on the far West Side in an area of abandoned docks and warehouses.

In the car Miss Leo said, "My poor brother works all day in his office. He's an inventor, you see. All day long he invents things." When Victoria located the address—from the outside it looked like a derelict packing shed—there was Miss Leo's elderly brother standing in the doorway waiting. Victoria then drove both Leos back to the Dakota. It was one of the few direct encounters anyone in the building had had with them.

The next morning a case of Dom Perignon champagne was delivered to Freddie Victoria's door.

The older Miss Leo got, the odder she became. A neighbor named Katz became concerned about a persistent banging on pipes in his dining-room wall, and blamed the Quinlans' children for the disturbance. When the Quinlan children were proven innocent, Mr. Katz had the entire wall taken out but was unable to locate the source of the banging. Eventually it was discovered. It was Miss Leo, next door, banging on the wall with her cane. She had already hammered a hole eight inches deep in the masonry. She passed her time that way, she said. She was persuaded to tack a piece of foam-rubber padding on her banging wall.

Miss Leo had an obsession about germs, and wore plastic Baggies on her hands to protect them from contamination. One of few outsiders ever permitted to enter her apartment was a plumber, called in to repair a broken pipe. The plumber found his work considerably impeded by the fact that Miss Leo insisted on following him about, wiping down everything he touched with Lysol. Gradually, Miss Leo moved into a world of dream. Her apartment was unusual in that it had its own stairway to the basement. One night, the night porters were startled to see a pale apparition moving slowly through the shadowy arches and were sure for a moment that it was another ghost. But it was only Miss Leo, singing happily to herself. She was stark naked.

Originally, Miss Leo and her bachelor brother had shared the big apartment with their mother. But Mother had departed long ago, and now it was just Miss Leo and Brother. No one ever discovered what Brother's "inventions" were, but he had a conspicuous hobby. He collected medieval suits of armor, swords, lances and maces. "The collection is priceless," Miss Leo used to say. "It is the most comprehensive collection of armor in the world. One day it will all go to the Metropolitan Museum." Long before, one of Miss Leo's favorite carriage horses had died, and she had had the animal stuffed, mounted and placed in her drawing room. He had then been fitted with a full suit of equestrian armor, and a suit of human armor was placed astride him, brandishing a lance. The stuffed horse and its rider were visible through Miss Leo's Seventy-second Street windows and became objects of curiosity to passers-by. After a while it became common to identify the Dakota as "the building with the stuffed horse in the window."

The only other member of the Leo household was Mrs. Fenton Maclay. Mrs. Maclay's role was as mysterious as the origins of the Leos. She was not a housekeeper, exactly—at least she received no salary for what she did. She was more like a companion, or family friend. And yet she was not really treated as a friend, either, because she never slept in the Leos' apartment, despite the many empty bedrooms. Mrs. Maclay would retire at night to her room beneath the eaves. In the old days Miss Leo and Mrs. Maclay had lunched together almost daily at the Plaza. But by 1961 Miss Leo had settled on a steady diet of mashed bananas which Mrs. Maclay prepared at home. Miss Leo also had her own theories about sleeping. She could not sleep, she explained, lying down, and so she always slept sitting upright in a canvas deck chair in her entrance foyer.

During the day Miss Leo sat in the dining room, next to her banging wall, where the telephone was, to be near the phone in case anything should happen. Her brother, when not in his office, preferred to sit in a tall tapestry chair in the drawing room with the stuffed horse. Mrs. Maclay disliked going into the room with the stuffed horse but one day, attracted by a strange, unpleasant odor, she entered it. Brother had died in the tapestry chair. He had been dead for several days. Miss Leo had known it but could not bear the thought of his leaving her. He was removed by the Board of Health.

Though everyone assumed that Miss Leo was well-fixed financially, when the building was in the process of becoming a co-operative she announced that she could not afford to buy her apartment. The Dakotans looked around for a smaller place for her; one was located in the northeast corner of the ground floor. One of the people who volunteered to help Miss Leo move was Henry Blanchard. He recalls vividly his first sight of the interior of apartment 17. All the rooms were painted the same institutional green. Closets were filled with piles of ancient newspapers and magazines that reached to the ceilings. One of the windows had apparently been left open for years, and a thick layer of black New York dust covered everything. "As we packed her things," Henry Blanchard says, "clouds of dust swirled around us like fine, black snow." While Miss Leo was being moved, the armor collection, including the stuffed horse and its rider, stood for several days in the Dakota's courtyard to be wondered at by all the neighbors. And when Miss Leo was finally moved to her new apartment she left everything in the center of the floor where the movers had put it, and she never unpacked the barrels and cartons. When she died—at the age, some people said, of one hundred and nine—the Metropolitan Museum was contacted about the armor collection. The Museum's Department of Arms and Armor turned down the gift. All the pieces, it seemed, were fakes, and the stuffed horse, by then a sadly deteriorated piece of taxidermy, was carried away to a grave in New Jersey. Mrs. Maclay lived on in her attic room. She lives there to this day.

Several years later apartment 17 was bought by Lawrence Ellman, a New York restaurateur and his wife. The Ellmans redecorated the apartment lavishly in a *belle-époque* style, covering the once-green walls with expensive fabrics. In the process of the renovation a plumber uncovered what appeared to be a sunken bathtub. As he dug in the floor the sunken tub got bigger, wider and deeper. "How much more should I dig?" he asked the Ellmans. "Dig till you get to the bottom of it," Mr. Ellman told him. When the plumber finished digging he had uncovered what amounted to a small swimming pool, measuring about 8 by 10 feet and 5 1/2 feet deep. The Ellmans lined it with blue tile and installed a ladder. The pool, it turned out, antedated Miss Leo. It had been installed by an early tenant whose wife, so the story goes, liked to fill it with milk for baths. "When he was about ten years old," Elaine Ellman says, "my stepson went through a period when he didn't like to take baths. But when we uncovered the little pool he wanted to take baths all the time. We told him he could, provided he used plenty of soap."

Even more mysterious, as the Ellmans redecorated, were the silver-dollar-sized indentations in the floors of certain rooms and corridors. "We couldn't figure out what caused these strange holes," Elaine Ellman says. Then it dawned on them. The holes had been where the various heavy swords, sabres, maces and lances had stood on display.

Not far down the hall from Mrs. Maclay lives Jimmy Martin in a room with his elderly nephew George. Jimmy Martin celebrated his ninety-third birthday in May 1978, and is therefore of roughly the same vintage as Mrs. Maclay. Jimmy Martin and Mrs. Maclay do not get on. Mrs. Maclay had been using what had once been a maids' kitchen to do her cooking, and since the kitchen was on a communal hallway, Jimmy Martin asked whether he could use it too. Mrs. Maclay flatly refused. There has been bad blood between the two nonagenarians ever since, and when Jimmy Martin is in the vicinity of Mrs. Maclay's room he will sometimes bang his fists on the walls or on her door just to rattle her up a bit.

In fact, there are not too many people in the building with whom Jimmy Martin gets on. A particular enemy is actress Ruth Ford. It started a long time ago when Jimmy Martin was coming into the building with an armful of groceries and was having trouble getting his burden through the door. Miss Ford happened to be coming into the building at the same time and held the door open for him. But Jimmy was still having trouble with his parcels, and finally, impatient, Miss Ford said, "I'm not a doorman, you know." "She's a bitch," says Jimmy Martin. "I said to her, 'You bitch! If you'd stop bleaching your hair, maybe some of it would grow back!'" Miss Ford feels no more generous toward Jimmy Martin, calling him "a seedy, disagreeable, pretentious little man. In the summer he goes up on the roof and sunbathes in his undershirt—sunbathing, at his age." "Ha! She was a chorus girl who worked for the Schuberts," replies Jimmy Martin, making light of the fact that Ruth Ford is also an actress for whom William Faulkner expressly wrote his only play, *Requiem for a Nun.*

Of other neighbors in the building Jimmy Martin is more charitable, referring to Roberta Flack as "a fine colored woman—she's going to give a birthday party for me." And he is even more enthusiastic in his recollection of his own theatrical career, which started in the synagogue of Rabbi Stephen Wise, where he was a choirboy, and carried him to Broadway and vaudeville. He appeared in the Ziegfeld Follies and in such long-forgotten shows as *Mary, The Wild Cat, The Wanderer, Molly Darlin'* and *Hoker Poker.* "See how I've kept my figure?" Jimmy Martin says proudly, and to show he has also kept his form, he executes a few quick dance steps and, in a fluty vibrato, sings a few notes from *Hoker Poker.* In one show, the name of which he has forgotten, one of the lead performers became ill. "I was in the chorus, and I jumped into the show. George M. Cohan said, 'Had it not been for the brains of Mr. Martin, I would have had to close the show'—I made two hundred and seventy-five dollars a week."

Jimmy Martin is still bitter about the fact that after his eye injury he was denied a pension by the Actors' Fund: "They're crooked people in the Actors' Fund," he says. When the building became a co-operative, and inherited such problems as what to do with people like Jimmy Martin, who was then well into his seventies and had no regular source of income, the Dakotans—not altogether cheerfully, and not exactly unanimously—agreed to chip in to buy him an insurance policy that would yield him a small annuity.

Today, Jimmy Martin's little room is hard to reconcile with a deluxe apartment house or a "tradition in elegance." It is cluttered with piles of old clothes, pillows that are losing their stuffing, an ancient sofa covered with a soiled sheet that serves as Mr. Martin's bed. The walls are cracked and peeling, in want of paint. There is one window. A small refrigerator holds soft drinks, which Jimmy Martin offers to visitors. For cooking there is an electric frying pan and a Roto-Broiler. "I love to cook," he says, stroking his full head of astonishingly black hair. "And I'm a very good cook. Tonight, for example, for my nephew and myself, I'm fixing chop suey. I have no regrets. I have wonderful memories of the theater and the people I knew—Mr. Cohan, Mr. Ziegfeld, Will Rogers, Geraldine Farrar, George E. Hale, Florence Eaton and Nance O'Neill. Now I sit here and enjoy my lovely room. We live a life of luxury."

Over the years, to be sure, some of Jimmy Martin's Dakota neighbors have become a little weary of his tart and acerbic appraisals of them. Of the Henry Blanchards: "They're nice enough." Of Mrs. C. D. Jackson: "Thumbs down on her!" (Grace Jackson sighs and says, "That poor insurance company—I'm sure they never thought that annuity we bought for him would go on so long.") Of Lauren Bacall: "She's had her face lifted." Still, he conceded that when the movie crew came to film *Rosemary's Baby,* Miss Bacall suggested to the producer that Jimmy Martin be hired as an extra, and he was. "You can even see me in the picture," he says. "I made forty-eight dollars!"

Financially, the Browning sisters are not in the same category as Jimmy Martin. Though not rich, the Brownings were left with enough money to keep them comfortable, and they live in their small, eighth-floor room with its closet-kitchen not so much out of necessity as out of choice. "It's easier in a small place, there's less to care for," Miss Adele says. Miss Adele is almost blind and very deaf. When architect Paul Segal, next door, was remodeling his apartment, he became concerned that the noise of hammering and electric saws might be disturbing the elderly Brownings. Segal rang the Brownings' bell, and when Miss Adele answered it Segal offered a lengthy apology for the noise. When he had finished, Miss Adele cupped her hand to her ear and said, "What?"

Miss Adele Browning still speaks in a clear, cultivated voice, however —the voice of a daughter of a leading educator of his time—and still gets out to do the marketing for herself and her invalid sister who fell and broke her hip in 1978. "My memory flickers . . . flickers," she says in that rich voice. "Let's see—what do I remember? I remember when women first got the vote, and I went out to vote with Dad. Dad said he wouldn't tell me who to vote for, I had to decide myself. In the summers we went up to a place we had in Ossining. Mother chose the place, and boys from Dad's school would go up there for weekends. Dad was very interested in racial equality, years ahead of his time. He wanted to experiment raising whites, blacks, yellows and reds together. Dad was a wonderful man, but Mother always had the last word when it came to raising us. Dad would say, 'Me for Mom'—the first woman governor had just been elected in the state of Texas and that was her slogan, so that was Dad's little joke, you see. I remember when the Eighth Avenue subway first came through—that was quite an issue. I remember we could see the Essex House across the Park, where Presidents used to stay. I remember the Theo Steinways lived next door, in apartment forty-six. His son went to the Browning School, and the son went on to invent the first upright piano. But when my sister and I took piano lessons, Mr. Steinway had to ask Dad to move the piano to another part of the apartment because he didn't like our playing. My memory flickers . . . Dad used to say, 'Blessed is she who expecteth nothing, for then she will not be disappointed.' Dad wanted us to be independent. . . ."

During World War II, Adele Browning served as an air-raid warden for the building, and she still likes to go up and down the long corridors of the eighth floor, checking on the security of everything. And she demonstrated her independence during the filming of *Rosemary's Baby*. "There were lights and cameras all around the building," she recalls. "I was coming home from an errand, and the policeman said to me, 'Lady, you'll have to go in through the basement.' " The officer may not have been able to tell from Miss Adele's appearance that he was addressing a woman of substance and culture. Like many older people, Miss Adele tends to dress in the same sort of costume day after day—a buttoned, brown wool skirt, several layers of sweaters topped by a woolen vest, woolen athletic socks over her stockings, and house slippers. Also, she has little time to spend at the hairdresser's. In any case, the policeman was unprepared for the very determined, self-assured and erect little lady who confronted him and, in that strong, well-bred voice said, "I will *not* go in through the basement. I live here. I was born here. This is my *home*. I will enter my home through my front door."

She was allowed in through the front door.

MISS ANNE IVES is still another kind of Dakota old-timer—a nonagenarian with a career. Miss Ives is an actress and, at ninety-two, manages to supplement her pensions by doing television commercials. With her petite figure, her carefully coifed white hair, her creamy-pink complexion and arresting purple eyes she could pass for a woman in her early seventies. Her looks make her the ideal candy-box-top grandmother type for television. Anne Ives is a graduate of the American Academy of Dramatic Arts (called the Sargeant School in her day) and, among other things, has played with Henry Fonda in *Point of No Return*, with Irene Worth in *Hedda Gabler* and in various stock companies in Stockbridge and Abingdon. For years she was a Sunday Bible-story lady on radio in Washington, D.C., and her most recent stage performance was as the little old lady in *Tobacco Road*, which she did in Lake Forest and for which she received a special award. Most recently, however, it has been television commercials.

"My AT&T commercial has been doing very well in terms of residuals," she says. "My Birdseye I did three years ago and that keeps coming back. My yogurt comes back, and I expect a lot from my cat food. I've done a couple of print ads, but the money is in television." Compared with the Brownings, Miss Ives, who moved to the Dakota in 1954, is a newcomer, and her relative affluence permits her to live on a somewhat grander scale. Her one-room-with-bath apartment is on the second floor facing seventy-second Street, one of the former guest rooms that were set aside for visiting friends of tenants. She was able to buy this space with no difficulty when the building became a co-operative. Her room has high ceilings, a fireplace, and is furnished in dainty antiques. A handsome Oriental rug is on the floor, and her bathroom is painted royal purple, a color she also favors in clothes because it matches her eyes. To be sure, her kitchen is also her clothes closet, but from it she is able to prepare dinners for friends and, besides, "I get asked out a lot."

The main difference in the building that Miss Ives has noticed over the years is that, "When I came here the people were all the age that I am now—now I'm one of the oldest ones here. There are so many young people here now, so many more children. But I don't feel old. I'm in excellent health. My mother lived to be ninety-four. One thing I have noticed, though, as I get older is that I spend a lot of time at my window, looking out at the street. People are always stopping across the street to look up at this old building, and sometimes they see me, and sometimes I get a little wave. I always wave back. Not long ago a fire truck came by, and the fireman who was standing at the end of the ladder was right at the level of my second-floor window. He passed my window and saw me standing there, and he smiled and waved. I smiled and waved back. He was almost close enough to reach out and touch."

Miss Ives never married. "That's my sad story," she says. "I was going to, but it didn't work out." With a smile, she adds, "As it happened, he never married either. As far as family goes, I'm almost the last leaf on the tree. I have one niece who lives in Rhode Island, but, my goodness, my niece is in her seventies! But I have my career. I've always worked, and with what I have now I'll be able to live comfortably here for the rest of my life."

In contrast to Adele Browning, who tends to feel unsafe on the eighth floor ("We have to keep our door locked and bolted all the time"), Miss Ives has no feelings of insecurity in the building. "My room isn't air conditioned," she says, "but because it faces south, I never get direct sun beating in. On warm days, I just open my window and open the door, and a nice little breeze comes through." To indicate that she is "at home," and would welcome visitors, Miss Ives places a bowl of fresh flowers on a little table just outside her door.

Among her social activities she has her membership in the Twelfth Night Club, a women's theatrical group that meets weekly in the annex of the Woodward Hotel at Broadway and Fifty-fifth Street, and which recently celebrated its eighty-seventh birthday. "It was formed as a club for 'nice young ladies of the theater,' " she says, "but not long ago we looked around and saw that we were all women of about my vintage. Since then, we've brought in a number of nice young ladies. We put on one-act plays, once a week."

Only one small annoyance grieves Miss Ives at the moment. "A few months ago, I was a little bit unwell. It was nothing serious, just a little thing, and I'm quite fine now. But you know how this business is. The gossip travels so fast. The word got out—Anne Ives is sick, Anne Ives is on her last legs. I stopped getting calls from agents and producers for commercials. Well, I intend to go on working as long as I can remember lines. So now what I've got to do, now that I'm better, is go around ringing doorbells again to let the industry know that Anne Ives is alive and well and ready for more jobs. In fact, I'm thinking of having a little dinner party and inviting the agents and producers over, just to show them how alive and well and ready for jobs Anne Ives is."

Part Four

BOYS AND GIRLS TOGETHER

Where else the bounty of an age
Where space was undivided?
Where else the stately Otis cage
By gentlewomen guided? . . .

FROM "Ballad of the Dakota"

Chapter 13

Nuts and Bolts

LIKE SMALL towns and large cities everywhere, now that the Dakota was a fiscal entity of its own, no longer able to rely on Clark benevolence, one of the biggest problems the building faced was how to pay for the services it offered. What it had cost to staff and maintain the Dakota had never seemed to matter to the Clarks at all, and when the new resident-owners looked at the figures they came as something of a blow. In 1961, for example, the building had forty-five full-time employees, including three resident employees, or roughly one employee for every two tenant families—a crew-passenger ratio that had once been the boast of the old *Queen Mary*. To be sure, these people individually didn't earn much in salaries—salaries seemed to have been frozen, like the rents, at an 1880's level—and were making only $64 to $108 a week. Still, their wages added up to an annual payroll of about $225,000 a year, which seemed a staggering sum. The number of staff, it was decided, would have to be slashed by about one half.

It was a difficult and painful moment. Dismissing an old and trusted employee is never a pleasant task, and many of the Dakota's staff had never worked anywhere else, had grown old along with the tenants, considered the Dakota their home as well and were more like old family friends. The Dakota's maids and porters had baby-sat for Dakota families in their spare time, had run special errands, had moonlighted as butlers, bartenders and canapé-passers at Dakota parties. Still, in the name of economy, something had to be done, and the Dakotans consoled themselves with the thought that, after all, these people would have their pensions to live on.

So it was still another blow when the Dakotans discovered that the Clark family had never instituted any sort of employee pension or retirement plan at all. Nor had the Clark Foundation. Once more, the Dakotans appealed to the Foundation on the employees' behalf.

American charitable foundations, it has often been pointed out, may be in the business of dispensing large sums of money to the needy and the deserving, but in terms of the people who work for them they are notoriously tight. The Clark Foundation turned out to be no exception. When it was brought to the Foundation's attention that these long-time employees had served the family and the Foundation well and deserved some sort of pension, the Foundation huffed and puffed. For weeks it dragged its heels, claiming that it had "no obligation" to the Dakota's staff. The Dakota again approached Stephen Clark's widow who, though she had no decision-making power, agreed to lend her influence to the cause. Finally, and with great reluctance, the Foundation agreed to establish a pension fund. It did so very begrudgingly and not at all graciously, writing to the Dakota's board that, though it had "no legal responsibility" to take care of the employees, it would "in light of its charitable purposes" do so, provided such employees had "served faithfully" fifteen years or more. At the time, fourteen of the Dakota's staff had been with the building fifteen years or longer; eight had served twenty-five years or more; twenty were over sixty years old, and nine were over sixty-five.

The first to have to go, of course, would be the Mary Petty elevator ladies in their bombazine dresses. True, the elevator ladies, like Miss Leo's stuffed horse in the Seventy-second Street window, had been one of the building's enduring trademarks. Over the years the ladies had formed what amounted to their own little private club, and in their hours off they liked to gather in one of the basement rooms for tea and then read each other's tea leaves. The doyenne of these women was

Adela T. Ward, by then in her eighties, who bore a marked resemblance to Queen Victoria. But by automating and electrifying the elevators, the building would save $30,000 a year in labor and $16,000 a year in steam.

In order to automate the elevators, the building now had to deal with the bureaucracy of New York City building, elevator and fire inspectors. The Dakota had supposed that even though the elevator ladies would have to go, the fanciful openwork mahogany elevator cages could be saved. They were the oldest residential elevators in New York. Also, they were most curiously engineered and operated on a system that involved, of all things, the radiators in individual apartments. The building was still heated by the original steam radiators, which were built under windowsills. The radiators operated on a conventional two-pipe system, but with a third, added line: under each radiator in the building was a metal pan to catch drippage, and from all the pans a mare's nest of drainage lines ran down through the Dakota's innards to the cistern in the basement. This cistern also collected rainwater from the roof through another network of drains, and this was the water that provided the elevators' hydraulic power. Arcane though this plumbing arrangement sounds, it had worked successfully for nearly eighty years.

To be sure, the elevators were extraordinarily slow, but they were also exceptionally beautiful examples of almost-lost cabinetmakers' and millworkers' arts, each detail meticulously hand carved, and they were genuine antiques. Architecture expert Paul Goldberger still insists that the old cages *could* have been saved. But a variety of city inspectors pronounced them unsafe at any speed (though they had operated without mishap for nearly eighty years) and decreed that if the elevators were to be automated, "modern" cages must be installed. Though Jo Mielziner did his best in designing the new cages to recreate the spirit of the old ones—reproducing the bronze Indian heads on the paneled walls—Dakotans were as sad to part with their elevator cages as they were to part with the ladies. The new elevators, it turned out, were as slow or even slower than the old, and were much more erratic in terms of stopping on wrong floors.

When the old elevator cars were removed, the C. D. Jacksons asked for one of them. The Jacksons placed it in an archway between two rooms of their apartment where, with its little benches, it became a sitting alcove. Susan Stein thought she might use one of the cabs in her apartment too, and her father, MCA head Jules Stein, said, "If they're free, take two." So Susan Stein and her movie-producer husband, Gil Shiva, now have two elevators side by side in their apartment. The Shivas use the elevators as their bar, and twenty to thirty people can sit comfortably inside them. With the three old elevators being put to such imaginative uses, there was a sudden scramble for the fourth one, which, inexplicably, suddenly could not be found. Somehow, the fourth elevator had made its way out of the building. How this happened, or where it went, has never been determined.

New York, meanwhile, was rapidly moving into the age of air conditioning. But at the Dakota, a building that was designed to resist changes of any sort, air conditioning turned out to present especially difficult problems. Apartments could be centrally air conditioned, but this was expensive and involved lowering ceilings, which Dakotans were loath to approve. Window units could be installed, but defenders of the building's aesthetics considered these unsightly, and besides, they dripped water on the building's façade and on the heads of passers-by on the street below. One of the earliest chairmen of the Dakota's board of directors was Admiral Alan Kirk, a military man and decidedly a traditionalist. One of the first tenants to apply to the board for permission to install an air conditioner was Freddie Victoria, and Admiral Kirk's response was, "I don't have air conditioners. Why should anyone else?"

An alternative to window units was through-the-wall air conditioning. These systems were less obtrusive since they fitted flush against the exterior walls of the building but they required the removal of masonry, some of it richly ornamental. Freddie Victoria applied again for a through-the-wall unit, pointing out that his apartment faced the back of the building where such an installation would be well away from public view. Once more his request was denied. Throughout the early 1960's arguments about air conditioners continued, and tempers soared with the thermometer in a battle between modernists and preservationists. Meanwhile, several tenants went ahead and installed through-the-wall units anyway, and some window units sprouted, particularly from windows at the rear of the building.

In 1969 the New York Landmarks Preservation Commission officially declared the Dakota a city landmark. In its designation the

Landmarks Commission said, "The Dakota . . . is one of the earliest and most distinguished apartment houses in the United States . . . Overlooking the northern end of Central Park, the Dakota simultaneously affords its residents a magnificent view of the Park and presents an impressive appearance to passers-by. Its richly varied skyline makes this building a prime example of late nineteenth-century picturesque eclecticism . . . With its massive load-bearing walls, heavy interior partitions and double-thick floors of concrete, it is one of the quietest buildings in the city. . . . "

The Dakotans were initially delighted; they had, in fact, actively sought the landmark designation. Believing, rightly or wrongly, that they had helped the building narrowly escape the wreckers' ball, the Dakotans believed that now that they were a landmark, the building would be preserved until the end of time. Besides, living in a landmark seemed to carry such cachet. A small bronze plaque was affixed to one of the Dakota's Seventy-second Street cornerstones attesting to its special, hallowed status.

But the Dakotans soon discovered that being a landmark was a mixed blessing, to say the least. Yes, the designation conveyed no small amount of intangible prestige to the address. But the New York City Landmarks Preservation Commission offered no guarantee whatever that the building would be perpetually "preserved." The Landmarks Commission had no budget from which to offer funds for the preservation of old buildings, nor did being a landmark entitle an old building to any sort of special tax relief. What it meant was that no exterior changes to the Dakota could be made without the commission's approval. Ward Bennett could never have created his dramatic pyramid-shaped apartment with its two-story-high slanting skylight had he not done so before the building was declared a landmark. Furthermore, the Landmarks Commission could do little to prevent the Dakota's eventual sale to a developer who might want to tear down the building and replace it with a modern, more efficient structure. If such a situation were to arise, the Commission would have just one year in which to find a buyer who was willing to preserve the building. Failing that, the Commission would have no choice but to allow the building's sale to the developer.

Other old apartment houses—including 810, 834 and 960 Fifth Avenue, and the San Remo and the Beresford on Central Park West

—had been offered landmark status by the Commission and had resisted the temptation to accept it. So had the Osborne, at 205 West Fifty-seventh Street. In many ways, theirs was the more sophisticated decision. For the Dakota, it soon turned out, being a landmark was more of a burden than a boon. (In recent years some New Yorkers have begun to think of the Landmarks Commission's activities as a series of dreadful jokes; in 1979, for example, there was outrage among certain of the city's citizenry when the Commission designated as a landmark the subway kiosk at the corner of Seventy-second Street and Broadway.)

The Dakota now had to deal with the Commission on every detail concerning its exterior, and the Commission was just another division of New York City's bureaucracy with a foundation mentality. Among others, the question of air conditioners persisted. Once more, Freddie Victoria, a gentleman of persistence and also a man who believed in going by the rules, petitioned the Landmarks Commission for permission to install a through-the-wall unit, pointing out that there were already seven such units in the building. Once more, permission was denied. He next tried pleading his case in the press; he told the New York *Times* that he could not afford central air conditioning and that he felt that window units, which many Dakotans now had, obstructed light and views and sometimes required original windowpanes to be destroyed. "What is the point of having landmark preservation if one cannot have creature comforts," he wanted to know, "and if there are no benefits from the stigma of its hardships?"

Beverly Moss Spatt, the Commission's chairman, replied that "in general" her agency would "not permit through-the-wall units where any architectural element will be destroyed." Mrs. Spatt added that she would not have permitted the existing units if she had been chairman when they were installed. Taking Freddie Victoria's side, Lauren Bacall was more outspoken. The Landmarks Commission's attitude, she said, was "absolutely asinine. There is nothing as ugly as a window air conditioner. Unless we are going back to the Middle Ages, we should make living in the city as practicable and as palatable as possible in this age of electronics."

Freddie Victoria then tried another tactic and asked the Commission to let him install Thermo-Pane glass in his windows. Thermo-Pane, he felt, would help insulate his apartment from the summer heat as well as the winter cold, thereby cutting his fuel consumption and conserving energy. He pointed to the fact that his bedroom windowsills were already rotting from rainwater that was seeping in around ill-fitting windowpanes. The bureaucratic response from the Commission to this request was bizarre: "If the original architect had wanted Thermo-Pane glass in the windows, he would have installed them with Thermo-Pane."

Now Betty Bacall decided to throw herself full force into the battle to cool her apartment. Since no one in the building now had more experience in dealing with the Landmarks Commission than Freddie Victoria, she went to him for advice. Freddie agreed to take her case to the Commission. When Freddie appeared at the Commission's offices at 305 Broadway, he explained that he had come on behalf of another Dakota tenant who wished to install through-the-wall air conditioning in her apartment. The commissioner looked bored and unreceptive to the idea. "The tenant is Miss Lauren Bacall," Freddie said, and suddenly the commissioner looked more interested. After riffling through some files of landmarks regulations, the commissioner said hesitantly, "Will I get to meet Miss Bacall?" Freddie assured him that Miss Bacall would be happy to discuss the matter with the commissioner, and suggested that the commissioner "drop by for drinks with her on Thursday."

Before meeting with the commissioner, Freddie Victoria advised Miss Bacall to dress for the occasion in her sultry, sexy, movie-star best, and when the commissioner arrived on Thursday he was not greeted by the earthy, salty, sardonic and self-mocking woman—New York housewife and mother of three who usually tossed an old sweater over her blouse and slacks when she went out to walk her dog in the park—that the Dakotans knew as a neighbor. He was greeted instead by a radiant Lauren Bacall, the Hollywood Legend. She received permission to install her through-the-wall unit. To be sure, there were a few strings attached. She had to agree to save and store and catalogue and label all the bricks and stone removed to make way for her air conditioner, and to promise that if she ever vacated the apartment she would either restore the façade to its original condition or else secure an agreement from the new purchaser that he or she would do so.

But she got her air conditioner—much, needless to say, to the disgruntlement of other tenants in the building who did not happen to be Lauren Bacall, and who continue to complain about how Miss Bacall got her air conditioner. Freddie Victoria, for instance, is still without air conditioning and still has rotting, leaking windowsills.

The Landmarks Commission quickly became the Dakota's albatross, and the ironies of the situation were not lost on the Dakotans. Earlier, various city agencies had insisted on condemning the splendid old elevator cabs as "outmoded," and had forced the building to install modern ones. Now here was another city agency that was refusing to let them modernize anything at all. In 1973 the Dakota's board decided that the building's intricate roof was badly in need of repair. Slates had loosened and fallen off. The copper trim had come loose and, in some places, had corroded. There were leaks. Cast-iron chimney caps had broken off and finials and statuary needed attention. A roof is obviously an exterior detail, and so the Landmarks Commission's approval was needed before any work could be undertaken.

The Commission was nothing if not solicitous in the matter. It pored over the Dakota's original plans and brought in experts and technicians from a variety of fields—architectural, structural and historical. It spent months inspecting the roof, and when all the outside studies had been gathered and collated and cross-indexed, the Commission came up with its recommendation: a full restoration was what was needed. It would cost about a million dollars, which would amount to an average assessment of roughly $10,000 for each of the building's tenant families. Collectively the Dakotans groaned. Ultimately, and only after a great deal of heel-dragging, the Commission agreed to a more modest patch job—one that would only cost about $160,000.

But the roof was only the beginning. The new elevators were already in need of repair, and so was the central plumbing system. Altogether, an additional $500,000 was needed to attend to these urgent matters, and no one knew where the money was to come from.

Some Dakotans argued that through the Landmarks Commission city funds should be made available to keep up at least the exterior of the old building. Restaurateur Warner LeRoy says, "I'm a great believer that the city should keep up the façades of landmarks. If the façade of the Dakota were sandblasted, it would be absolutely fantastic, one of those things that would keep the city alive." But Commission chairman Beverly Spatt, while conceding that the tenant shareholders couldn't afford to spend the kind of money needed, said that if funds were granted for the Dakota "then maybe two hundred other requests would come in, and I don't think the city is prepared to handle such a situation."

Others suggested that a tax abatement would help give the building funds with which to do its own restoration. Economists pointed out that as the maintenance and operating costs of a building rise, a building becomes a less attractive place to live. In a spiral of rising costs the building could "succumb to success," and would eventually have to be sold to a developer and destroyed—the very thing the Landmarks Preservation Commission was designed to prevent.

One thing was certain. Between 1969, when the Dakota had received its landmark designation, and 1972, the tenants' maintenance charges rose 42 percent to $439,988 a year, and there was no indication that they would not rise still higher. Clearly, to be a landmark was expensive. The Lawrence Ellmans, who bought Miss Leo's old apartment, considered it "grossly big," and sold off 40 percent of it. Soon, however, their maintenance charges were more than when they divided the apartment. Rex Reed, who watched his monthly maintenance bills nearly double in four years' time, describes it as "an incredible nightmare. The mechanics are impossible. Repairs and alterations cost five times what they cost in an ordinary building. The financial feasibility of the building boggles the mind." He adds, somewhat weakly, "But it's worth everything you go through—I guess."

But the question began to be, how long would it be worth it? At the point when the Landmarks Commission seemed to be absolutely insistent that the Dakota install a million-dollar new roof, some Dakotans wondered if there might be a way to have the building *un*declared a landmark. But that, it seems, is not the way things work down at New York's City Hall. A landmark designation is not reversible. Once a building is declared a landmark, the Commission feels, a landmark it must remain—even though the little bronze plaque seems to carry with it the kiss of death.

Part Five

PROBLEMS
AND SOLUTIONS

Nay, not for us the steel and glass,
The click of automation—
In our mahogany and brass
Is true luxuriation—

And we in our Dakoterie
Are stalwart in defiance
Of all that tokens slavery
To the parade of science.

from "Ballad of the Dakota"

Chapter 14

The Park

CITY DWELLERS everywhere tend to be passionately chauvinistic about their parks, and it is not hard to see why. Parks remind urban men and women that the metropolis has not forsaken the countryside, and that greenery can coexist with asphalt and concrete. San Franciscans are fiercely proud of Golden Gate Park, Bostonians of the Common, Washingtonians of Rock Creek Park, Londoners of Hyde Park and Parisians of the Bois. Central Park is unquestionably one of New York's greatest civic centerpieces and showplaces. Simply, appropriately and unpretentiously named, and elegantly laid out, the Park is one of the things that makes New York life possible and gives it an oasis. To the Dakotans, the Park is even more: it is their front yard.

When the city purchased the acreage for Central Park in 1856, it did so not a moment too soon. Had it waited just a few more years it would have been too late. The land would have become far too valuable as commercial real estate, and what is now preserved as Central Park would be covered with asphalt and masonry.

The concept of Central Park was grandiose in scale, considering the fact that in the 1850's the Park was by no means "central" to city life. It was, however, placed in roughly the center of Manhattan. It was an even half-mile wide and two and a half miles long which gave it over eight hundred acres, or more than twice the size of London's Hyde Park, which, prior to Central Park, had been the epitome of big-city parks. To Londoners in 1856 the size of New York's new park seemed outrageously pretentious. New York was a city of less than 700,000 people; London's population was 2,363,000, more than three times as large. The park took nearly ten years to build and cost over nine million dollars, a staggering sum in those days. By the end of the Civil War, most of the work on the park had been completed, though the problem of squatters' shacks—particularly in the park's northern reaches— would continue for a number of years.

When the city commissioned Frederick Law Olmsted to design the park, it displayed a rare genius and sensitivity. Hardly ever before in the history of the United States had the principles of art been applied to the embellishment of nature or the landscape in a public park. Olmsted laid out walks, fountains, lakes, formal gardens, five miles of bridle paths, vistas, great grassy areas and a wide quarter-mile-long Mall leading into the park from its main entrance at Fifty-Ninth Street and Fifth Avenue. Other sections were left wild and wooded with a ground cover of wildflowers. As one of the great landscape artists of the century, Olmsted went on to design Prospect park in Brooklyn, Morningside and Riverside parks in Manhattan, Fairmont Park in Philadelphia, South Park in Chicago, Mount Royal Park in Montreal and the campus of Stanford University in California. But he always considered Central Park his most important achievement.

The Park's effect on the social habits of New Yorkers was immediate and profound. For one thing it brought the city's rich and poor together for the first time. To be sure, in those decorous days the sense of class differences was deeply ingrained, and the rich and the poor, when they entered Central Park—the rich in their smart carriages and the poor on bicycles or on foot—maintained respectful distances. Before the completion of Central Park it had been unthinkable for a lady to ride horseback in the city. Well-bred ladies rode, but only in the privacy of their country places. Just ten years earlier Fanny Kemble had scandalized the city by riding her horse down Broadway. But then Fanny was an actress, and a certain amount of unorthodox behavior was expected of her. Now all that was changed, and for a lady to ride her horse in the Park—accompanied, of course, by her groom or riding master—was suddenly *comme il faut*. The fashionable riding hour for ladies was in the morning, before breakfast. That was when scores of society women trotted out in their gray face veils, high-buttoned jackets and long riding skirts, riding sidesaddle or "the Queen's seat" as it was called. Members of *real* society, of course, had their own private stables. But the Dakota, not to be outdone, maintained a stable for tenants at Broadway and Seventy-third Street, two blocks away.

In good weather a feature of New York life became the afternoon carriage parade, between four and five o'clock, along the Mall. For this, everyone turned out—the old rich, the *nouveaux* and members of the demimonde. Throngs of curious onlookers and tourists lined the entrance to the Mall to observe this unique phenomenon and to catch glimpses of Mrs. Astor, Mrs. Belmont and Mrs. Vanderbilt in their elegant carriages. One could also usually spot this or that famous actress of the day, a celebrated courtesan or two, and Josephine Wood, the mistress of New York's most expensive fancy-house. One of the snappiest equestrian outfits belonged to the notorious Madame Restell, society's most popular abortionist. The seats of her barouche were covered with rabbit fur, her tack was of sterling silver, her coachmen wore gold epaulets and on her horses' heads were cockades of ostrich plumes.

Status was conveyed by the sort of carriage one drove. The Old Guard enclosed themselves behind the closed and curtained doors of the broughams. Landaus, which could be either closed or opened to display their occupants in their finery, were for the more daring and sophisticated. The young smart set, along with ladies with "evening occupations" and others whose social credentials were less than impeccable, flaunted their fashionable outfits and hairdos in open barouches and victorias. The dogcart never managed to gain much fashionability. This curious vehicle with two parallel seats, one facing front and one facing rear, was what Mr. C. F. Bates of the Dakota drove, another indication of the Dakota's independence from the dictates of society.

The Central Park Mall, it was soon decreed, was the one place in New York where proper young ladies and gentlemen could stroll without a chaperone. At the end of the Mall was the lake, and here the young people met their friends and formed boating parties or fed the swans. Also at the head of the Mall were the Casino restaurant and the band pavilion where, on Wednesday and Saturday evenings in fine weather, concerts were presented. The wealthy arrived for these performances in their carriages, and listened from the Casino terrace near the "carriage concourse." The non-carriage trade rented folding chairs or sat on the grass.

In winter the lake and the pond at Fifty-ninth Street quickly made skating the most popular cold-weather pastime for rich and poor alike. When the public horse carts and omnibuses sported colored flags it meant "The ball is up in the Park"—a balloon that was raised to indicate that the ice was safe for skating. Tens of thousands of New Yorkers flocked to Central Park to waltz and figure skate on the park's frozen waters. At night the ice was lighted with calcium lamps to illuminate the Currier and Ives scene.

When Frederick Olmsted was laying out the Park, it was assumed that all sides—north, east, south and west—would one day be lined with the mansions of millionaires. By 1910, however, this had not happened. On Central Park West the Dakota had set the pace, and this wide thoroughfare was now lined with large apartment houses, presenting much the same skyline as it does today. On Central Park South, as Fifty-ninth Street had been renamed, apartment buildings had also risen. Central Park North, 110th Street, was where the squatters had moved as the city (and, indeed, the creation of the Park itself) had relentlessly pushed its poor northward as well as southeastward into the Lower East Side. The poor occupied a kind of a no man's land, or buffer zone, between lower Manhattan and Harlem, which had become a middle-class (and predominantly white) suburb. A small black colony had formed along Seventh Avenue, between Thirty-first and Thirty-eighth streets, in the heart of what is now the Garment District; it was not until after World War I that Harlem began to blossom as the largest black city in the world. In the early 1900's if one lived in Harlem, one did one's shopping along 125th Street, Harlem's main artery, and Harlemites had few reasons to venture downtown.

Only along Fifth Avenue—"The Queen of Avenues"—had the millionaires consented to build their private palaces. By 1899 the mansions along Fifth Avenue had become a tourist attraction of major proportions, and these houses of the rich were touted to sightseers that year in a full-page article in the Sunday *Tribune*. Headlined, "Houses at Which Visitors to the Metropolis Look With Interest," the *Tribune* story contained not only photographs of some of these houses but went on to list, in what would be considered very questionable journalistic practice today, the names and addresses of some two hundred rich New Yorkers under a subcaption, "Names of the Owners of Homes Along Fifth Avenue Where New York's Millionaires are Domiciled." Ten years later the idea of apartment living on Fifth Avenue was still repugnant.

By 1910 New York was effectively out of the Gaslight Era, and this was the year that the first luxury apartment building was erected on the Park's Fifth Avenue flank. Designed by McKim, Mead and White, it was a grand, twelve-story granite affair, built around a central court, at 998 Fifth Avenue, facing the Park on the corner of Eighty-first Street. The vast floor-through apartments offered, in addition to the customary living rooms and dining rooms, octagonal salons and reception rooms thirty-six feet long. Each apartment had eight master bedrooms and nine maids' rooms. Unlike the generation-older Dakota, bathrooms abounded. Each apartment had ten, each with what was then the world's most modern plumbing.*

For all its amenities, 998 Fifth Avenue was not an immediate success. Renting it was painfully slow, and it was clear that members of New York society were still unwilling to live under the same roof as others, even when they were people of their own kind. Then the rental agent, the young Douglas L. Elliman, hit upon a novel idea. If one member of Old Guard society could be persuaded to move into 998, perhaps others would follow. Elliman approached Senator Elihu Root, very definitely Old Guard, and offered him a cut rate—a $25,000-a-year apartment for only $15,000 a year. Root was sold, gave up his big brick town house at Seventy-first and Park, and moved into 998. One by one, others of Senator Root's social circle joined him at the Fifth Avenue address, and Mr. Elliman's successful real estate career was launched.

Still, Fifth Avenue did not experience the apartment-building boom that Central Park West had undergone earlier. The next apartment

---

*New Yorkers' puritanical sensibilities, however, would still not accept the bidet, considered sinfully European. In fact, it was against the law to install a bidet in New York until very recently. Also, for some reason, health laws dictated that all toilet seats must be of the open, U-shaped design and not of closed, oval shape.

house on Fifth Avenue did not appear until 1916, and it was not until the halcyon years of the 1920's that Fifth Avenue began to become the apartment-lined street that it is today.

The rest of New York, meanwhile, was changing with incredible speed. By 1910 New York and the entire country had entered the era of internal combustion. Mass production of automobiles had begun in 1900, and at an automobile show held at the old Madison Square Garden that year, more than fifty makers of "horseless carriages" displayed their models to enthusiastic audiences. The new cars were steered with tillers, like boats, had to be started with cranks and, like the carriages they were replacing, featured a great deal of brass to polish. Still, the following year at an Automobile Club meet in Long Island, one of these contraptions reached the astonishing speed of a mile a minute. At the Dakota, Mrs. Steinway refused to buy a horseless carriage; Mr. Bates, however, bought a Simplex, becoming the building's first auto-owner.

By 1910 the population of New York had jumped to over two and a half million, and the horse population had declined to 108,036, as more and more Scottish coachmen were being trained as chauffeurs. Electricity had eliminated the dirty and noisy steam locomotives. Gasoline-powered taxis and buses—including the exciting new double-deckers (introduced from France) on Fifth Avenue—were rapidly replacing the horse-drawn public carts and omnibuses. In 1900 tunneling for the first New York subway had begun. Four years later, following the mayor's ribbon-cutting ceremony, thousands of New Yorkers poured into the subway for the thrilling trip from City Hall Station up to Grand Central, then west to Times Square, and finally to the suburban reaches of 145th Street. For months afterward New Yorkers would spend their days off underground, riding back and forth on the nickle ride. One by one, the old elevated lines would disappear, to be replaced by the subway system.

Ladies who observed the laws of fashion still spent their weekdays carrying out the elaborate ritual of dropping calling cards. But now a much more exciting and efficient way of communicating with one's friends and neighbors had presented itself—the telephone. In 1880 not one in a thousand New Yorkers had owned one of these new devices, but by 1910 one out of ten New Yorkers had a phone, and the shroud of telephone and electric lines above the streets threatened to shut out the sun as effectively as the elevated trains. Along with the subway, the popularity of the telephone made New York seem suddenly much smaller and easier to reach. Gossip traveled with amazing speed over the telephone. As in any social ritual, rules were quickly established—the hours for telephoning were in the morning between eight and noon, and a woman considered herself unfit for afternoon shopping or other household chores until her morning telephoning was completed. The average New York woman, it was reported, "looked absolutely drawn through a knothole" when she emerged from her telephone duties.

Meanwhile, though some people bemoaned the loss of the horse-drawn carriages, others pointed out, with a certain amount of truth, that Central Park now provided a refuge for some of New York's beloved horseflesh. Horseback riding in the Park was still enormously popular, and horses that had once pulled carriages in the streets were now stabled on or just off the Park for early morning and weekend recreation.

FREDERICK OLMSTED MAY have been wrong in his vision of what sort of residences would one day surround the Park, but in other ways he was remarkably foresighted for his time. He was concerned, in addition to the Park's design, with its having ethnic harmony. He worried about security and about inevitable problems in sanitation, care and maintenance. He wanted the Park to be accessible to all and yet, at the same time, aloof and distant—not *too* accessible. Aware of New Yorkers' feelings about privacy, he wanted the Park to be a private sort of place as well as a public one, where privacy could be enjoyed. He wanted the Park to be a special place, to be entered with pleasure but also with a certain amount of respect and a touch of awe. For this reason Olmsted did not design a park that could be entered from any point along the street. He surrounded it with a high stone protective wall, pierced by carefully placed entrances. It was to be open at all times, but to create the impression, psychologically, that the Park was a particular province of its own, a little effort was required to get inside it. The device of the wall was intended to give New Yorkers an extra sense of *appreciation* of their Park, and extra pride in it.

TODAY, ON A summer weekend afternoon, when Dakotans—and other Park-facing New Yorkers—look out, they do not just see a great green rectangle of trees, grass and shimmering water, though all that is still there. They also see great throngs of people funneling into the Park through one or another of its entrances—one of which directly faces the Dakota. In their new, co-operative spirit of understanding and love, it was natural that the Dakotans, who had come to think of themselves as a particularly sensitive band of people, should begin to focus their concerns on their immediate environment, which included the Park. But there was more to it than that. Just as the "Dakoterie" on West Seventy-second Street had become very possessive about their building, they had also become very possessive about Central Park. It was *their* Park, and, just as the Dakotans were a bit elitist in their feelings toward their address, they were also elitist in their sentiments toward the Park. As they watched the invasion of their sometimes scruffily dressed fellow New Yorkers on the average Saturday and Sunday, the Dakotans began to wonder whether Mr. Olmsted's vision of the Park had been usurped or even lost.

The Park was still lovely, there was no question about that. But the people who were frequenting it sometimes were not. A section of Mr. Olmsted's wall was being used by male prostitutes for solicitation. The Park was being misused and, furthermore, the city seemed to be en-couraging its misuse. The villain behind all this, in some Dakotans' minds, was Mr. Thomas Hoving, the Park's commissioner. "Tommy Hoving," said Frederic Weinstein, "was out to do for Central Park just what he later did for the Metropolitan Museum when he became head of that"—that is, to overpopularize the Park, and to promote it with show-biz press-agentry. In the process, in the view of some New York-ers, the Park had begun to attract all the wrong people.

By the early 1970's the Park had become generally unsafe at night. Still, to the dismay of her neighbors, Lauren Bacall routinely walked her dog there, even late at night—though Miss Bacall's bold stride suggested a woman who might give any muggers a run for their money.

By daylight, meanwhile, the Park had become to some people—well, *unattractive.* The city, in the person of Mr. Hoving, had begun to boast that Central Park was a "people park." Indeed it was, and on most good days Central Park was the most densely populated public park of any in the world. The city had also begun scheduling more and more Big Apple Events in the Park, more plays, more operas, more symphony performances, more rock concerts, more ethnic festivals, all of which attracted greater hordes of people. Perhaps the city operated on the theory that in numbers there was safety, but it overlooked the corollary that with so much use, the Park deteriorates. The events in the Park attracted pushcart vendors—some of them licensed, some of them not —who sold everything from toys and balloons and cheap jewelry and post cards to hot dogs, bagels, soft drinks and ice cream. The vendors, on a good day, have managed to turn Central Park into one of the city's largest commercial centers of the junk-food trade, surely something Mr. Olmsted could never have foreseen. The vendors point out that they carry with them their own containers for used paper napkins and other trash. But food is carried away from their carts, and napkins wind up in the shrubbery, pop cans in the lake. Helium-filled balloons escape from children's tiny hands and festoon themselves high in the branches of trees, where they hang limply out of reach of the Park's overburdened sanitation staff.

The electronic age brought with it the transistor radio, and these devices are played, at high volume, throughout the Park, making it at times seem noisier than the streets. (In London, by contrast, it is illegal to play radios in the royal parks—Hyde Park, Green Park, St. James's Park and Kensington Gardens—and punishable by a £5 fine.)

The Central Park Zoo, though it is not a close Dakota neighbor, has long been something of an embarrassment to the city. Though the Zoo's indoor-outdoor cafeteria is still a pleasant place to lunch, even the Zoo's administrators admit that it is one of the worst animal parks in the country. With the exception of the always-playful seals, most of the Zoo's animals, in their too-small cages and enclosures, look listless and unhappy.

Tall weeds of lethargy and indifference seem to have grown in the Park, a sense of fatalism, and a feeling that nothing can be done. Olmsted's dream that the Park would be a place that would be entered with a sense of reverence and respect for nature seems far short of coming true. Grassy areas are turned to dirt from the soles of too many sneakers. The great variety of wildflowers that used to bloom there has diminished steadily over the years. Shrubs, plants and flowers are routinely pulled up and carried away. Branches are occasionally snapped from trees for games of stickball, and statues and monuments have been sprayed with graffiti—a practice which, fortunately, seems on the wane. The Park was conceived as a place where New Yorkers could escape from the sounds, tensions and bustle of the city—a peaceful, bucolic interval in the city's life. At times, though, it seems almost the opposite.

And just when New Yorkers are about to concede that the Park may be "getting a little better," something dreadful happens. A group of joggers is randomly attacked and bludgeoned by a band of hoodlums wielding bats and clubs and branches torn from trees. When apprehended the young men admitted that they were "out to get faggots," whom they hated as a breed. While this is an isolated instance, and though the Park is generally considered a much safer place than it was, say, in the 1960's, it hardly provides the kind of calm it was designed to engender. Meanwhile, maintaining this great natural resource seems to be of low priority in New York City's scheme of allocating scarce public funds.

To be sure, Frederick Law Olmsted was designing for an earlier generation of New Yorkers. The 1850's was a genteel, sentimental period in America, and New York was a decorous community of women in gauze dresses holding parasols and young men in polished boots communing with Nature. Olmsted certainly wanted to make his park available to New York's poor also, but he was thinking of the poor as they were then—polite and respectful to their "betters," and well-behaved. In the nineteenth century the less well-off tended to emulate the good manners of the wealthy. At the same time the rich were more serene, less edgy, and kinder to the poor. Olmsted lived in an era of the Grateful Poor, while in our more egalitarian age we have the Arrogant Poor, the Demanding Poor. His Park, walled like a medieval city-state, reflects the values of that older, more naïve, all-but-forgotten time, and, like the Dakota, it was really created for the nineteenth-century leisure class. The new egalitarianism—the youth revolt and the black revolt of the 1960's—and the feeling that *everyone* deserves his share of whatever public property exists, and has the absolute right to use it as he wishes—are things that Mr. Olmsted would never have understood, much less foreseen.

There may also be something primal in humans' feelings toward public places. The concept of sharing, as every parent and teacher knows, is a most difficult one to instill in children. At Rutgers, Professor Myra Bluebond-Langner, an anthropologist, recently reported on a study she is making of children between the ages of two and five,

ABOVE: Edward Clark
BELOW: Isaac Merritt Singer

The Dakota apartment house, c. 1895
INSET: Henry Janeway Hardenbergh

FROM FRANK LESLIE'S *Illustrated Paper*, SEPTEMBER 7, 1889

ABOVE: Looking south from the roof of the
Dakota in 1887
OPPOSITE: The Dakota as seen from the south

The Singer Seam
UNITES TWO CONTINENTS.

NORTH AMERICA

SOUTH AMERICA

ABOVE: Illustration from a Singer
advertising brochure, c. 1901
BELOW: Edward Severin (Severino)
Clark
OPPOSITE: Steinway and Sons

THE MEMBERS OF THE HOUSE OF

Steinway and Sons.

Skating on the lake near the Dakota, c. 1890
INSET: Five skaters in the Park, c. 1894

Carriages on the drive in Central Park, 1895
INSET: The drive in Central Park with the
Dakota in the background

OPPOSITE: The main gate
BELOW: Michael I. Pupin, left, at Union
College commencement day ceremonies

ABOVE: Staircase in the Dakota
BELOW: Detail from the Dakota
OPPOSITE: One of the original elevators

showing their "extreme respect for property rights." In her preliminary findings Professor Bluebond-Langner notes that children's disputes over private property ("That's my crayon") never last as long as those over communal property ("It's our turn to use the swings.") The more communal—and populous—a public place becomes, the more difficult it is to share, and the more it becomes a battleground.

Some Dakotans feel that the new egalitarianism of Central Park, which the city has encouraged, represents a perversion of Democracy. Not long ago a band of tenants spent a Saturday afternoon cleaning up the litter from that area of the Park immediately facing them. They succeeded in cleaning the Dakota's own front yard, which was just the tip of the iceberg and, of course, a few summer days later, the area they had cleaned was just as littered as it was before. Not long afterward, Frederic Weinstein watched from his third-floor window with dismay as a Sunday picnic group tore up a park bench to provide firewood for its barbecue.

Perhaps, some people feel, the trouble is that the city has tried to make the Park too many things to too many people. Perhaps, in this era of specialization, what is needed is a variety of parks, each with its own specialty—a park for rock concerts, another for noisy sports, another for playing transistor radios, and another for nature lovers—for quiet, solitude and contemplation.

A picture postcard that the Metropolitan Museum sells depicts the turn-of-the-century Dakota standing solitarily against the sky. In front of it stretches Central Park in winter, with well-dressed skaters comporting themselves gracefully on the frozen lake. They skate with hands joined—dancers, really—the gentlemen in their tall hats, the ladies in their long skirts and bonnets. Clearly those long-ago folk were enjoying their park, and were also treating it with respect and kindness.

Such scenes in Central Park are not just wistful memories today. The majority of New Yorkers still treasure the Park. On summer evenings, well-dressed people still turn out for symphony concerts and Shakespeare in the Park, often with elaborate picnics spread out before them on the grass. Joggers and cyclists abound, and in warm weather, teams from *The New Yorker* magazine and other New York publishing houses gather for lunch-hour or after-work baseball games. On winter afternoons and evenings, on the lake and on the pond, in the Wollman and

Lasker rinks, hundreds of skaters still create a scene out of Currier and
Ives.

IT WOULD BE IMPOSSIBLE not to note that many of the people now
enjoying the Park are black and Puerto Rican, reflecting the enormous
expansion of Harlem following World War II. Today, New Yorkers
tend to think of "Harlem" as anything north of Ninety-sixth Street,
where the Penn Central Railroad emerges from its tunnel beneath Park
Avenue into the open air. Strictly speaking, however, Harlem was the
area between 130th Street and 143rd Street, between Madison and
Seventh avenues. In the late nineteenth century, as huge migrations of
Russian and Polish Jews flooded into the city, fleeing the pogroms of
Eastern Europe, Harlem became primarily Jewish. Russian Jews dominated the 1910 census figures of the area, and next came the Italians,
the Irish, the Germans, the English, Hungarians, Czechs and others
from the Austro-Hungarian Empire. In addition, there were 75,000
native whites, and only 50,000 blacks. Blacks did not arrive in New
York in large numbers until after World War I, and, following the lead
of the foreign immigrants, they moved to Harlem. Most were from the
rural South, and most were poor. As the blacks moved in, the Jews
moved out—north into the Bronx or, if they could afford it, to the
South Shore of Queens and Long Island.

Following World War II there was a new infusion into Harlem from
Puerto Rico, and the new Spanish-speaking arrivals and the older-
established black Harlemites made tense and uneasy neighbors. Harlem
ceased being a jolly tourist spot which had offered "stompin' " at the
old Savoy Hotel and lively black entertainment at the famous Cotton
Club. Now it was more like an armed camp, looked on with fear by
New York's white population. Furthermore, the limits of Harlem were
bulging southward, particularly on the Upper West Side, down into the
West Nineties and West Eighties.

In the 1950's and 60's there was a certain sense of panic on the West
Side, and a feeling that the West Side would eventually "go black." (As
it turned out, this did not happen, and the West Side is currently
enjoying a sort of renaissance—not in fashionability, of course, but in
terms of rising rents.) During those uneasy decades, a number of white
families retreated to the East Side. The Birch Wathen School, fearful
that the West Side would soon be dangerous, moved its headquarters

across town. During this period also, the Trinity School on West Ninety-first Street formed an alliance with the upstate Pawling School in Dutchess County, partly as a hedge against being forced out of the neighborhood by an influx of black and Hispanic poor people. (This didn't happen either, and Trinity and Trinity-Pawling disassociated themselves from each other in the summer of 1978.)

At the Dakota, however, the mood was more serene, and there was no mass exodus from the building. The Dakotans, after all, had more important matters on their minds—preserving their precious parkside principality, their "fortress of delight." Also, after going co-op, the new mood at the Dakota involved not only love, but a certain longing to turn back the clock. In the elegant old relic of a building, the new commonality contained another important ingredient. It was nostalgia.

Of course some people were more nostalgic about the building than others. And just how nostalgic, in terms of preserving the romantic past, would become the center of another controversy. *Some* people, it seemed, were treating the Dakota just the way *some* people treated the Park.

Chapter 15

Dust

FREDERIC WEINSTEIN was furious. He and his wife had just returned from a holiday and, entering their apartment, found their rugs, furniture and books covered with a thick film of plaster dust. It had apparently filtered up through the chimney and spewed out of the Weinsteins' fireplace, the result of extensive renovations being done by the Bernard Rogers' in apartment 21, immediately below the Weinsteins. Dust wasn't all of it. Within an hour of their homecoming, plumbers from the floor below advised the Weinsteins that, as a result of a pipe that had burst during the renovation of 21, the Weinsteins would be without cold water for an indefinite period and that in order to correct the situation it might be necessary to tear up part of the Weinsteins' bedroom floor. Eventually, the problem was solved from below, without requiring such drastic measures. But Weinstein composed a cross letter to Wilbur Ross, the board's president, about the situation and, as was his right, submitted a house-cleaning bill to the Dakota.

One of the many reasons why tenant maintenance costs keep going up is that the Dakota is required to pay many such bills, for which the

Dakota maintains an expensive insurance policy, and the bills are often to correct the various unpleasant and unexpected side effects of someone's renovation. In his letter Frederic Weinstein raised an interesting question: Just how much interior renovation to the Dakota was, in the long run, a good idea? Just how much pounding away at the building, how much tearing down of walls, should be permitted? The Landmarks Commission prohibited any alteration to the building's exterior, but it had no jurisdiction over whatever inner surgery individual tenant-owners wished to perform. There was more involved here than just aesthetics. It was possible that, as more and more tenants removed and rearranged the building's bones and other organs, the Dakota's shell might eventually collapse. This actually happened to one heavily renovated building in Boston, though there were extenuating circumstances. One sub-zero day during the renovation a fire broke out in the building. The fire brigade was called and drenched the building with its hoses. After the fire, building inspectors pronounced the building's exterior sound, and the interior renovation continued through the winter. Then, on the first warm day of spring the building caved in. What had been holding it up, it seemed, was ice.

At the Dakota the renovation of apartment 21 involved the removal of a partition. Before that was done, Suzanne Weinstein swears, her apartment never trembled when the Eighth Avenue subway rolled by underneath. Now it does. Floors that didn't use to squeak now squeak.

In the Dakota's basement caves are stacked all sorts of interior architectural details that have been removed from Dakota apartments in a long series of renovations. There is a roomful of old doors, another of moldings, another of cornices, another of mantelpieces, another of hardware. They are intended to be labeled and catalogued, indicating from which apartment each item originated, so that, if some future tenant wished, these details could be restored. But in the dampness of their basement morgue, many fine pieces are crumbling into rot and decay. Items, too, have had a way of disappearing, as one of the old elevator cages disappeared. If an apartment is being restored, one is not supposed to go to the basement and just take a pretty door. But this has happened. Like most old buildings, the Dakota has had a long series of superintendents, and there is always the suspicion that at various times superintendents have been tempted to sell certain items. A while back a truck filled with old mantels was seen departing from the

Dakota's basement service entrance. Where these pieces of cabinet-work were bound, no one knew, but it is quite certain that they never came back.

Frederic Weinstein and others—for he is not alone in his sentiments—feel that the time has come to call a halt to renovations that require structural or near-structural changes in the building. Modernizing kitchens and bathrooms is one thing, these people feel (one basement room is filled with nothing but old bathtubs and sinks). But ripping out walls is quite another. Weinstein is painfully reminded of "the virtual collapse of the White House during the Truman Administration as a consequence of generations of uncoordinated renovation."

But Dakotans like Weinstein were also concerned about matters other than the fact that repeated renovations—involving removal and relocation of walls and beams and ceilings—might eventually weaken the building's skeleton to the point where it would topple. There was also the knotty question of aesthetics and taste. Architectural purists at the Dakota were nervously reminded of the "desecration" that was committed upon such buildings as 910 Fifth Avenue. That gracious Italianate apartment house was put up in 1920 and then, in 1959, was completely gutted and stripped to its steel skeleton, losing in the process its handsome friezes, cornices and balustrades. What stands at 910 Fifth Avenue today has been called a "dreadful parody" of what the building once was. At the Dakota the building's elaborate interior details were part of its special history and its special character. Some renovations were so extreme that they violated the Dakota's history, raped its character. Where did interior decoration leave off and dese-cration begin? Then there was a legal question. Certainly an individual who owns an apartment has certain rights to alter and renovate it to suit his needs, tastes and wishes. But the Dakota was different; it deserved special consideration. It was sacrilege, some people felt, to tamper with the Dakota's gracious old rooms and their elaborate, Old World details.

A great deal of tampering, meanwhile, had already been done, and many of the building's interior spaces bore little resemblance to the fin-de-siècle chambers they had once been. In the name of moderniza-tion a number of Mr. Hardenbergh's extravagant and fanciful touches had been removed, and, in some cases, his very concept for the Dakota's interior had been arrogantly defied. It had occurred to some tenants, for example, that if a big room could be divided vertically, it could also be divided horizontally. If one had a fifteen-foot ceiling, why not build a loft, or platform, with stairs leading up to it, thus creating an additional room under the ceiling. One of the first people to do this was Betty Friedan, who was then married and who decided to build sleeping platforms for her children. This was innovative, but it turned one high-ceilinged room into two low-ceilinged ones. Was this right, aesthetically? Instead of a sense of space one achieved a sense of claustrophobia. Was this right, morally, to do to the Dakota? If one didn't want the Dakota's high ceilings, perhaps one should live some-where else. If one wanted lofts, why not build them in Greenwich Village? Mrs. Friedan also did other things, such as paint over marble fireplaces, which struck her neighbors as sacrilegious. But a number of people copied her sleeping-loft idea.

By the mid-1970's the building became aesthetically divided be-tween the traditionalists, who wanted to preserve the old details, and the revisionists, who wanted to change things around. One tenant painstakingly, and at great expense, had the woodwork in her apart-ment stripped of the layers of paint that had accumulated over the years, and taken down to its original, natural golden glow. But when she sold her apartment the new owner promptly covered the old wood-work with paint again. One of the building's many committees was the Aesthetics Committee, which deplored such doings, but with no real power to enforce its aesthetic standards, all it could do was cluck its tongue when they occurred.

Lauren Bacall is decidedly on the side of the traditionalists, and her apartment, which she has decorated herself, recalls the stately apart-ments on the Avenue Foch in Paris. She has furnished it with antiques. "Furniture has to be old and good," she says. "I love French Re-gency, Provincial, and pieces from India and Morocco. When it comes to decorating, I prefer to do it myself. I have never been able to find a decorator I could communicate with in terms of me." In her front hallway a chest from Damascus houses a collec-tion of Oriental monkeys, along with opaline and old pewter pieces. Her apartment, the traditionalists say, is what a Dakota apartment *ought* to look like. So is Leonard Bernstein's. In fact, Bernstein's late wife was so in favor of turning back the clock that for years she waged an unsuccessful campaign to have the electric street lamps outside the Dakota replaced with gas fixtures.

Freddie Victoria, as would be expected of a man who deals in art and antiques, has carefully preserved his sculptured-plaster "birthday cake" ceilings, and one of the remarkable features of his living room is the way he has treated his windows. At a glance they seem to be framed with festoons of flowing silk. But the effect is *trompe l'oeil,* and the "draperies" are not draperies at all but lambrequins made of hand-carved and painted wood—executed by craftsmen in his own shop. The apartment also contains Mr. Victoria's extraordinary collection of antique clocks—some seventy in number and all in perfect working order—including a spectacular clock chandelier (one must stand beneath it and look upward to read its face). The clocks tick and chime peacefully throughout the apartment.

Judy and Gyora Novak straddle the fence somewhat between the traditionalist and revisionist point of view, but most Dakotans feel that the Novaks have treated their apartment splendidly, considering what they had to work with. When they bought the building's old dining room on the ground floor it lacked baths, a kitchen, closets, and even walls where it opened from the public corridor. The marble floor of the big main room had been layered with so many years of wax that it was almost black. The Novaks had the marble cleaned and restored to its original white, with a colored border. From what were pantries and storage rooms, the Novaks created a kitchen-pantry, a guest bathroom, and a combination library-guest room off the main room. What was originally the "little" dining room, designed for private parties, became the Novaks' bedroom, with a master bath, dressing room and closets.

At Philip Johnson's suggestion, the walls of the apartment were upholstered in oyster-white carpeting to deaden the sound of the subway below and to provide a soft backdrop for the Novaks' paintings and sculpture. The mahogany doors and coffered ceiling, which had been of a light-brown color, were cleaned and rubbed a black-brown to avoid casting reddish reflections on the paintings, and the old brass hardware was blackened to avoid glitter. All glossy surfaces were toned down. The white marble floor was given a no-gloss finish, and a non-shiny finish was applied to the snuff-colored leather with which the benches, sofas and dining chairs were covered. Modern touches included big globe lighting and can-shaped spotlights that are adjustable on ceiling tracks. Outside light is controlled by adjustable vertical louvers of heavy oyster-colored fabric at the windows. From the main apartment a staircase leads down to an area the Novaks reclaimed from the Dakota's basement. This includes a small reception room for Mr. Novak's clients, and a huge, white-walled studio lit by powerful lights, where Gyora Novak sculpts, paints, and designs jewelry and mens' clothing.

Upstairs, on the sixth floor, Dr. and Mrs. Scott Severns have retained their apartment's original amber-colored mahogany doors, moldings, window frames, its heavy brass hardware, fireplaces, parquet floors and carved ceilings. Otherwise the Severns' decor is starkly modern. The long, wide living room is sparsely furnished, dominated by a grand piano from which Mrs. Severns gives occasional lessons. A huge abstract painting, some twenty feet long and ten feet high, covers one wall. The room is furnished with Mies van der Rohe's famous Barcelona chairs, but Mrs. Severns likes to point out that "the really comfortable pieces" were designed by Philip Johnson, who happens to be her brother. (The apartment also affords a view of a new Philip Johnson building across the park.) The Severns' library is called the Andy Warhol Room, and its walls are hung only with paintings by the artist—the Marilyn Monroe, the Jackie Kennedy, the poppy pictures and so on. One room that Mrs. Severns has not chosen to modernize is her kitchen. Though large and comfortable, it is decidedly old-fashioned.

To Theodate Johnson Severns the Dakota's connotations will always be romantic. Mrs. Severns is a small, peppery person with boyishly cut gray hair, an emphatic manner, and a collection of Siamese and Abyssinian cats. "The Blanchards called me in late August of 1961," she says. "They said, 'Come, come quick, there's an apartment available.' I came, and I brought Scott with me. I had been married before, and it hadn't worked out. I hadn't really thought much about getting married again. I looked at the apartment, and it seemed enormous. Everything was painted a hideous elephant gray. I thought, how can I ever fill this up with furniture? I said no, no, it's just too much apartment for me. Then Scott looked at me and said, 'Who said you had to take it alone?' And he handed me the deed to apartment sixty-four. We were married three days later—to take advantage of the long Labor Day weekend.

"It had been Emmett Hughes's apartment. The Andy Warhol room was a bedroom which he had rented out to a paying guest. There are so many reasons why we love living here. It's more than just the space and the four-inch thick doors. It really *is* like one big family. Oh, we have our little spats and differences. But even when we fight we fight like a family. No one entertains without including some of the Dakota neighbors—that's something that never happens in most New York buildings. The other day we had a party for Virgil Thomson. First there was a screening of a film in Warner LeRoy's movie room. Then everyone came back for cocktails and dinner here. It's a real *community.*

"Of course we pay for it. We pay more maintenance than the most expensive rental buildings in the city. It's a question of: If you have to ask how much it costs, you can't afford it. But it's a good investment. This apartment has tripled in value since we bought it. But it's more than that. It's the funny little things that happen. The other day I got into a taxi and gave the driver my address, and he turned around to me and said, 'Lady, can I ask you a question?' I said I'd try to answer. He said, 'Is it true that in that building they even have fireplaces in the bathrooms?' And the old people, like the Brownings. The other day I had a note from Adele Browning, and it was written on the back of a 1914 letter. There's a sense of continuity here, a sense of life, a sense of *fertility.* Take the Novaks' parrots, for example. The Novaks have some rare parrots which, they were told, would never lay eggs in captivity. They never did lay eggs, until the Novaks moved here. When they got to the Dakota, the parrots started laying eggs right away! It's something in the air. . . ."

Downstairs, on the first floor, in what is roughly 60 percent of what was once Miss Leo's old apartment, the Larry Ellmans have chosen to go the traditionalist route, keeping the original details and covering walls with rich fabrics, decorating with antiques to create a turn-of-the-century mood. Larry Ellman, however—the former owner of Longchamps and now the proprietor of the Cattleman Restaurant—has gone all out on his kitchen, fitting it with every modern appliance conceivable. Next door, in the remainder of what was Miss Leo's apartment before the Ellmans divided it, actor Michael Wager occupies the Dakota's only "maisonette" apartment, with its own private entrance from the courtyard. Wager, too, is a traditionalist, decorating with antiques and covering his walls with Fortuny fabric to create an effect, as he puts it, of "instant Old Money."

Princess Mona Faisal, whose father founded the Arab League, is married to Mohamet Faisal, the son of Saudi Arabia's king. She and her brother Issam Azzam share a large Dakota apartment that is all done in pale desert colors and is considered one of the loveliest and most peaceful in the building. Some think it amusing to note that Michael Wager, an ardent Zionist whose father headed the Chaim Weizmann Institute, lives directly below the Arab princess.

When King Faisal was visiting the United States, the story goes, there was no time on his schedule for a personal call on his son and daughter-in-law, but the king was driven past the Dakota. "Ah," he said, looking up at the building, "I see that my son has bought a castle." Of course the story may be apocryphal. Many Dakota stories are.

UP IN THE southeast corner of the third floor, Frederic and Suzanne Weinstein have left intact all the architectural and decorative details that were there when they moved in but, like the Scott Severnses, they have chosen to furnish the apartment in a severe, contemporary style. A woven-to-order rug in an abstract design provides the only real color in the living room, a long sectional sofa, also custom-made to fit the room, is covered in a light coffee-colored fabric, and the walls are painted flat white. Adding to the feeling of airy lightness in the Weinsteins' apartment is the fact that the Weinsteins prefer to keep their white walls bare of art or any other decoration. "We wanted the rooms themselves to be the only decorative statements," Suzanne Weinstein says. Everything else is subordinated to the rooms' scale.

The largest apartment in the Dakota belongs to restaurateur Warner LeRoy, the son of movie director Mervyn LeRoy and the nephew of all the Warner brothers. Originally, the LeRoys' apartment consisted of only ten large rooms on the sixth floor, but when another apartment of the same size became available on the floor immediately above, the LeRoys bought that one too. They persuaded the building to let them construct a staircase between the two apartments, giving them the Dakota's only duplex, unless one counts Ward Bennett's split-level pyramid on the roof, the Novaks' basement studio, and the various sleeping-lofts and balconies that have been inserted between floors here and there. The LeRoy apartment, as might be expected, has been decorated in a theatrical style that one might call Hollywood High Camp, featuring Tiffany glass chandeliers like the ones used to adorn LeRoy's popular restaurant, Maxwell's Plum. The LeRoys have become the building's most ambitious host and hostess, and toss four or five big parties a year for as many as two hundred guests, plus numerous smaller dinners. To help her bring these large entertainments off, Kay LeRoy, a cook of some note, has a kitchen—or kitchens, really, since the kitchen area consists of several rooms—furnished with all the latest equipment, all of it hotel-size. In fact, Mrs. LeRoy got into a bit of trouble early in 1978 when it was learned that she was preparing certain dishes in her kitchen for the Tavern on the Green, another of her husband's restaurants just down the street. This, it seemed, violated some city health code. In addition to kitchens that a luxury hotel might envy, the LeRoy apartment also contains a screening room for movies.

Though not the largest, certainly the most spectacular apartment in the Dakota belongs to Mr. and Mrs. Peter Nitze. Peter Nitze is a lawyer and chairman of the board of Nitze-Stagen & Co., Inc., financial consultants. He is also a descendant of Harry Pratt who, along with a man named John D. Rockefeller, helped put together Standard Oil. His grandmother Pratt was New York's first woman alderman. The Nitze apartment on the sixth floor contains the building's largest room, the colonnaded salon measuring 24 by 49 feet with twin facing fireplaces at either end, originally intended as a ballroom. The Nitze apartment was the "bachelor flat" of Edward Severin Clark, and the ballroom is said to be a facsimile of a similar room in the old Clark mansion off Washington Square. Later it became the C. D. Jacksons' apartment. The Jacksons divided it, and part of it became the apartment of Edward R. Murrow. When the Nitzes bought it, they undivided it and as a result now have two kitchens. In addition to the kitchens and the ballroom there are some fourteen other rooms, but that is only counting the rooms that have windows. In all, there are eight working fireplaces.

The Nitzes undertook a complete restoration, as opposed to a renovation, of the apartment. Generations of paint were stripped from doors, moldings and paneling, uncovering the original mahogany and heavy brass hinges, which even had brass plates to conceal their screws. In the process of stripping one heavy door, the restorer asked Peter Nitze, "Do you really want this door put back into its *original* condition?" Certainly, said Nitze. The workman than pointed out what appeared to be traces of sterling silver in the corners of the panels; the panels had originally been edged with silver. The Nitzes stopped short of replacing the silver trimmings. Grace Jackson had taken one of the old elevator cages and placed it in a vestibule, intending to later install it as a powder room. The Nitzes kept the elevator where it was, and use it as a cozy setting for childrens' tea parties. Though it is the only part of the apartment that was not there in 1884, the Nitzes feel that the elevator belongs there for sentimental reasons.

Other tenants have been less scrupulously respectful of the Dakota's innards. The traditionalists who deplore sleeping lofts are somewhat at cross-purposes with Paul Segal, the architect, who has lived at the Dakota since 1969. Segal is a red-headed, enthusiastic and immediately likable young man, and has helped redo a number of Dakota apartments. He supervised the renovation of Paul Goldberger's new apartment, helped the Ellmans divide Miss Leo's old place into two apartments and helped Michael Wager create an apartment out of his end of that division. He oversaw the renovation of the Wilbur Rosses' apartment and designed a superkitchen for John and Yoko Lennon. He was also responsible for the renovation of the Bernard Rogers' apartment (the dust from which filtered up into the Weinsteins' place on the floor above).

In the process of this work, Paul Segal has familiarized himself with every nook and cranny of the Dakota, from the basement crawl spaces to the mazelike corridors of the eighth and ninth floors, and to the narrow walkways on the roof. He once won a bottle of Scotch on a bet with a fellow Dakotan who said that it was not possible to walk completely around the building through the various eighth-floor hallways. It was possible, and Paul Segal showed his neighbor how to do it through what amounted to a secret door. Also, in the process Paul Segal has gained the unofficial title of the Dakota's "house architect."

Paul Segal's architectural style is very contemporary, and though he boasts that he has "never completely gutted" an apartment, he has brought a number of apartments up to date. He favors sleeping lofts and had one built in his own apartment, though it is used as a study and not for sleeping. The construction of a mezzanine, with a curved balcony extending over the living room, was part of Segal's design for the Bernard Rogers' apartment. Planned as a library-study, the mezzanine certainly added floor space, though it cut the ceiling height in half. Segal's design was considered sufficiently innovative to be given a four-page color spread in *House Beautiful* in 1978.

But purists in the building, Frederic Weinstein in particular, feel that some of Paul Segal's designs are seriously eroding the building's inner personality. Weinstein has watched sadly as one by one venerable interior details have disappeared—the corridor globes on the second floor replaced by more "modern" fixtures, the steady removal of old mantelpieces, doors, cornices, the growing pile of architectural detritus in the basement. Weinstein raises another question in terms of the Segal renovations. To renovate an apartment according to the building's Hoyle, all plans must be approved by the outside architectural firm of Glass & Glass. They must then be approved by the building's board of directors. Finally, building permits must be obtained and specifications reviewed by whatever city inspectors are involved. When the C. D. Jacksons divided their apartment they had to tear down and rebuild the wall three times before the city inspectors were satisfied with it.

Paul Segal, meanwhile, is a member of the building's board and has served two separate three-year terms. He has, however, been very scrupulous about not participating in those architectural and remodeling decisions which involve his own work or his recommendations. In fact, Segal makes a point of physically absenting himself during many of these discussions.

Frederic Weinstein clearly does not approve of Paul Segal's architectural style and insists that this has nothing to do with the fact that Segal's renovations on the floor below inconvenienced him.

Weinstein later commented: "In my opinion the Dakota stands as a tragic landmark to a skin-deep conception of landmark conservancy. While its façade is now protected, throughout its history renovations of apartments have been undertaken which in some cases have permanently distorted the interior architectural context and ambiance of the building. I am not a blind antiquarian sentimentalist. Reasonable and functional renovations have been and are necessary adaptations to each era and have kept the Dakota a living building rather than a museum piece. But there is a distinction between this kind of renovation and profound, irreparable and irreversible surgery. Paris and London, while also experiencing grave landmark crises, have so much more margin for error. In Europe, buildings like the Dakota, while not commonplace, are nevertheless not uncommon."

Weinstein went on to say, "The Dakota is a poignant document precisely because we all subsist in a society here which perpetually erases itself. We have so much more to lose because we have so much less to begin with. I believe there is still time to practice landmark conservancy from the skin inwards. Not as a matter of antiquarian preciousness. The Dakota's survival as the Dakota is itself at stake—survival as something more than a gutted interior with a quaint façade.

"I say all this without any criticism intended of my fellow tenants of previous eras or those living here now. Everyone who has lived here respects this building and is captive to it and to its ineffable presence. And I'm fully aware that I've entered the shapeless and inscrutable area of taste as well as those vast ambiguities relating to the rights of the individual to create a personal environment against the somewhat fragile rights of the society to preserve its heirlooms. Unfortunately, perhaps tragically, which is where I began, great buildings do not share a protected status along with great canvases and great poems."

Frederic Weinstein is by nature a worrier. Though his fiftieth birthday is behind him, he is attempting to embark on a new career as a writer, and he frets that he may be getting too late a start. Fortunately, he has his coolly beautiful, long-legged, level-headed wife to offset his worrying side. When Freddie Weinstein worries aloud, Suzanne Weinstein just gives him a long, slow, sideways look with her enormous eyes, and Freddie responds with a little smile. Freddie worries about the Dakota, and its future.

"If this building is a microcosm of New York," he says, "then the Dakota's board is a microcosm of a microcosm. There's always the feeling that the board is 'out to get' everybody.

"There are a lot of strange folk here, a lot of people who indulge in what I call 'quotation mark' behavior—people acting cute, campy, ditsy and quaint. This used to be a place where people could breathe. Now we have what I call the Beachboy Syndrome—the fact that on an average Saturday night half the building seems to be in drag. The smell of marijuana and poppers wafts under the doorways, and you hear the falsetto echo of laughter in the halls, like sparrows chirping in the niches. There are people like Leonard Bernstein, who are true celebrities, versus people who are playing at being celebrities, playing at being gay. New malignancies have crept in, like this theory of rolling indebtedness that the building seems to operate on. The place is rife with improprieties, and everybody is winking at what goes on. It's part of what is happening in New York, of course, but shouldn't the Dakota be above all that? It's acquiring the quality of a keep, or fortress—it's a prison, and it's captured all of us.

"There's hostility from within. Suzanne just went on the board and asked if she could serve on the Aesthetics Committee. She's a member of the Victorian Society and interested in preservation. Ruth Ford said, 'No outsiders on the Aesthetics Committee.' She seems to think of herself as a kind of Madame Pompadour.

"Some people are very withdrawn. There's Virginia Dwan, for example, who used to have a famous gallery. No one really knows Virginia. She's very rich, radical and chic, and her whole apartment is like a vast art gallery, full of beautiful things. She's been in the building a little longer than we have, but it wasn't until a month ago that we had her in for tea.

"Meanwhile, everyone is circling around and sniffing each other, and each person seems to be leading some secret life. There's a Chaucerian aspect to life here—a *Canterbury Tales* quality. . . . We live at the Tabard. . . ."

DISRESPECT FOR the building—that is considered a cardinal sin at the Dakota. But respect and disrespect become fuzzy terms when one is dealing with individual tastes, preferences and needs, and when, as in the operation of Central Park, one is trying to run a facility as a model democracy that will keep everybody happy. One tenant who certainly took a different "path" in renovating her seventh-floor apartment was Roberta Flack. She wanted ceilings lowered, walls removed, mantels and moldings ripped out. Her plans were initially rejected by the board.

She and her architect then agreed to modify their plans for the ambitious renovation, and work proceeded. There was a great deal of backing and filling between Miss Flack and the board and, even after the work was finished, the controversy continued. Some tenants claimed that walls and moldings had been removed, which her architect promised would be saved. Roberta Flack feels she went along with everything the building required of her. In any case, although legally the Dakota's board could require Miss Flack to undo the renovation, it obviously has not done so.

Miss Flack is a famous star—one gold record after another, and now a platinum one. One does not give orders to famous stars. For another thing, she is black—the first and, to date, the only black tenant in the building. The Dakota is a little touchy on the subject of blacks. Miss Flack's application to come into the building in the first place was not exactly greeted with universal cheering. But what was the Dakota to do? In their modern mood of democracy, communication, tolerance and love—to a group of people who had reacted with horror to the thought that the Dakota should discriminate against homosexuals—it was unthinkable that the building should appear to bar anyone on the basis of race.

"She won't let me come to see her apartment," Rex Reed says. "She says I'll hate it." A lot of others in the building feel just as strongly about Roberta Flack's apartment. But there is little that they can do about it except sit and quietly wring their hands.

Miss Flack, meanwhile, defends what she has done to her southwest corner of the seventh floor. "I think my apartment is the prettiest one in the building," she says. "My architect, Myron Goldfinger, is one of the best in the business. When I bought this place in 1976 it was very dark. There was a lot of fancy inlaid wood design and stuff, and a lot of marble basins in the closets—all that had to go. I wanted everything soft white and contemporary, with clean lines, to go with my contemporary Italian furniture." What Miss Flack liked most about the apartment was that it was big enough to house her Bösendorfer piano—a huge 9'6" concert instrument with four extra keys in the bass register —considered the Rolls-Royce of pianos and worth, according to Miss Flack, between $45,000 and $50,000. "It had to be hoisted up with a cherry-picker, and now there's no way to ever get it out." To make room for the piano the partition between the living room and dining room was removed, "though they had to leave one column standing because there was plumbing in it or something." Ceilings in all the hallways were lowered, and central air conditioning was installed. The entire apartment was wired for an elaborate quadrophonic sound system, and four speakers were built into Miss Flack's bed. Bathrooms were enlarged—one so that it could hold a marble Jacuzzi whirlpool tub big enough, according to Miss Flack, "for four people to take a bath in, or for two people to have fun in—you know?"

Miss Flack had her kitchen made smaller, "to try to control my passion for cooking—and eating." Miss Flack admits that the building's board gave her "quite a hassle" over her renovation plans but insists that now "They're all my friends."

One decorative detail in the Flack apartment is the Buddhist shrine in the living room. "But a lot of people have those," she says. "I don't worship in front of it as much as I should, but the house is full of Bibles so we're covered for ghosts." Miss Flack has not seen a ghost in the Dakota yet, "But I won't go down in the basement. I believe in extraterrestrial beings, and I've had experiences. I saw my grandfather's ghost once, when I was a little girl. There was this hole in our backyard with a cardboard lid on it, where we dumped the garbage. I was dumping the garbage one day, and I looked up and there was this *thing*. It was my grandfather's ghost. He stood looking at me for quite a while. I wouldn't be surprised if there are ghosts here, too. After all, this building has been occupied by a lot of strong people. They stay, they have memories. They come back."

Chapter 16

Winnie's World

OVER THE YEARS, as happens in the case of most old, well-lived-in houses, the Dakota has acquired its own characteristic smell. One notices it the minute one enters the building—a faint, fruity pungency that fills the air. The Dakota's smell would seem to be a particular blend of odors—linseed oil and wax, brass and marble polishes, old varnished wood and weathered stone, along with the thin, papery scent one encounters when untying a packet of old love letters. The Dakota's private smell suggests the many hands that have tended to its upkeep throughout its history, and it is also a fragrant reminder of the special privacy the building has provided its tenants. For despite its boast of communality, the Dakota sometimes affords a privacy so complete that Warner LeRoy did not realize he had a first cousin living in the building until after she had moved out. For nearly twenty years author and critic Marya Mannes, daughter of violinist David Mannes and niece of Walter Damrosch, lived at the Dakota. So did her first husband, Jo Mielziner. Neither was aware that they shared the same address, since their apartments were on different elevator stems.

For some crises, of course, the Dakota is specially well equipped. In a blackout, for example, there is no chance that the building will be without elevator service. The Dakota's service elevators, which are water-powered, go right on working with or without electricity. But for other situations the Dakotans have had to equip themselves.

On May 3, 1976, the Building Service Employees International Union, AFL–CIO, New York Council No. 11, went out on strike, and picket lines appeared in front of every New York apartment house. Residents of high-rise apartments which still had manually operated elevators were sorely inconvenienced and found themselves having to learn how to be elevator operators. But the strike had not progressed for long before New Yorkers found themselves pervaded with a spirit of high adventure. The strike was just the sort of thing New Yorkers liked to have occur from time to time—like a great blizzard—to remind them that for all New Yorkers' fierce feelings about privacy, New York was really a one-for-all community. The strike was turning out to be great fun, as tenants learned how to staff and run their buildings. Every building in the city had its favorite strike stories. It was like London during the blitz, but even better because no one was being killed or injured. It was more like pretending to be poor, and there was a feeling in the air that New York was really just a village after all, where everyone looked after his neighbor.

A sense of camaraderie and sharing pervaded. The spring weather was balmy and pleasant, and the forsythia was in full bloom in the Park. A duty roster was sent around the building, volunteers were solicited, and tasks were assigned and eagerly taken up. It was like being at summer camp, as the gentry "Upstairs" discovered what life was like "Downstairs." "The most popular job, on the part of the wives," Wilbur Ross recalled not long ago, "was sorting the mail, so that they could read the post cards and see who was hearing from whom." The most popular job on the part of the husbands turned out to be collecting garbage—a more muscular form of nosiness, since garbage can be tattletale too, and reveals how many empty liquor bottles one's neighbor tosses out each week, among other things.

Another popular chore was manning the desk in the front office, answering the phone and screening visitors—particularly on nights when there were large parties. In addition to the fun of seeing famous people toting garbage, there was the fun of announcing famous guests who came to call on famous people, and being able to note how long their visits lasted. Identification cards were printed for all tenants so that those not immediately recognizable could come and go without interference, and a number of night owls were discovered in the building who were delighted to man the desk on the midnight to eight A.M. shift. Mr. Godfrey Flaker took the night shift and spent the wee hours hooking rugs.

Outside on the sidewalk the striking Dakota staff seemed a little awkward and embarrassed as they walked up and down their picket line, responding somewhat sheepishly to the cheerful greetings of the tenants who regarded the staff as their friends. But one member of the staff had not gone on strike, and her loyalty to the building came as a surprise to no one. She was Miss Winifred Bodkin, and the night before the strike was called she quietly moved into the Dakota from her apartment in Astoria, so that she would not have to cross the picket line. The tenants took turns shopping for her groceries.

Winnie Bodkin's title at the Dakota is a little vague, but she is more or less the building's concierge, and she is indispensable. She normally arrives at the Dakota at the stroke of eight in the morning, and departs at four in the afternoon, five days a week. Her principal duty is to manage the desk, but she does much more than that. She is the building's heart, some people say, its very soul. Through the slow attrition of the staff over the years, Winnie Bodkin has remained. She has seen superintendents come and go. Some of them she liked, and some of them she didn't like at all and made no bones about it. Still, Winnie has remained. Most Dakotans today cannot remember a time when she was not at the desk. And since Winnie is assumed to "know where all the bodies are buried," some people are terrified of her. After all, Winnie likes some of her tenants better than she likes others.

Winifred Bodkin came to the Dakota on November 11, 1930, not long after her arrival in America from the little village of Tuam in County Galway. She was a lass of twenty then. Though she has never been back to her native Ireland, her soft voice, some fifty years later, still carries a trace of a brogue. In the beginning she worked as one of the Dakota's elevator ladies, but by the early 1940's the Clarks had realized that Winnie Bodkin was a young woman capable of assuming more than routine responsibilities, and she was promoted to the front desk where she has remained.

Today, Winnie Bodkin is a trim, erect, bespectacled woman who wears simply cut dresses and keeps her short white hair carefully coifed. In appearance she reminds one of a high-school English teacher, and her customary expression is stern and somewhat preoccupied. When one of her favorite tenants walks into her office, however, her eyes and her whole face light up. For her pets Winnie Bodkin will perform all sorts of special favors. When photographer Peter Fink is too busy to go to the bank, for instance, Winnie will go down the street and cash a check for him. Still, Winnie has her standards. When Fink married his French wife Monique a while back, he neglected to apprise Winnie of this fact. For several weeks afterward Winnie insisted on announcing the new Mrs. Fink to her husband, as she would a guest, whenever Mrs. Fink entered the building. This continued until Fink made his marriage official by telling Winnie about it.

In addition to screening and announcing visitors, Winnie's job involves receiving and sorting mail and packages, answering the telephone and operating the switchboard, but she also keeps track of other matters. If, for example, a tenant's weekly cleaning woman has a free day, Winnie usually knows of another tenant in the building who is looking for someone to clean. When a tenant plans to entertain, Winnie is nearly always notified, and she will, if need be, line up off-duty members of the building's staff to moonlight as waiters and bartenders. There are some things she will not do. In 1962 Winnie was asked if she would write out the building's payroll. She declined. She was then told that if she would do the payroll, she would be given a raise. Though her salary was only $82 a week, she declined the raise and the payroll job. It was, she said, just too confusing.

Winnie Bodkin dislikes change.

As every apartment dweller knows, the only proper Christmas gift to an employee of a building is cash in a white envelope. Or, if not cash, a check will do. Several winters ago Ruth Ford decided to give the building's staff more personal Christmas gifts, and her gift to Winnie was a bottle of perfume. Winnie returned the gift politely, saying that it was not her scent.

Over the years Winnie has seen the building change more than a little. "It used to be like one big happy family," she says. "It was strictly a family place. Now it's become commercialized somewhat, and there are all the show-business people. There was a period in the thirties and forties when the building didn't want show people, and there was a period when it didn't want Jews. Then in the middle forties the times started to change, and now it's every other one. Before that there were *families*—families like the Charles Grayson Martins, he was a leading real estate man. And the Charles J. Hardys—the head of American Car and Foundry, and the William Arbuckle Jamisons of Arbuckle Sugar. They were wonderful people, and it was easy to control the children because everyone had servants. Nowadays, there are so many people who work out of their apartments, who use their apartments for business. In the old days this was not allowed. Nowadays, I have to announce business callers. And so many people are doing renovations now —each one of those workmen has to be announced. So, the older I get, the harder I have to work."

Paul Segal, meanwhile, thinks that Winnie secretly enjoys announcing business visitors. "I admit," he says, "that this is supposed to be a *residential* building. But for a while I used my apartment as my office. When I finally had to have a bigger place I moved my office to 730 Fifth Avenue. I told Winnie that she wouldn't have to be announcing my clients any more, and she actually acted a little hurt and disappointed."

It is also possible that Winnie secretly enjoys the new breed of celebrity tenants and their celebrity friends who come to visit them, and finds conspiring with John Lennon to avoid the *paparazzi* an exciting part of her job. "There was a truck with cameras parked across the street for days and days, just waiting for him to come out," she says. "But he escaped through the basement when I warned him. The phone is a nuisance, though. I get between fifteen and twenty calls a day from people trying to get through to him. People try to leave messages, and they try to leave gifts. We don't take the messages, and we don't accept the gifts."

But times may be changing. Not long ago Warner LeRoy became concerned when he noticed that a group of teen-age girls was going up and down the street, talking to various doormen. He asked one of the doormen what the girls were after. "They're trying to find out which building Rex Reed lives in," he was told.

In terms of renovations Winnie Bodkin is decidedly a traditionalist. "I feel terrible when I see the beautiful paneling and mantels being shipped out," she says, "or when I hear that someone is painting over the lovely mahogany. People never used to do things like that." She is also disparaging of the building's elaborate new security system. New York, in Winnie's opinion, began to get security-conscious in the late 1950's and 1960's, and by the 1970's people had become obsessive about it to the point of paranoia. "In the old days there were no burglaries," she says. "Now we have an electric door and an electric gate. What good does it do? If a burglar wants to get in, he'll get in. The trouble with people nowadays is that they don't want jobs, they don't want to work. People just work a few weeks so they can collect unemployment."

Winnie Bodkin remembers the names of all the Dakotans, past and present, along with their apartment numbers. But if she knows of any family skeletons, or where any "bodies are buried," she is too discreet, too protective of what she still occasionally refers to as "my people" to reveal them. Actually, she doubtless considers it part of her duty *not* to know too much about her tenants' private lives, and if she was ever privy to any juicy secrets, she says, "When I started here, I was too young to pay attention, and now I'm too old to remember."

She does remember Mr. Edward Severin Clark, though. "He lived upstate and didn't come down much. When he did, he'd sit in a chair just outside the office door—a little bit of a man—just watching the people come and go."

That is what Winnie Bodkin enjoys doing, too. She also has a startlingly clear mental picture of the building's labyrinthine floor plan —something that even the oldest of the old-timers in the building have never quite managed to grasp. Visitors are always getting lost in the Dakota's corridors. Not long ago Mrs. Edward Sherrick heard her front doorbell ring. Though not expecting a visitor and still in her robe and slippers, she assumed that the caller must be someone from the building's staff. She opened the door to face Jacqueline Kennedy Onassis in all her glory. Mrs. Onassis, who had come to call on Jean Stein vanden Heuvel, had rung the wrong bell. She would not have got lost had she followed Winnie's directions to the letter: "Cross the courtyard to the window with the pink curtain, turn left, go up three steps, turn right . . ." At the same time, Winnie Bodkin has never set foot inside most of the apartments in the Dakota. People have asked her in from time to time, but she has politely refused. That, she feels, is not her place.

As for ghosts in the Dakota, Winnie Bodkin says, "We did have one watchman who took it seriously. He used to say he heard fantastic noises—voices and sounds of people walking about. As for me, I never saw one worse ghost than myself."

When Winnie Bodkin declined to join the strikers' picket line, and chose instead to slip quietly into the building and remain there for the duration of the strike, she was not only expressing her loyalty to the Dakota and her people but was also saying something about her attitudes toward work and strikes in general. She enjoyed herself during the strike along with everyone else, just sticking to her routine. The building ran itself without a hitch and everyone cooperated—or almost everyone. Lauren Bacall insisted on having a service elevator (manned by a tenant volunteer) at her disposal, to the annoyance of some people, since most tenants were using the stairs and Miss Bacall lived only on the fourth floor. Roberta Flack was also somewhat demanding. She had not bothered to have an identification card made up for herself, and, one day when Theodate Severns was at the front desk, a black gentleman came into the building and asked for Miss Flack's key. Miss Flack had asked him, he said, to go up and feed her cat. Mrs. Severns was reluctant to admit him but, to avoid a scene, finally let him in. A short time later, a black woman appeared and asked Mrs. Severns to buzz her in through the front gate. Mrs. Severns, who did not recognize the singer, asked for identification. "I am Roberta Flack," said Miss Flack. "I don't need identification."

IN ONE OF the rooftop storage rooms of the Dakota stand a number of ancient and empty filing cabinets. Several years ago Edward Downes was surprised to encounter in the hall one of the building's handymen with his arms full of bulging old file folders. Downes asked the porter what he was doing with them. "Throwing all this old stuff out," said the porter. Hastily, Downes managed to retrieve a few random documents—old bills, rent records, correspondence between Edward Clark and his superintendent—perhaps a dozen pieces of paper in all. But the rest of the building's records, eighty years' worth of its history, were all destroyed that day. Records of who had lived there and where, who had complained about what, who had been born, who had died, who had moved on, were all gone. Jo Mielziner, during his lifetime, had collected bits and pieces of Dakota history and kept them in files and scrapbooks. But Mielziner's executors have been unable to uncover that collection of Dakotiana, and so that also must be assumed to be gone.

Only one person has preserved a scrapbook on the Dakota and its history—Winnie Bodkin. Her scrapbook, a frail volume of yellowing and tattered clippings, is one of her most fiercely guarded possessions. Since its pages are in such a fragile state, she entrusts it to almost no one. In it are collected news items about the Dakota and its people, many of them obituaries of past Dakotans whom Winnie knew and worked for. Here one can read that William Arbuckle Jamison left an estate of $7,318,545 when he died in 1926. We read of George T. Wilson's death in 1933, and of how, from a $3-a-week lunchroom worker for Equitable Life, he rose to become the company's second vice-president at $24,000 a year; obviously an imposing salary in those Depression days. We read of the wedding in Old Westbury, Long Island, of Mr. F. Ambrose Clark, a brother of Stephen C. Clark, to Mrs. Jennifer Miller. The bride was sixty, the bridegroom seventy-seven. We read of sixty-eight-year-old Patrick Feehan, a Dakota elevator operator, who fell dead of a stroke at the lever of his elevator car. The elevator stopped automatically on the ninth floor. When Rosa F. Huyler Cooke, an heiress to a candy fortune, died, we read that, LUNATIC GETS SHARE OF HUYLER ESTATE. The lunatic was her husband, an inmate at the State Insane Hospital in Middleton, New York, and he was willed $50,000, his wife's jewelry and the life income of his wife's residuary estate. It was Mrs. Cooke who installed the swimming pool which the Larry Ellmans uncovered, and it is clear that the Cookes preceded Miss Leo in apartment 17.

One puzzling clipping is headlined ADJUSTING FLUSH TANK EASY IF YOU KNOW HOW. What follows is a lengthy and detailed description of how to fix a leaking toilet tank. There is no mention of the Dakota in the piece. One can only conclude that the author of the story, written for the old *Herald Tribune,* was then, or at one time, a Dakota resident.

And so it is clear that Winifred Bodkin is more than just a concierge for the building, more than a helpful screener of callers and runner of errands. She is also one of the few remaining caretakers and custodians of the Dakota's random memories. Looking around her high-ceilinged office just inside the main gate, she says, "It's a grand old building. In the old days, this building *was* New York."

Chapter 17

Old Guard vs. New

IN 1965, NOT LONG before she moved out, declaring that the place had simply become too expensive, Marya Mannes commented with her customary asperity that the Dakota just wasn't what it used to be and that she simply didn't understand the new breed of people that had moved in. "Now it's getting to be all Café Society," she said. "I just don't run with this new set. There's a great emphasis now on show biz, on 'in' people. There are people now who belong to the extremely up-to-date group of op art and Courrèges fashions and all these fads. It's all quite new here."

To her, the gulf between the old and the new, between elderly matrons and young socialites, had become as wide as their differences in ages, styles and tastes. Though, as in every neighborhood, a few dowagers in black velvet suits and heavy pearl earrings still gathered to sip sherry in their apartments at four in the afternoon, most of the new Dakotans, it seemed to Miss Mannes, now darted in and out of the building in white shaggy furs, short skirts or blue jeans. And though none of the *old* Old Guard ever lived at the Dakota, this is the same change in the "texture" of the building's clientele that is mourned by Winnie Bodkin.

The average age of Dakota tenants had already declined by at least twenty years, and the numbers of the aging few were more than offset by the increased numbers of couples with little children. In the old days, of course, the building had not attracted couples with children, and as recently as 1930, when Mrs. Charles Quinlan (mother of the rebellious William) moved into the building with her brood of three, Mrs. Quinlan remembers that hers were the only children there. During the thirty years that the Quinlans lived there, Mrs. Quinlan was able also to observe a decline in the building's amenities, and in manners as well. Her sons had been taught to bow from the waist; now youngsters wheeling bicycles barged into the elevator ahead of her.

Mrs. Quinlan also remembers the particularly gracious character of the building and its management. When in 1933, at the age of forty, her husband suddenly died of food poisoning, Mrs. Quinlan decided to move to slightly smaller quarters—five rooms and one bath on the third floor. The building helped her move, and then sent in painters, carpenters and electricians to re-do the apartment to her specifications. Bookcases were constructed, and in the process of this work the carpenter suggested to Mrs. Quinlan that she ought to have a storage cabinet for her "papers," and so he built one. A rather awkward passageway led between the living room and one of the bedrooms. This was replaced with an additional bathroom. The kitchen was in a curious state. It had apparently once been a bathroom, or perhaps two bathrooms, because it contained two toilets which sat side by side. These were removed. All of this was done at no cost to Mrs. Quinlan.

"If you didn't feel like cooking, and didn't want to dress up to go down to the dining room," Mrs. Quinlan recalls, "you could phone down and have your meal sent up. Everything came up in huge warmers. They would even set the table for you, and serve you if you wanted. If you got a special-delivery letter, a porter with white gloves brought it up on a silver tray."

The dining room was nothing if not solicitous. Once, Edward Downes recalls, when his father had returned from a fishing trip with a large tuna he had caught, the Dakota's chef cleaned and cooked it for him, and served it on a huge wooden plank. "I'd never known what the expression 'planked fish' meant until then," Downes says. In the old days there was a newsstand across the street that was open twenty-four hours a day, and porters delivered New York's then-multitude of dailies to Dakota tenants as the papers hit the stand. Though the only children in the building were the Quinlans,' a special city policeman was detailed at the corner to escort the children from the Dakota across the street into the Park. "I remember his name was George, and he was so kind," Mrs. Quinlan says. It was an era of politeness and gentility that New York may never see again.

When apartments changed hands in the old days, they did so graciously and with a flourish of gentlemanly considerateness. In the summer of 1907, when Colonel George Harvey was turning over apartment 67 to Mr. Frederick J. Lancaster, Colonel Harvey wrote to the new rentor:

My dear Sir:
Of course I am quite willing that you should take possession of the Dakota Apartment at any time you see fit. I think all of our things have been removed excepting possibly the wall covering of the Reception Room, but I will ask Mrs. Harvey to communicate immediately with the house people regarding that, so that the way will be clear for you.

Yours very truly,

Even the tradespeople with whom the Dakota did business were decorous and courtly. For instance, the Dakota purchased its butter from Fenimore Farm in Cooperstown, which, by no coincidence, belonged to Edward S. Clark, and one would assume that a change in the price of butter would have no effect on this arrangement. Still, in 1906 Mr. Johnston, the agent at the farm, felt it necessary to write to Romer Gillis, then the Dakota's manager, to advise him of a price increase:

On account of the increase in the market value of butter, I am authorized to advise you that commencing January 1st, 1907, and until further notice, the price of butter furnished you from the Fenimore Farm will be at the rate of 35¢ per pound.
Thanking you for your patronage in the past and hoping for a continuance of same, I am, with the compliments of the season,

Very truly yours,

By the summer of 1907 Mr. Gillis had been replaced at the Dakota by Mr. C. B. Knott, and Samuel Couch & Sons, Elevators, Supplies & Repairs—whose letterhead also announced the company as "Manufacturers of Best Lubricating Compound, Peerless Air Checks, Sensible Grease Cups, and United States Flax and Vulcanized Packings"—felt it wise to write to Mr. Knott and say:

We are in receipt of formal announcement . . . of your appointment as Manager of the Dakota Apartment House, and hereby tender our congratulations.

We have, during the past fifteen years attended to the wants of the Clark Estates, when the elevators in the Dakota required attention, and sincerely trust that the same cordial relations will continue to exist. Should you at any time desire any information concerning the elevators, we would be only too willing to give you our expert advice, and assure you that we are at your command at any time you may desire us.

Trusting to have the pleasure of continuing our business relations and soliciting your valued patronage, we are,

Very truly yours,

The Oriental Tea Company of Boston supplied the Dakota with its coffee, and Mr. William North of that company also wrote a solicitous letter to the new manager:

I have your favor of Sept. 18th at hand.* Let me assure you, first, that I appreciate your loyalty to me much more than I do your business. The letter, however, is very gratifying and I shall do my best to see that your weekly shipment of coffee is kept up to standard from first to last; in other words, I shall do all I can at this end to make that part of your work as easy and as pleasant for yourself and your guests as possible.

I shall probably begin shipping Tuesday, October 1st, and that being as good a day as any for me, will continue shipping on that date. I presume you want the coffee ground fine, same as I sent it to you before, and will carry out that idea unless I hear from you to the contrary.

Once more thanking you, I remain,

Very truly yours,

---

*This letter is dated September 19, revealing the interesting fact that in 1907 it took no more than a day for a letter to travel between New York and Boston.

One would not have supposed that this letter would have called for a reply, but Mr. Knott, not to be outdone in the arena of courtesies, sent off the following day this communication to Mr. North:

I am in receipt of your favor of the 19th inst., and note same and thank you for your very kind expressions. In return let me congratulate you on the method you have always pursued in the conduction of your business, that it is possible for one to deal with the head of the house without being always cast off onto a salesman, who in all probability is working for a commission and whose solicitations cease on the booking of the order, when with him the whistle blew twelve and there is absolutely nothing on his mind except dinner, or another order and any instruction in regard to yours "can go hanged." This state of things is very disagreeable to the purchaser. I never found it in your concern, so you see you have yourself to thank for the loyalty of your customers.

Yes, I want the same fine grind as you sent and the date selected by you will be eminently satisfactory.

Best wishes.

Yours very truly,

Perhaps, once upon a time, Americans were a gentler breed of folk.

Certainly the Dakota, when it was a building of somewhat older, properly married, for the most part childless people—the kind of people Winnie Bodkin feels made it seem more like a "family" building —was a considerably quieter, less disputatious place. Though it didn't project the kind of glossy glamour that it does today, it projected continuity and calm. The building had its share of well-known tenants, but they were people whose celebrity did not depend on press agents. As a result, some of those older people, distinguished in their day, have not exactly lasted as household names into the late 1970's.

For example, Mr. Frederick Coykendall, the chairman of the board of trustees of Columbia University, died at the Dakota in 1954, a few days short of his eighty-second birthday. It was Mr. Coykendall's board that was responsible for a historic mix-up in 1948, when the university was scouting for a new president. The board had voted to approach "Eisenhower," intending this to be Dr. Milton S. Eisenhower, the educator. Somewhere down the line, however, there was a misunderstanding, and the Eisenhower approached was Dr. Eisenhower's brother, Dwight D. Eisenhower. The former President promptly accepted the post. Though it got the wrong Eisenhower, there was not much the university could do under the circumstances, and Frederick Coykendall officiated at President Eisenhower's installation, proffering to him the historic charters and keys. Mr. Coykendall was in charge of the same ceremony again in 1953 when Dr. Grayson Kirk assumed the presidency of Columbia.

Frederick Coykendall was originally from Kingston, New York, where the Coykendall family had been prominent for several generations. He was graduated from Columbia in the class of 1895, and for a time he headed an informal social group which called itself "The Last of the Forty-Niners," men who had graduated from the old Columbia at Forty-ninth Street and Madison Avenue. In 1926 Mr. Coykendall received the Class of 1889 Gold Medal for Achievement at Columbia, and in 1940 Hamilton College gave him an honorary degree of Doctor of Laws.

The Coykendall family had long been prominent in Hudson River shipping, and, following college, Frederick Coykendall became secretary of the family-owned Cornell Steamboat Company (which operated a fleet of tugboats on the river) and later became the company's president. As a businessman, he was a member of the New York State Chamber of Commerce, the New York Board of Trade, and Commerce and Industry Association, and the Maritime Association of the Port of New York. Still, he was essentially a scholar and a bibliophile. For years his 6,000-volume collection of poetry, early periodicals, and seventeenth- and eighteenth-century romances lined the walls of his Dakota apartment. Eventually, most of this collection went to Columbia.

"Professor" Coykendall, as he was often called, was a gentle-mannered gentleman with a full head of white hair, and was once described by a contemporary as a "quiet man who says but little, but when he does speak has already made up his mind and states it with a force that instantly brings to him the concurrent support of his associates." When Mr. Coykendall died his Dakota apartment on the courtyard was one of the few that had remained in its original state, its doorways draped with heavy portieres and tassels, its walls all hung with dark-green velvet. Windows and over-doors were of stained glass and, just inside the front door, was a stuffed bear that carried a silver card tray in one paw. After his death the New York *Times* editorialized, "Frederick

Coykendall did not use his excellent taste in letters and the arts as a refuge from the storms and responsibilities of life. Instead, he projected them into many years of able service to Columbia University. Combined with a talent and industry that made him a force in the business life of New York State, they were of great importance to the university." During his funeral service, Columbia suspended all classes.

Another distinguished Dakotan of the past was Dr. Michael Idvorsky Pupin who lived at the Dakota until his death in 1935. His was a Horatio Alger success story—a Serbian shepherd boy, the son of illiterate parents, who came to America, became one of the most famous scientists and inventors of his day, won the Pulitzer Prize and numberless other honors and degrees, and died a millionaire. In his autobiography, *From Immigrant to Inventor,* Dr. Pupin wrote of how, at age fifteen, he persuaded his parents to let him immigrate to "the land of infinite opportunity," taking with him only a small bundle of food and clothing. When he arrived at Castle Garden in the autumn of 1874, he had only five cents to his name. He immediately spent his fortune on a slice of prune pie that, when he bit into it, seemed to contain mostly prune pits. On his voyage from the old country he had lost his hat, and when he stepped out into the streets of New York he was wearing a fez. This marked him as a foreigner, and he was immediately set upon by a group of young hoodlums. In the end, Pupin won the fight but lost both the fez and the piece of pie. Still, despite this unfriendly welcome, he cheerfully set out to make a name for himself in the New World.

For a while he worked as a mule driver in Delaware City, Maryland. He also worked in a cracker factory, in a grocery store as a shipping clerk, and as a laborer on farms in New Jersey. By 1879 he had saved $311 from these odd jobs, which was sufficient to permit him to enter Columbia. He passed the entrance examinations with high honors, and four years later graduated, again with honors, as president of his class. Michael Pupin then went to Cambridge for a while, where he studied mathematics and physics, and then to the University of Berlin, where he studied thermodynamics. In 1901 he returned to Columbia where, until 1931, he was Professor of Electro-Mechanics.

It was during these years that his genius as an inventor became apparent—with inventions in electrical wave propagation, electrical resonance and multiplex telegraphy. He discovered secondary X-ray radiation and invented a means for short-exposure X-ray photography by means of a fluorescent screen. This produced a method of photography that shortened the time of exposure from about an hour to a few seconds. During World War I he invented an X-ray device for spotting submarines, which he donated to the United States government. His most celebrated invention, however, was the Pupin Coil, which greatly extended the range of the long-distance telephone. This he sold to the Bell Telephone Company and to other foreign telephone interests. The Pupin Coil made him a rich man.

For the rest of his life Dr. Pupin went on inventing devices in telephone, telegraphy and X-ray technology, collecting, as he went, a long string of medals, awards, honorary degrees and prizes. His book, when he won the Pulitzer Prize in 1924, was cited as "the best American biography teaching patriotic and unselfish services to the people." When he died, at age seventy-six, the huge Cathedral of St. John the Divine overflowed with mourners, and among those who sent flowers were King Peter II of Yugoslavia, John D. Rockefeller and J. P. Morgan. Bishop Manning eulogized: "Michael Pupin was a noble and illustrious American whose life was an honor to his adopted country."

Michael Pupin was a plump, cheerful man with a walrus moustache and round, steel-framed spectacles that perched on the tip of his nose. Though his scientific inventions had, for the most part, practical human uses, Dr. Pupin also had a strong faith in God, in a divine plan and in a life of the human soul and intelligence beyond the grave. In an interview with the New York *Times* he once said, "Science gives us plenty of ground for intelligent hope that our physical life is only a stage in the existence of the soul. The law of continuity and the general scientific view of the universe tend to strengthen our belief that the soul goes on existing and developing after death."

His first intimations of immortality, he said, came to him on nights as a boy in Serbia, where he guarded his father's sheep and cattle from wolves and thieves, when he gazed at the stars and listened to the tolling of distant church bells. "It seemed to me then," he said, "that light and sound were divine methods of speech, and so two questions: What is light? And what is sound? filled my waking thoughts and penetrated my dreams. The more I have thought of these things as a scientific man, the more do I realize that my boyhood fancy was correct. When I hear a great musician play Beethoven or Brahms on a violin, I feel he is making the vibrating strings speak a language that is a true message from Heaven."

He was asked to explain his concept of Heaven. "It is what scientists call the real world and of which this world is only a picture. All scientific work and investigation are directed toward further revelation of the world beyond. All of this world—the present world—that we know anything about is perceived through the senses. We see a sunset, a rainbow, the new green of spring. We hear the songs of the birds, we smell the perfume of the rose, we taste, we feel, but it all leads to glimpses of another world. Wherever science has explored the universe, it has found it to be a manifestation of a coordinating principle, a definite, guiding principle which leads from chaos to cosmos. I choose to believe in this coordinating principle as a divine intelligence. There is dependability, continuity everywhere present in the universe."

Finally, Dr. Pupin was asked what sort of state the soul would occupy when it progressed to what he called the real world, and he answered this question with another question. "The soul of man is the highest product of God's creative handiwork. Now, after God has spent untold time in creating man and endowing him with a soul, which is the reflection of his image, is it reasonable to suppose that man lives here on earth for a brief span and then is extinguished by death? That the soul perishes with the physical body? That it existed in vain?"

OF COURSE, NOT all the early Dakotans were philosophers, humanitarians, scientists and educators. Those more serene, less harried days also saw people who almost made it a point to do very little with their lives. There was Mr. James King Hand, for example. Though he served as a lieutenant in the Navy during World War I, stationed comfortably in Washington, Mr. Hand's only other real occupation was as "perpetual president" of the James King Hand Walking Club. The James King Hand Walking Club was started in 1894, when Mr. Hand was thirty-seven and was in the habit of going to Sunday worship at the old Holy Trinity Church, which was then at 122nd Street and Lexington Avenue. One of Mr. Hand's contemporaries in the congregation was Mr. J. Oakley Hobby, Jr., who later became treasurer of the American Locomotive Company. Another friend was Theodore Bridgeman whose father, the Reverend C. DeWitt Bridgeman, was pastor of the church.

The Sunday before Christmas of that year, young Bridgeman advised Messrs. Hand and Hobby that a visiting clergyman, whose sermons were considered less than stimulating, would be in the pulpit that day. Bridgeman suggested that the trio might find something more amusing to do than sitting in a pew. Mr. Hand suggested a walk in Westchester County. Hand had grown up in Ossining, knew the countryside well, and that Sunday the three young men hiked from Ossining to Yorktown, about twenty-five miles. The three had such a wonderful time on their walk that they decided then and there to make it an annual pre-Christmas Sunday tradition.

Theodore Bridgeman eventually dropped out of the Walking Club, but Hand and Hobby continued to observe the yearly ritual, and some twenty new members were taken in. The club became very exclusive, and it was not long before it had closed itself to new members. As the years went by, this had the effect of gradually thinning the numbers of hikers. By the late 1920's only a handful remained, and the distance of the yearly walk had been cut down to three and three-quarters miles, from Chappaqua to the Campfire Club in White Plains. By the early 1930's some of the members had become so enfeebled that they actually covered this distance by automobile, and met the others at the club for dinner. In 1932 Mr. Hand was too ill to join his group at all. Still, as he had done for forty years, Mr. Hobby went out the day before the hike and blazed the trail, stashing in advance a supply of snacks and spirits here and there so that the hikers could pause and refresh themselves during the course of their ordeal.

The little group had become very touchy about publicity, and members were irked by the fact that for some time the local press had been having a bit of sport with the annual activities of the James King Hand Walking Club. For several years, newspaper photographers had taken to concealing themselves in the shrubbery along the trail in order to get pictures of the elderly members observing their rite. This grew so irksome to the group that in 1933 the perpetual president announced that that year's hike was being cancelled, due to the advanced age of the members. Of course it was only a ruse to throw the newspapers off the scent. The group met clandestinely, and carried out the rite in secret.

In 1934 the perpetual president died in his home at the Dakota, and what remained of the James King Hand Walking Club disbanded.

MR. HAND, a bachelor, liked to entertain at small "gentlemens' dinners" at the Dakota, and was celebrated among his friends for his original cocktail recipes. With his effects were found several of his private formulas from the Prohibition era. One favorite was called the Last Resort, consisting of one-part gin, one-part grapefruit juice, one-part orange juice, and a teaspoon of grenadine. This was served in a glass rolled in granulated sugar. Then there was the Three-Mile Limit— two-thirds brandy, one-third Bacardi rum, a teaspoon of grenadine and a dash of lemon juice. But considered the most delicious was the Lady Corday—two-thirds gin, one-third vanilla ice cream and a teaspoon of grenadine. This concoction was then shaken until the ice cream liquefied.

What, a short generation later, would the likes of Mr. Hand and his contemporaries have made of the 1970 party tossed at the Dakota by a thirty-two-year-old record-company executive named Robert Crewe? His apartment blazed with flashing strobe lights and rocked with noisy music. There were three hundred guests, including such people-of-the-moment as Mrs. Leonard ("Baby Jane") Holzer, Andy Warhol, Christiana Paolozzi and the Rolling Stones. Among other things, the guests heard a singer called Tiny Tim sing "Tiptoe Through the Tulips" in a squeaking falsetto.

Against such a frenetic background and harried life-style, even the bizarrely dressed John Lennons seem like creatures of another, gentler era. Lennon isn't very active in the music world anymore, though he does operate something called Lennon Music, Inc., with offices on Sixth Avenue, and a telephone, which is an answering service. In our fast and frenzied world of today—an era which seems characterized by a terribly short community, and national, memory—the Beatles seem suddenly quite long-ago.

David Marlowe, a novelist (*Yearbook*), can look from his eighth-floor living-room window down into the Lennons' seventh-floor kitchen in the Dakota. Sometimes he sees John Lennon sitting in the kitchen, alone, strumming his guitar. If the window is open, faint music drifts up. The old Beatles songs, with their wild bursts of melody, which once seemed so exuberantly cheerful ("Yeah, yeah, yeah"), and which were about love as much as anything, now sound sad from David Marlowe's window listening-point. The tunes fill Marlowe with a curious feeling of melancholy, a wishful wistfulness for the old days when, it sometimes seems, everything (including people) was a little nicer.

Chapter 18

The
Palace Revolution

I<small>N THE LITTLE</small> town of Coventry, Connecticut, not long ago, a local lawyer's Irish setter got into a neighboring farmer's chicken coop and killed some broody hens. Though the owner of the offending dog fully compensated the farmer for his loss, bad blood remained between the farmer and the lawyer. Some time after the incident the lawyer was named for a government post that required top-secret security clearance, and, as it routinely does in such cases, the Federal Bureau of Investigation interviewed a number of the lawyer's fellow townspeople. The FBI learned nothing of a security-threatening nature until the neighboring farmer was interviewed. From him the agent learned that the lawyer was not only a scoundrel and a rogue but, to boot, a drunkard and a wife-beater and a member in good standing of the Communist Party. Fortunately for the lawyer's future, further checking revealed that what was at issue was not politics but poultry.

Sophisticated New Yorkers, of course, would not stoop to such small-town stuff as Hatfield-McCoy feuding. And yet, quite recently, in a luxury co-operative on the West Side, a similar controversy developed over the issue of storm windows. The windows chosen by the incumbent board of directors had been of the single-panel variety. Another faction in the building, however, favored two-track aluminum-frame windows. The controversy reached such a degree of intensity that at a basement caucus convened to discuss the matter, a fistfight broke out between members of the opposing factions. At the same time, two young people in the building, meeting for the first time and discovering themselves both to be impassioned defenders of the two-track aluminum-frame devices, fell in love and were married.

Of course this all took place in another building—not the superso-phisticated Dakota.

"HERE AT THE Dakota, we're like kids at a summer camp," says Mrs. Henry Blanchard. Some people think that Mrs. Blanchard tends to view Dakota life through rose-colored spectacles, but she may be stating the situation aptly. Kids at a summer camp, one remembers, fight a lot. The Dakota had not been a co-operative long before it became apparent that some people were more co-operative than others. Still, in 1969 few people realized that storm clouds were gathering in the building that would bring on another important crisis in the building's history, the worst since Zeckendorf-Glickman *et al.*

It all began innocently enough when Mr. and Mrs. Gordon K. Greenfield agreed to sell their Dakota apartment to Mr. and Mrs. Wilbur L. Ross, Jr. The Rosses and the Greenfields had much in common. Both Wilbur Ross and Gordon Greenfield were men in the prime of life, successful businessmen, handsome, with slim, attractive, dark-haired wives. Gordon Greenfield was in real estate and was the son of the millionaire Albert M. Greenfield, a legendary Philadelphia real estate man. Wilbur Ross was an investment banker at the time, a partner in the New York firm of Faulkner, Dawkins & Sullivan. Both men were able, responsible, bright and tough—and knew it. For the Greenfields it was a within-the-house move of the kind that so often took place under the Dakota's roof as apartments became available and were shuffled or traded off, and tenants moved up or down in search of larger or smaller spaces. The Rosses were moving into the Green-fields' old place, and the Greenfields were moving to another floor.

There were, however, in Greenfield's eye, certain subtle differences between the Rosses and the Greenfields involving social class, not unlike the differences that had kept Edward Clark and Isaac Singer at arms' length throughout their business careers. Gordon Greenfield, a graduate of Lawrenceville and Princeton, had grown up in Philadelphia, where the Greenfields were almost if not quite accepted as part of Philadelphia society, and he considered himself a philanthropist and patron of the arts. To Greenfield, Wilbur Ross's New Jersey origins were more humble. Furthermore, in terms of the Dakota the Greenfields considered themselves among the building's Old Guard. They had lived there since before the building went co-operative. The Rosses had been in the building since only 1969 and were therefore, in the literal sense, parvenus. Finally, when Ernest Gross had retired as president of the Dakota's board, he had selected Gordon Greenfield as his heir. Greenfield ran the building, and, it had to be admitted, he ran a tight ship.

The Greenfields had agreed to move out of their apartment the day before the Rosses were to move in. In many ways moving can be a shattering experience in itself. Not only are there the heavy chores of packing and supervising packers; there are also the attendant fears of breakage and loss of cherished objects. Added to the trauma of moving day are its emotional connotations, the wrench of leaving a familiar place and its memories. Psychologists have pointed out that moving day, while it can be a nightmare for everyone, can play particular havoc with a woman's psyche. It is the nest she has built for her brood that must be moved. Thus it was with considerable dismay that Judy Ross and her movers arrived at her new apartment on the appointed day to find the Greenfields still in bed. They had not even begun to move out. "I really hit the ceiling," says Mrs. Ross. What followed was a scene of the first order, and in the end the Greenfields moved out the back door while the Rosses moved in from the front.

Ill feeling had already been brewing between the two families. After buying the Greenfield apartment Wilbur Ross had been heard to mutter to someone in the building that Greenfield had charged him more than the apartment was worth. Word of this had gotten back to the Greenfields, who resented the implication that they had been guilty of sharp practice. According to the Greenfields, however, this was not why they had not moved out of the apartment on the date promised. There had been, Harriet Greenfield says, a subway flood the previous day, and the Greenfields' movers had been unable to come as sched-

uled. Still, the Greenfields had neglected to tell the Rosses of this
change of plans. To make matters between the two families worse,
when all the moving was finally completed, Gordon Greenfield telephoned Wilbur Ross to say that some of Mrs. Greenfield's jewelry was
missing; he suggested that the Rosses' moving men might have taken
it. "I hit the ceiling all over again," says Judy Ross. The two women
never spoke again, and a certain chilliness developed between the two
men—though the jewels later turned up.

Meanwhile, from its earliest days as a co-operative, there had been
grumblings in the building about how it was being run. As to the
Dakota's management, the building was operated, some people said, by
an "elite cadre"—by men like C. D. Jackson, Ernest Gross, Admiral
Kirk, by the men who owned the largest apartments and the largest
blocks of voting shares. The little guy was being ignored. From Ernest
Gross the mantle of stewardship had passed to Gordon Greenfield, who
directed the building in the same high-handed way, as though it was
his building and not everybody else's too. Greenfield, they said, was
autocratic, dictatorial. He was uncommunicative, secretive, and when
his rulership was questioned, his responses were abrasive. Year after
year, for the seven places on the building's board the same seven names
appeared on the ballot. A palace guard was in command, and the voices
of young Turks went unheard. Gordon Greenfield was compared with
Napoleon, with Louis XIV, with Hitler, with Captain Queeg, with
Richard Nixon. Late in 1970 a movement began to get underway to
dethrone him—led by Wilbur Ross.

In fairness to Gordon Greenfield, he loved the Dakota and had its
best interests at heart. He was also a shrewd businessman, and his
primary objective was to keep the costs of maintaining the building in
check. Others, notably from the Dakota's "artistic" community, had
suggestions that, Greenfield maintained, would make the Dakota a
more expensive, less desirable place to live and were, moreover, "crack-
pot and spendthrift." The Dakota's vaulted basement wine cellar, for
example, had been empty for years. Someone thought that this space
could be converted into an exciting restaurant and discotheque. Another large basement area seemed ideally suited for a squash court, and,
without even measuring the space, plans were drawn up. (When it was
finally measured the area turned out to be too small.) Then there was
a proposal to turn the subterranean water tank, which held the water

that ran the hydraulic elevators, into a swimming pool, and in this connection a scheme for an elaborate basement health club was proposed. Someone else wanted to restore the tents and awnings and gazebos that had long ago adorned the Dakota's roof. Greenfield and his board said no to all these fun-and-games notions.

Gordon Greenfield's eye was on the bottom line. Except where absolutely necessary, he wanted to cut expenditures, not increase them, because—and it was indeed a fact—the Dakota was already walking on very thin ice financially. Why, Greenfield was asked, couldn't the building borrow money for some of these pleasant improvements? Greenfield, in the brusque manner that was typical of him, replied that the building was heavily enough in debt as it was.

Greenfield would dispose of what he considered trivia in a regal manner, keeping stockholders' meetings brief and to the point. Lauren Bacall, for example, did not often appear at tenant meetings, but she did have a habit of sending memoranda in which she complained about everything from bicycles blocking the driveway to the fact that she had difficulty understanding what some of the building's Hispanic staff were saying. At meetings Gordon Greenfield would say, "I think we can dispense with the usual Bacall memorandum," and it would be dispensed with. To some people this seemed quite wrong. Miss Bacall was a tenant and shareholder in good standing, too. Regardless of what was on her mind, she deserved to have her say.

What Gordon Greenfield may not have realized was that by 1970 New York—and the country—had been invaded by the Love Generation. Greenfield, who believed that a stern no-nonsense helmsman was required to steer a vessel of the Dakota's size and costliness, may have failed to see that what many people in the building now wanted were Communication, Sharing and Love. Love had become one of the most overused and, in the process, least understood words in the country. Some people, it seemed, were ready to kill for Love. At the Dakota a passionate Love faction girded itself to go into battle against Hate, which had come to be personified by Gordon Greenfield.

No one could fault Greenfield on his thoroughness, his honesty, his tough-minded efficiency. The Dakota and its vicissitudes consumed hours of his time, for which he received no remuneration, and, indeed, some people wondered why he seemed devoted to such a thankless job. To be sure, he may have enjoyed the power that he wielded—in fact, comparing him with Captain Bligh, some people called him power-mad. But in the end it was really not anything that Greenfield *did* that anyone resented. It was his personal *style* that grated.

In addition to the Dakota's financial picture, Gordon Greenfield had also become concerned about what he called a "social problem" in the building. Let him describe it:

"After the building went co-op, a company called the Franchard Corporation was set up by Glickman. The purpose of Franchard was to sell the unsold apartments, and to sell them as quickly as possible. That, in my opinion, was the beginning of the deterioration of the quality of the tenancy, because a lot of sharks moved in and bought cheap apartments. A lot of wheeling and dealing went on within the building, and people were trying to get a bigger slice of the pie. I know that ——— bought a big apartment for $5,000, then divided it and sold off half of it for $55,000. Other questionable things went on such as when ——— bought an apartment for $10,000 and sold an antique mahogany and marble mantelpiece for $35,000. We wanted conservative types as tenants, we wanted good, solid family types, we didn't want riffraff. We had always had an interesting group of theatrical people in the building—people like Robert Ryan and his wife, who were solid family types. The Lennons bought the Ryan apartment, and you just can't put John Lennon in the same category as Robert Ryan. The Carter Burdens bought an apartment, and they were the sort of people we wanted, but then they sold to Freddie Mates who ran the Mates Fund, which folded, and Freddie Mates moved out. He started out with a Rolls-Royce and now he runs a bar. At the time I pointed out that it was dangerous to sell to stock speculators. But then there was what I call a special 'social problem' in the building. There was one couple who used to have terrible domestic fights, and the police would have to be called. Another woman was an alcoholic and used to slide down banisters. There were two young men who liked to pick up male hustlers in Central Park and bring them into the building. There was a man named——— who became a homosexual, and his boyfriend set a fire. Another man wanted to move in with his boyfriend, and we turned him down because of his life-style. One tenant bought several rooms on the eighth and ninth floors, and rented them out to young men. Before I sold my apartment to Wilbur Ross I'd had a higher offer from a well-known homosexual. I turned it down. There were more fires, wild parties. Finally the board said, 'We don't want to show any more apartments to homosexuals.' Things were building up to a head of steam."

The board member in charge of interviewing and screening prospective tenants in those days was Mrs. Eileen Carlson, a lawyer who supported Mr. Greenfield's views. In her interviews Mrs. Carlson began asking what to some people seemed rather nosy questions related to "life-style." "Are you married?" she asked one man who wanted to buy an apartment. "Well, I'm getting a divorce," he replied. "Can I still join the club?"

When the gentle-mannered, bespectacled playwright Mart Crowley applied to the building, he was vigorously sponsored by both Rex Reed and Ruth Ford. Crowley had become a New York celebrity as a result of his Broadway and motion-picture homosexual drama, *The Boys in the Band*. Crowley was turned down by the Dakota. "I really felt terrible, afterward, about sponsoring Mart," Rex Reed says, "because it opened such an ugly vein."

In taking a stand against homosexuals in the building, the Dakota's board was touching an extremely sensitive nerve. It was not that the Dakota was the first or only New York apartment building to discriminate in this fashion. A number of buildings, particularly on the East Side, routinely denied applications to partners of the same sex, just as they turned down theater people, who kept irregular hours, and musicians who practiced on noisy instruments. But that this should happen at the *Dakota* seemed particularly repugnant. The Dakota had long provided a safe harbor for the gifted, the brilliant misfits, the different. This was not the East Side; it was the West Side, where the fresh breezes of intelligence, enlightenment, tolerance and freedom blew. At the same time, all over the country homosexuality was being regarded much more openly and liberally, and homosexuals were demanding— and getting—more respect. Writers such as Tennessee Williams and Truman Capote were making no bones about it. Frank and sympathetic books were being published on the subject, and in some cities, notably San Francisco, groups such as the Gay Activists Alliance were becoming a political force. It had become something of a joke at the Dakota to say, "Some of the most distinguished homosexuals in New York live here."

To people in the theater, homosexuality was considered a commonplace not even worth mentioning, and a person's sexual orientation was a topic less interesting than the weather. And in a city that cherished privacy over all other blessings, sexual preference was deemed the most private realm of all—nobody's business but the individual's. When it was learned that the Dakota's board was investigating and weighing such matters in terms of prospective tenants, hackles rose in alarm.

Still, to give Gordon Greenfield credit he did have a certain point. Just a block north of the Dakota, as we have seen, a section of the stone wall that encloses Central Park had become known as "the meat rack." The wall was a favorite perching place for young male prostitutes soliciting their clients. At least a few of these young men, it was safe to assume, had other things on their minds than sex—robbery, burglary, blackmail and extortion, for example. They were considered dangerous, and bringing them into the building, as some tenants were suspected of doing, was a threat to the general welfare.

TO MR. WILBUR ROSS, meanwhile, there were more important things wrong with the Greenfield administration than its unwelcoming attitude toward homosexuals. Ross, who had received a master's degree with distinction from the Harvard School of Business, considered himself something of an expert in the field of finance. As a relatively new tenant in the building he had observed aspects of the board's operation that seemed to him improper, or at least unfair. It disturbed him, for example, that for seven places on the Dakota's board there were only seven candidates for whom to vote. To make the board more representative, Ross wanted an eleven-man board.

The board had also proposed a regulation to the effect that any apartment for sale in the building had to be offered through a particular real estate broker. This rule had been put up in an effort to put an end to private, inside deals, but it seemed wrong. Ross believed that most of the tenants in the building were not people like Gordon Greenfield, who was independently wealthy. Instead, they were people with high incomes but little actual capital. One of the attractions of owning a co-operative apartment is that a substantial proportion of each tenant's monthly maintenance—that which represents mortgage interest, real estate taxes and insurance—is tax deductible. The mortgage that the Dakota then had, allowed in Wilbur Ross's opinion, too much payment against principal and not enough in interest. If a new mortgage could be obtained that would cost the building more in interest and paid less in capital, each tenant's tax-deductible share of his maintenance cost could be increased.

Ross also felt that certiorari proceedings could be undertaken with the city in order to get a tax reduction for the building, based on its landmark status. He felt that the building was paying too much for insurance and should have a higher deductible clause in its contract. He felt that the building had not had enough preventive maintenance, that the roof, plumbing and electrical systems had been neglected under the regime of Gordon Greenfield.

But an overriding issue seemed to be Ross's belief that Greenfield and his board had ruled the building in a fashion that was "autocratic," and that it had ruled it long enough. It was time for new blood, new talent on the board, time for a new generation. Wilbur Ross, at the time, was a feisty thirty-three; Gordon Greenfield was fifty-five. It was time, Wilbur Ross decided, to throw the old fogeys out.

Early in 1970 Wilbur Ross drew a group of tenants together and urged them to get other shareholders active. They circularized the building with a complaint sheet, and then held a large meeting and wrote up a slate for the next annual meeting. They wrote to Gordon Greenfield and asked to appear before his board with their grievances.

Gordon Greenfield was furious. "To show you the kind of man Ross is," he says today, "he actually brought some business to me while he was plotting behind my back to overthrow me."

Wilbur Ross says, "It was not intended as a personal thing. Gordon chose to take it personally."

But Wilbur Ross had early on gotten the support of two of the building's most popular tenants—Jo Mielziner and Henry Blanchard. They brought with them others—Lewis Galantiere, a writer; Edward Downes, a music scholar and critic; Lauren Bacall, Ruth Ford, Rex Reed. But it was not just a conflict between practical business folk and less practical artistic types. On the dissidents' side were Richard Defendini, a doctor; Larry Ellman, a restauranteur; and Peter Nitze, a banker. Nor was it—despite all the talk of the need for "new blood"—strictly speaking a confrontation between a younger generation and the old-timers. Mrs. C. D. Jackson and even old Miss Leo declared themselves on the side of the insurgents. It was more like a political battle between Republicans and Democrats.

Some people in the building were merely confused by what was happening. Sheila Herbert, a young advertising woman who had practically grown up in the building, was baffled. "I couldn't understand it," she says. "I thought that Gordon Greenfield's board should have been *revered* for all they'd done, for all the time they'd devoted to the building. I thought the building should be grateful. But suddenly everybody was going around saying these perfectly dreadful things about them."

The building's rhetoric had indeed become quite martial, and what to an outsider might have seemed a tempest in a Victorian teapot was being discussed in terms that could have described a junta in a banana republic. Gordon Greenfield, meanwhile, and his incumbent board were convinced that their record of cautious, conservative economy and cost-cutting would speak for itself. They were certain that, since most of them had longer tenure in the building than Wilbur Ross, they had earned more loyalty and won more friends. "But if they wanted all-out war, we decided to give them all-out war," Gordon Greenfield says.

Chapter 19

"High Noon"

WILBUR ROSS has a theory that the Dakota itself—the very physicality of the old building—somehow manages to induce a certain amount of irrationality on the part of its tenants. Certainly Dakotans seem to get more exercised about events than ordinary New Yorkers. Early in 1979, for example, the building was up in arms again about a neighborhood coffee shop that proposed to call itself The Dakota. Once again, committees of protest were formed to fight the "outrage" and "insult" to the building, though it was hard for some people to figure out what the fuss was all about. Naming shops after nearby buildings is a common practice all over the world. (Hard by the Apthorp Apartments can be found the Apthorp Garage, the Apthorp Pharmacy, the Apthorp Hairdressers, and the Apthorp Laundromat.) But to the Dakotans, what the restaurant proposed to do seemed more of a sacrilege than taking the name of God in vain.

Feelings ran just as strongly during the winter of 1970–71 in what would later be referred to grandiosely as the "Palace Revolution." Gordon Greenfield still refers to what went on as "a cabal, a plot by a few mean-spirited people to take over the building and throw me out."

Actually, the revolt had been preceded by a number of minor squabbles and disputes within the building. There had been Jo Mielziner's fight to retain a stained-glass door panel, for example, which Gordon Greenfield and his board considered in violation of fire laws. "But glass doesn't *burn!*" Mielziner had cried indignantly. "That panel is a priceless antique!" Then, in 1964, there was blast damage to the building from the construction of the new Mayfair Tower next door, and nerves in the Dakota grew frazzled from the explosions and the general dawn-to-dusk din of the construction work. Ward Bennett had begun his renovation of his rooftop gable, but his plans had had to be approved by committee after committee, and the hammering of his builders added to the noise. The problem of what to do with the dining room had been solved, and in a way that was both ingenious and fortuitous for the building. But it had not been solved without a certain amount of haggling, arguments and suggestions for revisions from the building's board.

All through the winter there were secret meetings on the part of the revolutionaries as Mr. Ross tried to gather more tenants on his side. Now there were meetings nearly every night in one part of the building or another, and often these meetings went on into the wee hours. More and more tenants, it seemed, were against Greenfield, and when Greenfield attempted to invade one of the tenants' meetings that was being held in the Scott Severns' apartment, Dr. Severns told Greenfield that if he didn't leave, he'd throw him out.

It was a particularly difficult situation for Henry Blanchard, who had been a member of Gordon Greenfield's board, but now sided with Ross and was thus a member of both the Old Guard and the New. It was a great feather in Ross's cap to have Blanchard's support, but to Greenfield his old friend seemed a traitor. Even today, Gordon Greenfield is bitter about this switch of allegiance: "Harry started going around saying, 'Greenfield's got to go,' " he says. "He told lies, tales to stir things up—he did unspeakable things."

Henry Blanchard is no more charitable in his appraisal: "Gordon Greenfield did some inexcusable things, made inexcusable statements. At one point he said he would leave the board if I would leave too. But he'd said so many nasty, rotten things about my wife and me that I decided to stay. When my wife was in the hospital with a broken hip, he barged into her hospital room, didn't even take off his hat, and *demanded*—not asked—demanded that she influence me, demanded that I appear at his meetings."

At one point Henry Blanchard, who in demeanor resembles a country judge, stood up to Gordon Greenfield and, in an even voice, said, "You are a heel." At another point in their confrontations Greenfield shouted, "Harry Blanchard doesn't care what happens to the building —he's so rich!"

It was not long before the two men had stopped speaking to one another. They still do not speak.

LOOKING BACK from the distance of a few years, the Dakota's Palace Revolution may seem like much ado about very little. But a few things are important to remember about January and February of 1971. In 1969 and 1970 there had been a severe stock-market decline, the so-called "Nixon recession." Compounding this was spiraling inflation, and everything was costing more. At the Dakota monthly maintenance costs were rising alarmingly, and, in addition, the building seemed to be deteriorating. The New York *Times* had published an article which made it sound as though the building were falling down, hardly a good advertisement for life at the Dakota. If the building was on the verge of collapse, how could the tenants find a market for their apartments, which, in many cases, represented the major investments of their lives? Home- and apartment-owners were feeling the pinch all over the country. How long would the recession, coupled with inflation, go on? No one knew. The Dakotans, like property-owners everywhere, were frightened. Wall Street investment-banking houses were beginning to go under, one by one. To those who remembered it seemed like October of 1929 all over again. Their homes and their pocketbooks were threatened.

Wilbur Ross, meanwhile, who *was* a generation younger than Greenfield, offered what amounted to a panacea in his mortgage refinancing plan. As for Greenfield, he was independently rich, a fat cat. What did he care about the little fellow, the fellow who had to work for every penny he earned? In this atmosphere it is not surprising that more and more tenants joined the Ross faction and swung away from Gordon Greenfield.

Still the meetings went on, the petitions and platforms circulated, and the telephones rang throughout the day as each side tried to gather supporters. The insurgents complained that when they telephoned Greenfield with their complaints he did not return their calls, and Mrs. Greenfield stood up to declare that her husband answered every telephone call, without fail, always. In connection with the Greenfield board's stand on homosexuals, the Ross faction accused the incumbent board of "practicing apartheid," and compared the board with the government of South Africa. Another tenant complained that the Dakota was "run like Sing Sing." At one point Mr. Edward O. D. Downes, who had joined the Ross faction and was also a Distinguished Professor of Music History at Queens College, was awakened by a telephone call late at night and an anonymous voice that said to him, "I think you ought to know that Wilbur Ross wants to take over so he can tear this building down, and when that happens the wrecker's ball will come right through your window!"

But the most grisly moment of all came at a February meeting when one of the incumbent board muttered, "Wait until you see what we've got in the little black book!" The meeting went into a complete uproar.

The tenants had been aware, in a vague, uneasy way, of the existence of a little black book kept at the front desk that recorded the hours of departure and arrival of Dakota tenants. It also recorded with whom, and of which sex, each Dakotan had entered and left, as well as names, descriptions, destinations and arrival and departure times of all guests to the building. The little black book had been instituted as a security measure, but whose idea it was originally is unclear. The black book had always seemed like a form of snooping, a certain invasion of privacy. Now, however, with the Revolution in full swing, it was clear that it could be used as an instrument of exposure, embarrassment and blackmail. Mr. Greenfield and his board appeared to control the book, and this now threatened everybody. It guaranteed that the Dakota's Palace Revolution, like all revolutions in history, would not end on a note of logic, practicality or common sense. It would end in chaos.

THE SHOW-DOWN meeting, the final confrontation between the Greenfield board and Ross's Young Turks, was scheduled for March 15, 1971, in the dining room of the Olcott Hotel at 27 West Seventy-second Street at three o'clock in the afternoon. A court stenographer was hired to record the proceedings, so crucial did they seem, so high ran the tensions, though the presence of the stenographer greatly displeased Mr. Greenfield. Four hours later, there was still a great deal of unfinished business, but the meeting had to disperse because the Olcott had rented the room for another function from seven o'clock on. The impatiently waiting bar mitzvah group must have wondered what in the world the commotion among the well-dressed group of Dakotans was all about, with its periodic shouts of "Gestapo!" "S.S. tactics!" and other epithets.

During the course of the meeting both sides of the dispute accused the other of having "sinister" motives for wanting "power." At times the proceedings became so incoherent that, in her 127-page transcript of the meeting, the court stenographer could only helplessly record, "Voices . . . a voice . . . voices . . . voices." And she was at a loss to find stenographic symbols to convey the boos, the hisses, the catcalls, Bronx cheers, the shouts and the stamping of feet. But the meeting had not gone on for long before it was quite clear that the old regime was over, that the Wilbur Ross group of insurgents had won, that what Gordon Greenfield still refers to in military terms as the "coup" and the "take-over" was complete. Out of some 50,000 shareholder votes, the revolutionaries had gathered between 46,000 and 47,000.

Toward the end of the March 15 meeting, Mr. Greenfield made a long speech, admitting his defeat and submitting his resignation, but the court reporter's transcript can only partly convey the depth of his emotion, the voice that cracked and faltered several times, the fact that at moments he seemed close to tears. He said in part:

"I grew up in the Dakota . . . I worked very hard . . . long hours with many headaches, many trials and tribulations at some considerable expense, personal expense, for a long, long time . . . I am not the kind of individual who is patient enough to explain myself. I operate businesses, and I have a career which indicates that I know how to operate businesses successfully . . . I have no apologies to make for the job that has been done. I did it in the best way I could according to my life. However, I have one big complaint about it and that is the manner in which this situation was handled. I am not going to indulge in personalities and I could be critical of Mr. Ross. I am not going to be. And I could be critical of another individual in this meeting, but I am not going to take your time and bore you with what has been going on. This

Byzantine, this lethal type of politicking, and this character assassination of me because of problems in the building. You are not going to [have] . . . any improvement in the quality of life in this building that is material, unless you have the money. You haven't had the money to do it . . . It was sheer folly to think about refinancing at nine-and-a-half percent interest on the mortgage. It was a ridiculous thought to try to do it. I have some doubts that Mr. Ross can accomplish this plan today . . .

"My wife and I have been very hurt. We think we have been badly treated. Not by the community of the Dakota, but by the way this political campaign was launched. No excuse for it. Totally unnecessary. Now I have said it and I think you owe me an apology. I have served you. I have been honorable with it. I have been fair with you. Mrs. Scott is looking at me. She doesn't think I have been fair because we had a disagreement."

With that, Ruth Ford Scott interjected tartly, "Don't bring personalities into this. I am looking at you because you are speaking."

Greenfield continued, "What I did was in the best interest of the building and not to be harmful . . . I have been criticized and there are people in the building that don't like me as a result of what I have done, I thought, in the interest of all the tenant owners. I have never personally thought of myself first. I have never had special services . . . I am straitlaced on finance matters. I cross every T and dot every I. And I see that everything is accounted for and that is the stewardship that I have given you. I am not going to try to prejudice you . . . but I think that you are making a mistake to elect this slate because I don't think you entirely realize the outside attention . . . you are going to get. I think you may get something that you don't think you are getting in that . . . You should decide in this meeting largely whether or not that kind of atmosphere is the kind of atmosphere that should be brought to the board. People can create that kind of atmosphere. Take control of what? Take control who have nothing, not a dime in it.* So impor-

---

*This was probably a veiled reference to Henry Blanchard who, though he was one of the most popular people in the building, did not actually own any stock in it. The Blanchards' apartment was owned by their old friend John de Cuevas, who lived in Long Island.

tant to take control of it maybe for ulterior purposes. I don't know what they are . . . I am being booed. I withdraw the thought.

"In any event, I believe it is a serious mistake to the building. And I am very unhappy . . . I just feel it is not good and handled very badly. And you could have gotten some kind of compromise situation. I want to retire with nothing to do with it. Thank you very much."

Much later Wilbur Ross said, "We felt that the board had been in power too long. Gordon got sensitive. What I'll never understand is why Gordon wanted that job so badly. Long before that March meeting he must have known that he was bound to lose. From the signatures that we began to gather on the various petitions we submitted to him, it was obvious that the vast majority of the shareholders wanted a change. But he wouldn't step down gracefully. He seemed to want a *High Noon* shoot-out."

The new board that came in in 1971 was able to accomplish several of its objectives. A new mortgage was negotiated, at a higher interest rate, thereby increasing each tenant's tax-deductible share of maintenance from 30 percent to about 50 percent. The new board also had a certain amount of success in getting the building's taxes reduced, based on its landmark status—though the tax break was less than had been hoped. Most important, as far as the incoming board was concerned, was the rule that for the eleven seats on the board there had to be at least sixteen or seventeen candidates, and that no board member could serve for longer than three consecutive years at a time. This, it was felt, was not only more democratic; it would also ensure a new supply of blood and talent every three years and prevent the board from becoming the self-perpetuating body it had seemed to be in the Greenfield era.

When it was all over, Gordon Greenfield seemed to withdraw into himself. He rarely spoke to anyone he encountered in the building, and, in terms of the Dakota at least, he became almost reclusive. When tempers began to cool, a number of people felt sad about this, and a little guilty. No one, after all, really felt that Gordon was a bad person—a Captain Queeg or Bligh, a Richard Nixon or a Hitler. That had just been anger talking about what seemed Gordon Greenfield's "insensitivity" to the building's moods and needs at the time, and what seemed his "landlord methods." But it was clear that he was deeply hurt by the whole episode. "I really lost all interest in the building at that point," he says. "It took us seven or eight years to sell the apartment, but we finally did in nineteen seventy-eight, and we moved out." Robert and Eileen Carlson, who had been Greenfield's staunchest backers, also moved out.

Today, Wilbur Ross hopes that Gordon Greenfield has at least in part forgiven him. "After years of not speaking," he says, "Gordon suddenly approached me at Chatham, on the Cape, where he then had a house, and told me he was thinking of selling his house. He asked me if I'd be interested in buying it."

But Gordon Greenfield still feels bitter and betrayed by the events of the winter of 1970–71 and still speaks vociferously on the subject. "The first thing that happened when it was all over was that Larry Ellman started parking his 300D Mercedes in the driveway," he says. "Afterward, they were incredibly nasty at the board meetings— they'd hoot and jeer and boo and laugh when any of the old directors tried to say anything. They talked about 'communication' and they talked about 'love.' Their platform contained more promises than Jimmy Carter's. They had schemes for a restaurant in the basement, a squash court and all sorts of other sportsy things. They drew up elaborate plans for penthouses on the eighth and ninth floors. Paul Segal became sort of their house architect—he drives around town on a motorcycle. They planted trees in the courtyard, and the trees all died for lack of sunshine. They wasted money—money went down the drain. I could have gotten them a new mortgage at a lower rate, but they wouldn't wait. They took all their equity and now have a debt bigger than ever. The minute they took over, everybody's maintenance began going up. My maintenance went from eight hundred a month to seventeen hundred a month in the eight years the new regime ran the building. Freddie Victoria had placed some pieces of antique furniture in the hallways, and they threw them out. Jo Mielziner had hung some beautiful sketches of his set designs in the hallways, and the minute he died they threw them all out. I admit I had little patience with them. They didn't hire me for a love-in. I remember when I was a kid something that my father said to me. He'd just hired an ex-congressman to work for him, and Father asked me what I thought of him. I said he seemed like a nice fella. My father said, 'Nice fella, hell! We didn't hire him for breeding purposes!' You've got to be tough to run something like the Dakota, and I *was* tough. It's a jungle out there, and I happened to understand it. As for the rule that nobody can serve on the board for more than three years at a time, they call that *democracy*. Maybe it is, but with a turnover every three years how do you develop any *experience* on a board like that?"

Mr. Greenfield has a point, and it could be argued that a building cannot be run as though it were a village, a state or a nation. Because of the proximity of neighbor to neighbor, and the intensity of feelings about privacy that this closeness engenders, the fact that, no matter how thick the ceilings and walls, sounds can still be heard from next door and above and below—constant restive reminders that one is not quite alone (or not alone *enough*)—a big apartment house is best run by a benevolent dictator, like a ship at sea, where the captain has the final say on any matter. Perhaps even a co-op needs a "landlord," a benevolent despot to oversee things. That was the way the Clarks had run things. Mr. Greenfield apparently feels this way.

"Nobody gave me any credit for keeping maintenance in line," he says. "Nobody gave me credit for the things I had to do as president that were unpleasant. I had to handle all the complaints. Actresses who consider themselves big stars—Ruth Ford, Betty Bacall—are the biggest complainers about the littlest things. One time someone set fire to a car in the alley. I went out to see about it, and a drunk knocked me down. Jack Lemmon was making a movie out in the street, and there were all sorts of complaints about lights and noise—it was some sort of chase scene. I went out and spoke to a policeman about it. He said, 'I'm not a cop, I'm an actor. I'm in the movie.' Paramount paid the Dakota a thousand dollars a day to do *Rosemary's Baby*. I could have gotten them more."

It may be ascribed to bitterness, but Gordon Greenfield believes that "After the Revolution, the quality of the building changed. If they're not careful, the building could turn into a collection of second-rate show-biz types and restauranteurs. There are few people of real substance in the building anymore. It suddenly became 'mod,' a cult building for people indulging in atmosphere. It became a parody of itself. It became camp. It became Andy Warhol. Socially, it represented a kind of New York demimonde. It threw open its arms to the gay community. And everybody in the building got into deals with one another, buying and dividing and selling off apartments—like slum-lords."

AT THE CLOSE of fiscal 1977, Dakota, Inc. was $20,000 in the red. An employee of Douglas Elliman-Gibbons & Ives, the real estate firm that manages the building, says, "All they do now is complain about how the maintenance costs keep going up. But what can they do? Their payroll is $275,000 a year. The taxes were $66,000 a year, and now they're $300,000. The building went co-op in 1961, but by 1973 there were still a few old rent-control tenants from World War Two who wouldn't vacate their apartments, or buy them, even though they were owned by other people. People with high incomes want high-maintenance costs for tax reasons, but after a few years of pay-ing high maintenance they forget about that. Traditionally, a co-op with high maintenance has low prices for apartments, but from 1972 until just a year or so ago, you couldn't *give* those apartments away. Now the prices of apartments have shot through the ceiling. In my opinion, the old board knew what it was doing. Gordon Greenfield was a pleasure to work with. . . . Then these new people surfaced . . . They went out and borrowed $300,000. This was most unwise. It was bad business practice, in my opinion. They should have just in-creased the maintenance to balance the budget. Of course some peo-ple have ulterior motives when it comes to maintenances costs—wanting to keep it low if they happen to be planning to sell, for instance.

"When Greenfield ran it, there were only a couple of board meetings a year. Now they meet once a month, and the meetings go on for hours into the night. The new group then set up com-mittees galore—a hospitality committee, a bricks committee, a courtyard committee, an employees committee. This just confuses the employees. The employees don't know who's running the build-ing. When you have a board that gets involved in day-to-day do-ings, you get chaos, inevitably. Of course it's a crazy building. It defies every law—of economics and nature. But what have they got now? They've got tenants who are seriously in arrears with their maintenance payments. They've got a $2,700,000 morgage, and no working capital.

"What's going to happen," this real estate man wonders aloud, "when Judgment Day comes?"

WHEN THE REVOLUTION was over, someone commented wrily, "The winners were victorious, but the losers were lucky."

But out of all the anger and name-calling and heartache of the Revolution, a number of good things came to the Dakota like flowers sprouting out of the ashes of war. A certain community feeling was observed in the building in the Revolution's aftermath. "Before," says architect Paul Segal, "this was just a typical anonymous place where nobody really knew their neighbors. But during the heat and all the *sturm und drang,* we discovered ourselves. There might be ill will between old friends, but many more new friends evolved out of it." Today, few people entertain at the Dakota without including several of their neighbors in the building, a situation that never existed at the Dakota before and one that is quite unusual in New York City.

The Revolution was the beginning of the tradition of the October Courtyard Party, the likes of which had not been seen in the building since the celebratory party in 1961 when the building became a co-operative. The October Party is a sort of church supper affair, with each family bringing a separate dish. Rex Reed, for example, likes to cook his lemon icebox pies to go with Lauren Bacall's brownies. Eugenia Sheppard makes spinach salad, and Warner LeRoy supplies dishes ranging from chili to *blanquette de veau.* Each year courtly old Lewis Galantiere used to contribute a hundred fresh oysters from the Century Club. The John Lennons cook *sushi,* and one year handed out gift copies of a book on the virtues of organic food to everyone. Roberta Flack fixes spoon bread. At these parties there may be as many as twenty-five little children running about. Only once, since 1971, has it rained for a Dakota October Courtyard Party, and when that happened, the party simply moved under the spacious vaulted entrance archway.

Out of the Revolution, too, came the annual *Dakota Directory,* the Dakota's own telephone book and social register, listing home and office telephone numbers, wives' and childrens' names, and Dakotans' summer addresses and telephone numbers. The *Dakota Directory* is a valued document because it lists the very private and unlisted telephone numbers of quite a few famous people.

True, the new trees that were planted in the courtyard did not survive. The courtyard gets full sunshine for no more than an hour or so each day. But the stone planters in the center of the court were then planted with azaleas, and these have done well and afford a fine spring show of blooms.

Finally, once the dust of the Revolution had settled, one of the first pieces of business was what to do with the dread little black book. Unanimously, it was voted that it be destroyed.

The man assigned the task of disposing of it was lawyer George Beane. Naturally, when he had the book in his possession he could not resist a brief look at its contents. As a ledger, it seemed to him an indecipherable collection of hieroglyphics. Perhaps it was in code, and perhaps somewhere there was a key to it, but most of the writing in it was illegible. Later, when the Dakota's Palace Revolution would be spoken of in terms of Watergate, and the little black book would assume the proportions of the "smoking gun" in the Nixon tapes, it was hard for Beane to believe that the book contained that much of consequence. Still, he did as he was told and consigned it to the incinerator.

Chapter 20

Deals

To some of the older Dakotans, including Winnie Bodkin, one of the most striking changes that has occurred in recent years is the way the quality of conversation—or even gossip—has deteriorated. In 1922, for example, there was good subject for talk in the new traffic-control lights that had just been placed on Fifth Avenue. These were the objects of wonder, not only for their up-to-dateness but also for the rather shocking fact that each traffic light was topped with a bronze statuette of a naked man—the god Mercury wearing nothing but a World War I infantryman's helmet. And of course the uptown telephone circuits buzzed with the usual talk of mistresses, lovers, showgirls and scandal, but it was all quite harmless and inconsequential.

Today, however, talk at the Dakota has taken on a tougher, harder, less pleasant edge. When Dakotans meet, their conversation tends to fall into one of three general categories—money, and how much everything costs; parties, who is giving them and inviting whom; and how well—or poorly—the building is being run. "People don't seem to converse any more," says Winnie Bodkin, "they carp." Of course this could be a reflection of the way conversation in the city of New York has changed.

There is carping about the way some people have turned the Dakota itself into a business of sorts. A number of tenants have purchased rooms on the eighth and ninth floors which they use as servants' or storage rooms. (The Blanchards' cook lives up there, and so does Leonard Bernstein's housekeeper.) But others have bought rooms which they rent out to other people, and from which they derive income. Though this is not uncommon practice, some people in the building rather frown on this, but there is legally nothing wrong with it. Ever since the building went co-operative, there has been a certain amount of intramural wheeling and dealing in the building, with apartments being bought, sold and traded by tenants to one another. Since *Rosemary's Baby* "put the Dakota on the map" (even though only exterior shots of the building were filmed), it has acquired a spookily romantic aura. And particularly in the years since 1976, when the entire country began a real estate boom that sent costs of housing spiraling upward, Dakota apartments have turned out to be exceptionally lucrative investments.

When an apartment becomes available, the building learns it first, and quite often, the apartment will be snapped up by another tenant, refurbished and sold for a profit to yet another tenant. In 1976, for example, Daniel and Barbara Quinn bought apartment 212 for $14,620 —not to live in, since they already lived in apartment 55. A year later the Quinns were able to sell 212, which only has one room and one bath, to Patrick O'Neal for $18,000, a profit of roughly 25 percent. In the meantime the O'Neals had bought Joan Bingham's big apartment (ten rooms, four baths) for $115,000 to live in, and have since acquired three more apartments for extra space. One hundred and fifteen thousand dollars for that much space was a steal for the O'Neals in 1977, because by 1978 apartment 15 (seven rooms, two-and-a-half baths) went for $120,000, which was what the Quinns got when they sold it to Mr. and Mrs. Seymour Terry.

The temptation to parlay apartments and make big money in the process becomes understandable, in light of the way Dakota prices began escalating in 1976 and 1977. In 1976 a nine-room three-and a-half bath apartment, carrying with it 860 shares of Dakota voting stock, sold for $115,000. In 1978, a smaller apartment—eight rooms and three baths, and 780 shares of stock—sold for $150,000. Paul Goldberger bought his apartment in 1976 for $42,000, and fixed it up. By 1978 he estimated that he could sell it for at least $100,000. The same year, George Davison-Ackley estimated that his might bring a quarter of a million dollars.

Michael Wager is an actor who played with Ruth Ford in *Six Characters in Search of an Author*. In 1974 he was looking for an apartment, and Miss Ford suggested the Dakota. He bought apartment 53-C for around $50,000—it had five rooms and two baths—and redecorated it handsomely, covering the walls with Fortuny fabric, among other things. Downstairs, meanwhile, the Larry Ellmans were in the process of dividing their "grossly large" apartment, for which they had also paid around $50,000 in 1967, and were planning to sell off roughly 40 percent of it. By 1976 Michael Wager was able to sell 53-C to Robert Renfield for $100,000 and to buy the Ellman's 40 percent for $50,000. He even came out with one more room in the deal, and, naturally, he brought his Fortuny downstairs with him. He immediately began to redecorate, confident that he will be able to sell the maisonette and double his money again. For an actor, whose work is at best uncertain, buying and selling Dakota apartments can provide an important source of income. Wager claims that not long ago he saw a coffin being carried down the stairs. He immediately inquired, "Whose apartment is available?"

Nor are the Ellmans at all unhappy. They doubled their money too.

Of course there is nothing illegal or improper about all these in-house business dealings, but some Dakotans find them all—well, a little regrettable.

There are rumors, meanwhile, that John Lennon would like to buy the entire building, and Lennon does seem to require rather a lot of space for his relatively small family. By the early part of 1979 Lennon and his wife owned some twenty-eight rooms throughout the Dakota. And some business deals in the building have been less than profitable.

Michael Wager, who insists that you can "just take" doors and moldings from the basement in re-doing an apartment, likens the Dakota to "a kibbutz." There are two Israelis in the building—Gil Shiva and Gyora Novak—and Wager's late father was Meyer Weisgal, chancellor of the Chaim Weizmann Institute. "Gil Shiva's brother was my father's chauffeur," Wager sniffs, but adds, "It's all very cozy. The

Shivas call down to borrow dishes, Ruth Ford rings up to have me for dinner." And things other than apartments are traded back and forth. The Dale Kellers' two boys had outgrown their Japanese nanny, and so the Kellers gave the nanny to the Lennons for young Sean. A very courtly black gentleman named Vassal Thomas had worked on and off for Michael Wager, helping him with parties. Mr. Thomas is a figure of some social standing in Harlem, and helps run the annual "Evening of Elegance," a major fund-raising event of New York's black upper crust. When Lauren Bacall was looking for a cook-houseman, Wager suggested Mr. Thomas. Some time later Mr. Thomas announced to Mr. Wager, "I've just fired Miss Bacall." Wager asked how this had come about. Pointing to the enunciator call-button in the kitchen, Mr. Thomas said, "Do you see that button? Miss Bacall rang it once too often."

JUST AS THE quality of conversation has changed in New York, so has the quality of entertaining, and if George Templeton Strong were still around, he might be moved to comment again, "How New York has fallen off!" In the 1880's and 1890's, when the Dakota was young, New York was in the middle of an era of extravagant party-giving which will probably never be seen again. James Hazen Hyde gave his $200,000 ball at Sherry's, at which the ballroom was transformed into a replica of the Hall of Mirrors at Versailles. Suddenly every host and hostess of worth in New York was trying to outdo him—often with results that strained the imagination. Mrs. Stuyvesant Fish, for example, gave her famous Monkey Dinner in the 1890's, where the guest of honor, in full evening dress, was a monkey, who was solemnly introduced as Prince del Drago. This was followed by a Dog Dinner, at which the honored guests, wearing their mistresses' finest jewels, were canine pets. Perhaps the oddest entertainment of that blithe period was the Horseback Dinner given in 1903 by Mr. C. K. G. Billings. For this party, also at Sherry's, the ballroom was filled with live trees and shrubs to represent a forest glade. The floor was sodded, and all about the room "blue bloods of the equine world" were hitched at mangers filled with hay. Strapped to the flanks of each horse was a table. Guests, in formal riding attire, mounted their assigned horses and were served course after course of food by waiters dressed as grooms. From the shoulders of each horse, meanwhile, were slung two saddlebags, each filled with

ice and bottles of champagne. As they dined, the guests sipped champagne through nippled rubber tubes that ran down to the saddlebags.

And yet, if this sort of thing all seems a far cry from the disco doings
of the 1970's at such popular watering places as Studio 54, where
strange weeds are smoked and exotic chemicals sniffed, it would be well
to remember that on every fashionable lady's dressing table in the
1890's stood a bottle of something called Tilden's Extract. It cost six
cents for half an ounce and could be purchased at any drug store in the
city. It was recommended for "over-wrought hostesses," who were
advised to take a small dose before receiving guests or going out to
dinner, to prepare them for the "rigors" of the evening ahead. Tilden's
was pure extract of hashish.

The courtyard of the Dakota has been the scene of a number of gala
entertainments over the years—weddings, receptions, bar mitzvahs—
and each time one of them occurs the Dakotans remind themselves
that the Dakota is a cozy, one-big-happy-family sort of place, a community within a community. At the courtyard parties a spirit of neighborhood coffee klatch is usually encouraged, though sometimes things go
wrong. When Michael Wager was having a bar mitzvah for his son,
he asked his caterer to set up tables in the courtyard. A little later, he
noticed that, on someone's orders, the tables were being removed.
Wager stormed out. For week's he had been complaining to the board
about the courtyard's clogged drains. "If I own the courtyard," he said,
"put back the tables. If you own it, fix the drains." The tables were put
back.

The private parties given in individual apartments, meanwhile, are
something else again. "The annual tax-deductible party" has become
a feature of big-city life everywhere, and a number of Dakota parties
are given for publicity—to promote a person, a product or an event.
The number of publicity-oriented parties is another thing about which
Winnie Bodkin shakes her head. With his restaurants, which he likes
to keep filled with a snappy clientele, Warner LeRoy finds it wise to
toss two or three large parties a year—each for at least a hundred guests
—with all New York's snappiest people in attendance. George Davison-Ackley has an interest in a theater and dance company, and, to
draw attention to these interests, he too has embarked upon a career
as a Dakota host, closely rivaling the LeRoys.

He certainly has the place for it. His rooms are graced with ceiling-

high bamboo trees in red-lacquered wicker tubs, with Oriental rugs and
Chinese tables and garden stools, needlepoint chairs and cushions,
huge bowls of red tulips and white lilies. "The people who did the
Seagram Building" did the bookshelves in the library. In his apartment,
Mr. Davison-Ackley is able to accommodate as many as fifty people for
a seated dinner. For a cocktail reception he can handle as many as 450
guests—more than could be squeezed into Mrs. Astor's ballroom. Of
one of these gatherings he says, "It was the most eclectic group—
blacks, whites, gays and straights. The Cronyns came, and Myrna Loy
and Louis Falco. A little lady downstairs came up and sat with Myrna
Loy, drinking until two A.M. I'd invited a black clerk from my law firm,
and he was standing next to my mother. The next thing I knew, they
went off and had dinner together! I turned my bedroom into a disco-
thèque. It was noisy, but there were no complaints. Eugenia Sheppard
got the date mixed up, and showed up two days later."

George Davison-Ackley is the kind of fellow who complains that his
telephone rings so much that it drives him to distraction, and yet
maintains six separate listing ("Davison, G. W. Ackley," "Ackley, G.
W. Davison," etc.) in the Manhattan telephone directory, all for the
same number, so that his telephone friends will have no trouble locat-
ing him. He is also the kind of man who, each time he pours himself
a fresh martini, pours it into a fresh Baccarat glass.

He has made great social strides in New York, where one of the city's
leading social arbiters is unquestionably Earl Blackwell. Earl Blackwell
used to look straight through George Davison-Ackley when the two
encountered each other. But no longer. "There was a dinner party at
the Kennedy Gallery," George Davison-Ackley recalls. "Eugenia and
Earl were there. Jackie Onassis arrived and spoke to me, and Earl come
over and asked me to join his group. He had finally decided that I was
someone to know."

When Gil and Susan Shiva give one of their big parties, coat racks
are set up inside the building's entrance gate, and someone is stationed
at a table with a guest list to check off names as guests arrive, so there
will be no crashers. So many celebrities turn up that there are inevitably
photographers outside the gate to photograph the famous faces as they
appear. Susan Shiva cooperates with the press by notifying them in
advance that she is having a party. But she draws the line at letting the
photographers up into her apartment. Gil Shiva recently embarked on

a career as a motion-picture producer, and for the opening of his first film—Lina Wertmuller's *The End of the World in Our Usual Bed in a Night Full of Rain*, with Candace Bergen—the Shivas had a large party. Lauren Bacall, who shares a service elevator with the Shivas, came to the party through the Shivas' kitchen door, thus avoiding the photographers. But when Gil Shiva explained that the party was to publicize his movie, Miss Bacall agreed to go downstairs into the courtyard to be photographed. "It was very kind of her," Gil Shiva says.

Publicity, fund-raising, politics and business, after all, are what New York society in the late 1970's is all about. But the amount of business entertaining that goes on in the building annoys some Dakotans who prefer a quieter, less publicized social life. Friendships have disintegrated over this issue.

In the summer of 1967, at the time of the Six-Day War, the Shivas were scheduled to have a party for the benefit of the Alvin Ailey Dance Company. Sixty people had been invited, but at the last minute the Shivas were asked to host an Israeli fund-raising affair in their apartment on the same date. The Israeli fund-raising, they felt, took precedent over the dance troupe. On the afternoon of the party Susan Shiva telephoned her upstairs neighbor Theodate Severns to ask a big favor. Would Mrs. Severns be a substitute hostess and have the Ailey party at her place? After all, the fact that the party was to be at the Dakota was the party's main drawing card.

Mrs. Severns agreed to help Susan Shiva out, and then phoned downstairs to Winnie Bodkin at the desk to ask for an off-duty elevator operator to help serve. Winnie told Mrs. Severns that she was sorry, but all the elevator operators had been pre-empted by the Shivas for the Israeli fund-raiser. "She had taken *all* of them," says Mrs. Severns. "I was flabbergasted! I was going to have *her* party in *my* house—and with no help! The Shivas sent up wine and cheese, but I had to provide all the glasses and all the clean-up. I never even got a thank-you note! I was furious!"

Like eggs in a crate, the thin-shelled egos compartmentalized in the Dakota are easily cracked. But it should be remembered that the Six-Day War was an emotional time for all Jews, and so perhaps Susan Shiva can be forgiven for forgetting the thank you.

As a hostess, meanwhile, Susan Shiva is usually in full command of the situation, and her parties rarely get out of hand. At a party for

Prince Michael of Greece, for example, a certain number of guests were invited for dinner, and certain others were invited for after dinner. On the after-dinner list was Gianni Agnelli, the Fiat head, who made the mistake of thinking that he could bring along ten or so uninvited friends to the party. The friends included Countess Gioconda Cigogna, Prince George Vassichekof, Count Yash and Eva Gabronska, the Duke and Duchess de Cadaval of Portugal, Patricia Lawford, Kevin McCarthy, Yul Brynner, and Kirk and Anne Douglas. This was too much for Susan Shiva, who threw the whole lot out, titles and all.

But there are times at the Shivas' parties when the going does get a little rough. When Robert F. Kennedy was making his Democratic Senate bid in New York, the Shivas, who are ardent Democrats, threw a party for him in order to win the "intellectual vote" away from the Republican incumbent, Senator Kenneth Keating. Among the intellectuals invited were William vanden Heuvel, who was Kennedy's campaign manager (and, for a while, Susan Shiva's brother-in-law), Jacqueline Kennedy, Leonard Bernstein, Adolph Green, Gloria Vanderbilt, Zachary Scott, Jason Robards, John Gunther, Jules Feiffer, Allegra Kent, Paddy Chayefsky, Abe Burrows, John Kenneth Galbraith, Lillian Hellman, George Plimpton, Lauren Bacall and Arthur Schlesinger, Jr. All went well until Arthur Kopit, the playwright (*Oh Dad, Poor Dad* . . .), announced that he was for Senator Keating. He was pushed backward over a sofa, spilling his drink on himself, the sofa, the rug and the person who had shoved him. Getting to his feet, he said, "I see the Kennedy swimming-pool-shoving syndrome is still with us."

Because of the celebrity of the building's tenants and their friends and guests, episodes like this have a way of getting into the gossip columns which, less celebrated tenants feel, tends to give the Dakota a bad name, and makes it sound as though the building is the scene of nothing but wild parties. In fact, almost everything that happens at the Dakota gets into the papers, and this ruffles some Dakotans' feathers. The building is particularly proud of its security system. All visitors must be announced. The entrance gate is locked at midnight, and late-arriving guests and tenants must ring for a watchman to be admitted. All groceries and mail are delivered to apartments by the building's porters. Workmen and repairmen arriving on the service elevators will not be admitted to apartments until they have been identified by the owners. Many apartment owners, when they are at home, still do not bother to lock their front doors, but New York has become increasingly security-conscious. And there have been slip-ups. Not long ago, David Marlowe's doorbell was rung by one of the periodic groups of young girls who had somehow penetrated the system, and who were going up and down hallways trying to find John Lennon. David Marlowe fooled them by saying, "This is John Lennon's apartment, but he's in Europe for the summer." The girls departed.

And there are fears. "One thing that worries us," Wilbur Ross says, "is that if someone got into the building, how would we ever find him?" It is true that in some of the building's dark storage spaces and closets and rooftop lofts a person could conceivably hide out for months undetected. But once he was inside, a prowler unfamiliar with the building would also have a hard time finding his way out, since so many of the Dakota's doors and hallways open into cul-de-sacs.

And there have been a few burglaries. In 1971 Sidney Carroll's apartment was robbed, and Robert and Eileen Carlson vigorously protested a search of their maid's room by an employee and the police. A few years later Warner and Kay LeRoy's apartment was burglarized, but the LeRoys admit that it was their own fault. "We'd gone away for the summer and given keys to a lot of workmen," LeRoy says. Some time after that, Eugenia Sheppard reported the loss of some jewelry. Later on, the missing pieces turned up in a drawer where Miss Sheppard had forgotten she had put them. But the Sheppard "burglary" somehow found its way to Liz Smith's gossip column, where it was reported that Miss Sheppard had said that hers was one of a "rash" of burglaries at the Dakota. For a while, everyone in the building was very cross with Eugenia Sheppard. One burglary and one non-burglary did not seem enough to constitute a "rash." This was the sort of publicity that the Dakota did not need at all. It hurt the value of everyone's investment.

Still, if you are famous, people recognize you and comment on what you do. One of the perils of the publicized life is public embarrassment. One of the drawbacks of life at the Dakota is that its famous tenants keep the building in an almost perpetual spotlight. The Lennons, of course, are a special problem, but other celebrities have occasionally managed to strain the rules. One is not supposed to park a car in the

Dakota's carriage entrance, but when Jason Robards was married to Lauren Bacall, and living there, he once slept all night at the wheel of his car, parked there, and no one knew quite what to do about it.

Cars frequently betray the identity of their owners. When John V. Lindsay was Mayor of New York, everyone in the building—and in the neighboring buildings—was interested to see the Mayor's official chauffeur-driven limousine draw up in front of the Dakota one balmy evening. The tall Mayor stepped out of the car and entered the building, Who, everyone wondered, might the Mayor of New York be visiting? The car and driver waited outside.

And waited.

The next morning the question became even more intense. The Mayor's limousine, its driver dozing at the wheel, was *still there.*

"Oh, there have been some really *wild* parties," bubbles Ruth Ford. "One night there was a *particularly* wild party, with all sorts of electric guitars and amplifiers and a rock band. By around eleven or twelve at night, people began complaining. Everyone who complained was invited to the party. Finally the police poured in—and *they* were invited to stay. They stayed, drinking and carrying on with everyone else. It *worked.*"

It might not have worked a few years ago. One of Warner LeRoy's downstairs neighbors was a woman, since moved away, who was an heiress to a beer fortune. She called the police at the slightest sound of a party, and the police arrived and broke up whatever was going on. The lady herself was fond of giving opera recitals, which she considered properly dignified and civilized in tone. At one of her recitals an elderly Dakota neighbor had the poor taste to have a heart attack and die. The indignant hostess ordered her butler to drag the dead man back to his own apartment and deposit him there, where he belonged.

Chapter 21

The Bottom Line

ON TUESDAY, February 22, 1898, the dining room of the Dakota offered a special menu. The Dakota's menus were elaborate in those days, but this one was especially so. After all, it was George Washington's birthday. The first President would have been 166 years old. The cover of the menu depicted "The Dakota Behind an Old Rock in Seventy-second Street Looking from the Bloomingdale Road, 1884." The Bloomingdale Road was Broadway, from which the Dakota was once visible. The bill of fare announced:

DINNER

Oysters en coquille   Little Neck Clams

*Tortue Claire à l'Anglaise   Crème de Volaille
Consommé à l'Impèratrice*

*Canape Lorenzé   Lettuce   Tomatoes   Radishes   Olives
Celery   Salted Almonds*

Mousse of Salmon à la Victoria
Broiled Spanish Mackerel à la Mâitre d'Hotel

Cucumbers   Pommes de Terre, Dauphine

Boiled Capon à la Reine
Filet Mignon of Beef à la Cheron
Stewed Terrapin à la Maryland
Timbale de Gibier à la St. Hubert

Fricassee of Fresh Mushrooms en Caisse
Beignets de Pêches glacés au Kirsch

Ribs of Prime Beef   Spring Lamb, Mint Sauce

Punch Benedictine

Ballotin de Pigeon en Bellevue
Roast English Pheasant, Bread Sauce

Boiled Sweet Potatoes   Mashed Potatoes   Parisian Potatoes
French Peas   Asparagus   Plain Spinach   Squash

Pineapple Pudding, Sauce Madère   Washington Pie
Apricot Tartelettes   Petits Fours   Chocolate Eclairs
Port Wine Jelly, Glace Fantaisie

Stilton, Roquefort and American Cheese

Fruit in season

Coffee

The old menu politely listed no prices for any of the above delicacies, but it did note: "Dishes ordered not on Bill of Fare will be charged extra."

Eighty years later, almost to the day, the Dakota dining room was the Gyora Novaks' apartment and the month of February 1978—which could be considered fairly typical nowadays—showed that the Dakota's tenants' maintenance payments were in arrears in the aggregate sum of $21,912.45. Twenty-one tenants—roughly a quarter of the building—had not paid their February maintenance at all. Eighteen others had made only partial payments. The individual arrearages for

February ranged in size from $1.95 (doubtless someone's careless error) to $2,260.56. In other words, the building was trying to operate and maintain itself on a fiscal basis that would boggle the mind of even a professional accountant.

How long can such a state of affairs continue, and what ever can be done? At the same time, an eleven-room, three-and-a-half bath apartment was for sale at an asking price of $312,000, and another had just been sold at $10,000 *above* the asking price. In the topsy-turvy world of New York real estate, the Dakota is a topsier, turvier place than most.

"The best thing about living here is that they don't hassle you about not paying your maintenance," says Pauline Pinto. "I mean, they know they'll get it *eventually*. You can live here and do unconventional things *and* not pay your maintenance. Right now I'm writing an analysis of President Carter's welfare plan—it's not like reading Kafka or Rilke or William Gass. The public knows *nothing* about Carter's welfare plan. It makes me feel that I'm in a minority, writing about the poor, working at a mental-health center. The Pintos are an old Sephardic Jewish family from Morocco, but I'm a WASP with plenty of money. I feel estranged, I feel different—I feel there's a wave length I'm not on. I feel ambivalent, like a cop-out, because I'm rich—*and* a liberal— there's a feeling of guilt. Here I am in my beautiful apartment at the Dakota, writing about poverty. Still, I feel better here than I would on Park Avenue. It's better for my conscience. . . ."

The rich, it has often been pointed out, are funny about money. In San Francisco the late Mrs. Adolph B. Spreckels, after giving away more millions than she could remember to create the Palace of the Legion of Honor and to other art museums, was approached by a member of the Legion of Honor staff. The staff had organized a softball team, which proposed to call itself the A. B. Spreckels Memorial Baseball Team, in honor of Mrs. Spreckels's late husband. The team, however, had found itself about fifty dollars short of the money it needed to buy uniforms. Could the Legion of Honor's wealthy benefactress help out? *"What?"* cried the outraged Mrs. Spreckels. She flung open her reticule and poured its contents—lipstick, emery boards, matches, a few coins, a handkerchief—on the table. "Where do you expect *me* to get fifty dollars?" she wanted to know. "You people have got my skin. Now you want my guts!"

The rich, as Pauline Pinto indicates, are often quite cavalier when it comes to paying bills. In Locust Valley, Long Island, for example, one woman routinely goes through her morning mail in bed with her breakfast tray. Anything that appears to be a bill she simply stuffs under her mattress. Only when the pile of bills reaches a size to threaten her sleeping comfort does she pull them all out and ship them to her husband's secretary for payment.

The rich, furthermore, are provided with certain privileges when it comes to bill paying—privileges which are denied to ordinary mortals. If one is rich enough, one can arrange with the telephone company and the utilities concerns to pay one's bills once a year instead of the more boring and time-consuming once a month. But the trouble is that many rich people fail to grasp the difference between AT&T, which can afford such liberal credit, and the corner drug store, which cannot. A number of years ago, for instance, the pretty Berkshire Hills around Williamstown, Massachusetts, began attracting a number of rich people, including Mrs. Alta Rockefeller Prentice, Mrs. Lillian Sanford Procter (Procter & Gamble) and Mr. and Mrs. William H. Vanderbilt; later came such successful folk from the literary and theater worlds as Sinclair Lewis, James Gould Cozzens and Cole Porter. The town's tradespeople, it was suggested, should be delighted with the important new infusion of money, but, as it turned out, they were far from sanguine about it all. True, their sales figures jumped appreciably, but so did their amounts of accounts receivable. The same problem besets Park Avenue florists who get thousands of dollars' worth of business from their carriage trade, while they hover on the brink of bankruptcy waiting to be paid. The Dakota has the same problem with some of its wealthy tenants.

Meanwhile, it has long been apparent that one of the great financial —as well as social—drains on the Dakota has been represented on the eighth and ninth floors.

As recently as 1973—a dozen years after the building became a co-operative—there were still a few rooms on the top two floors that tenants would not vacate, or buy, even though the rooms were technically owned by other people. In 1977 there was a serious effort to co-op the eighth and ninth floors, and it was stipulated that these rooms could only be purchased by people who already had apartments in the building. About $100,000 was realized from the sale of rooms on eight and nine—a rather small drop in the bucket for a building whose monthly operating budget is $130,000. The maintenance charges, meanwhile, for some of the smallest rooms—many of which are without windows —had to be set low, as little as forty dollars a month in some cases. And so the top two floors, which represent roughly 22 percent of the Dakota's available floor space, account for less than 4 percent of its monthly income.

One recent notion that has been proposed has been to turn the eighth and ninth floors into a series of luxury duplexes. To do this, of course, the Dakota would have to buy back the various rooms that it sold to tenants in 1977. Then the two floors would have to be completely renovated, and the new duplexes resold.

The idea would seem to have some merit. It could all be done within the limits proscribed by the Landmarks Commission, without tampering with the building's façade. To carry out such a scheme, of course, a number of things would have to happen. Some provision would have to be made for the oldsters—for Jimmy Martin, Mrs. Maclay, the Browning sisters. Most important, however, would be the Dakotans themselves, who would have to back the idea, unanimously, in *spirit.* The Dakotans would have to act together, as a family, as a community. Unanimity of spirit, however, has not exactly been an outstanding characteristic at the Dakota.

A certain amount of human lethargy and apathy would have to be overcome. Many Dakotans take the attitude that, though the cost of living in their building keeps going up, Judgment Day is not *quite* here. Perhaps the fact that the building closes its books $20,000 in the red each year isn't all *that* bad. The building continues to amortize its mortgage, "rolling it over," as the accountants say, with cheaper dollars, thanks to inflation. It is not like Christmas of 1960, they say. And they are right. There is no real cause for panic. But for economic pessimists there might be cause for a certain amount of nervousness.

Such an ambitious undertaking as the duplexes would have to come out of a sense of real need and immediate urgency—a feeling that unless something is done and done soon, their building will sink and the Dakotans will lose everything they own. This crisis mentality has not emerged yet, though such pessimists as Frederic Weinstein feel that some sort of crisis is very close at hand.

A strong leader would have to take the Dakota's helm to carry out such an ambitious plan, a benevolent despot who would run things—a Franklin D. Roosevelt who would lead the country out of the Great Depression.

But then the final question arises: Where would the Dakota, which has a small working capital, find the necessary hypothetical three-and-a-quarter-million dollars to implement such a scheme? A case could be made for the fact that there is a difference between mortgage financing and redevelopment financing. The 1972 refinancing was undertaken for different reasons. A new loan would be for building something that would increase the building's revenues and add to its value.

But because no real crisis yet exists, the Dakota sails on into the wind with business as usual, and the eighth and ninth floors remain in the same state as they have always been.

THERE IS AN important difference between buying a co-operative apartment and a condominium. When buying a condominium one buys one's living space, and only one's living space, outright, and gets a deed and title to it. Costs of maintaining common areas—hallways, roofs, plumbing and so on—are shared by everyone in the building. A co-operative, on the other hand, is a corporation with shares of stock to sell. The Dakota is owned by the Dakota, Inc., and when buying an apartment one buys a certain number of shares of Dakota stock based more or less on the apartment's cubic footage. Furthermore, one does not get a deed to a co-operative apartment; one gets a lease from the corporation—in the Dakota's case, a lease for forty years, with a six-month "escape" clause.* In other words, owners of co-operatives like the Dakota do not legally "own" their apartments, but they do own their buildings, which condominium owners do not.

Co-operative ventures are considered far riskier than condominiums because, theoretically, if 90 percent of a co-operative building de-

---

*If a tenant must default on his lease, he must give the corporation six months' written notice. He thereupon loses all privileges and rights to the apartment, and his shares in the building revert to the corporation. When the documents of incorporation were being drawn up, someone scribbled nervously in the margin beside this clause, "Is this standard?" It is an indication of the state the building would be in if tenants started exercising their escape clauses in large numbers.

faulted, the entire burden of maintaining the building, paying its taxes and its mortgage, would have to be borne by the remaining 10 percent. For this reason co-operatives are particularly choosy about whom they take in as tenants. Financial requirements are extraordinarily stringent. Quite often cash is required to pay for a co-operative apartment. Condominiums are comparatively easy to buy and can be financed the way houses can.

New Yorkers, living in a financial city and accustomed to buying and selling stock, are partial to co-operatives. In the Middle West and West—where more psychological importance is attached to having a deed as proof of one's ownership of property—condominiums are much more popular. Socially, too, a vast difference exists between the owner of a co-operative and the owner of a condominium. Condominiums, with their connotations of Miami Beach and retirement communities in Arizona, are considered much more middle class. To own a "co-op" is sophisticated and chic; to own a "condo" is not.

But the After-all-I-own-the-building syndrome, which co-op owners tend to develop, can lead to problems other than the Sin of Pride. With each tenant believing that the building is "his," each tenant has his own ideas as to what should be done with it, and how the building should present itself to the world. That such attitudes should prevail at the Dakota is no surprise. Different people have different ideas about what the Dakota's priorities should be—if, somehow, money should appear with which to attend to them.

For example, *Rosemary's Baby* may have made the Dakota nationally famous, but that may have been a mixed blessing. The motion-picture company selected the Dakota for its dark, gloomy, forbidding exterior appearance, and not for the large, airy, sunny apartments within. Associating it with the movie, many people feel that from the outside the Dakota looks rather sinister—a place to be avoided at all costs. At the height of the movie's popularity it was not uncommon for audiences to scream when the Dakota's grim image first flashed upon the screen.

And yet the sinister appearance of the Dakota's façade is simply the result of years of compounded dirt. It has never been cleaned, and needs a face-washing badly, or so some people think. A faction in the building, led by the Shivas, periodically campaigns for cleaning at least two sides of the building—the sides facing Seventy-second Street and Central Park.

It would be wonderful, the cleaning enthusiasts say, if the Dakota's bricks could be returned to their original pale jonquil-yellow color and the cornerstones to their original rich reddish brown. But questions remain as to how best to accomplish this. Traditional sandblasting, it is feared, could seriously weaken the mortar between the bricks and stones, and the entire building might have to be recaulked and re-pointed. A steam-cleaning method, developed in Europe, was success-fully used to clean a number of old buildings in Paris, but apparently New York grime is different from the grime of Paris and does not respond to the European treatment.

Moreover, there are those in the building who like the Dakota's blackened façade and feel that this is part of the building's special character, just as the sooty streets of Edinburgh give that city a special look and feel. The building carries its stains with pride, the anti-cleaning group feels, the way an old fighter carries his scars.

And while the cleaning and anti-cleaning factions debate, there is again the problem of money. Estimates to clean the Dakota have run as high as half a million dollars, and the longer the building waits to be cleaned, the higher the cost will no doubt go. If the cost of cleaning were equally divided among the ninety-odd tenant families, the cost would be roughly $5,500 per family. Some people would be willing to chip in that much, but others are not.

Still, despite its chronic shortage of ready cash, the Dakota's future seems reasonably secure. Even Gordon Greenfield, from his new loca-tion on the East Side, says, "As long as the building retains its cachet as an address for famous and successful people, it will survive. It doesn't have much old money, and it doesn't have much big money, but a lot of people who live there make a lot of money. As long as there are people who can afford to live there, the Dakota's future isn't bleak. Of course, as maintenance costs get higher, people with less money may be squeezed out and they'll have to be replaced with people with money. The people on the eighth and ninth floors may be squeezed out eventually, and then the building will have to do something about those floors, to make them attractive to rich people. The building may well become a building exclusively for the rich. But after all, that's what the Dakota has always been all about—apartments for the affluent. That was old man Clark's original idea. The building was built to appeal to snobs, and it still has the cachet and snob appeal. Of course if there ever were to be a serious recession, the building would be in trouble —in worse trouble, probably, than the more stable expensive buildings on the East Side, simply because the money at the Dakota isn't as stable as East Side money. It's a bit too heavily weighted toward show business and restaurants, businesses which are the first to suffer in a recession. I sold my apartment to Peter Yates, a movie director. As a businessman I don't foresee any serious recession in the near or even middle future. But fifty years from now, who can say? Nobody has a crystal ball."

Gordon Greenfield, upon whom the Dakota turned its back, still thinks, despite his sanguine outlook, that he could have run the building better than it is being run today. "I'm sorry to hear that they have a problem with arrearages," he says. "In my day, we were always very strict about collections."

Chapter 22

Faith

THE OCTOGENARIAN Miss Cordelia Deal once said, "My family moved to the Dakota because Father knew Mr. Edward Clark. Father said, 'Anything that Edward Clark's behind is sure to be successful.' We rented our apartment before the building was finished, and Mr. Clark let us change certain things. We didn't move up here because it was fashionable because, goodness me, it wasn't fashionable. It was too special. Fashionable to me implies conformity, and the Dakota didn't conform to anything in the city at the time. Some people want to be in fashion, and some people don't care. We didn't care. I used to read about Mrs. Astor's parties, and I thought they sounded rather silly, all the same people over and over again. I used to see Mrs. Astor in her carriage, and she looked like a very silly woman to me. There were stories about her, that once she got on a bus and the driver passed the fare box to her. She said, 'No thank you, I have my own charities.' What a silly thing to say, if the story's even true. What would Mrs. Astor have been doing, getting on a bus? We called those people 'the butterflies.' We laughed at them. We thought of ourselves as—well, solider. We weren't interested in fashion, but we were interested in form. Goodness me, Mother used to worry about whether or not it was good form to pick up an olive with a fork. That's what's missing nowadays, if you ask me. Good form, and good manners. Now everybody's doing everything in the *moderne* style because they say it's chic. They say the Dakota has gotten very chic. In my day we didn't worry about what was chic. We worried about form."

That was said in 1932, and it is interesting to note that Mr. Greenfield believes in 1978 that cachet—a quality of elitism—and not merely chic, is what must be maintained if the Dakota is to survive. Others, of course, have different notions of what the Dakota's life-giving ingredient must be. Some are proudest of the building's ethnic coziness—the fact that Jews, Arabs and WASPs live more or less peacefully under the same roof. And there is the generational coziness—the number of children at the courtyard parties, and the fact that when Albert and Gillian Maysles attend building meetings they bring their small daughter Rebekah with them. Paul Goldberger maintains that the building will endure because is is "a true democracy." But democracy and elitism would seem to be quite different concepts, at least on the surface.

It is certainly true that at the moment the Dakota is a perfect example of contemporary New York chic. And so, in pondering the Dakota's future, it might be helpful to consider what New York chic consists of—particularly since New York has become the standard for chic all over the country.

The West Side, for example, is not New York fashionable, but it is New York chic. The fashionability that was planned for it never came to be, and it remains the wrong side of the tracks. In New York it is not fashionable, but it is chic, to look for good goods at bargain prices, and that is what West Side apartments offer—more space for less money (though the Dakota's peculiar economics make it sort of an exception.) Everything is cheaper on the West Side. A 46-ounce can of tomato juice costs 89 cents at an East Side Gristedes, only 75 cents at Fine & Shapiro's Delicatessen on West Seventy-second Street. Dinner at an elegant West Side restaurant, such as the dining room of the Hotel des Artistes, will cost less than a smilarly appointed establishment on the East Side.

In New York it is chic for people who have money to live in close proximity to people who are poor. To be sure, if the Dakotans were to ring the doorbells of some of their near West Side neighbors, they wouldn't much like the looks of some of the people who answered the door. Some of their neighbors would turn out to be bright young professionals, men and women living together with or without benefit of clergy, many of them industriously restoring and remodeling nineteenth-century houses and apartments in formerly run-down neighborhoods. But they would also encounter people in *yarmulkes*, sporting phylacteries, people who spoke Spanish or broken English and whose apartments smelled of cabbage and garlic. Nor would Dakotans enjoy spending an afternoon sipping pop with Jimmy Martin in his tiny, untidy upstairs room. Still, it is somehow comforting to know that such people are there, in the abstract, nearby, without having to come into contact with them. One feels superior—elitiest—toward such people, but just having them there makes one feel democratic.

In New York it is chic to have money, but not too much money. Big money, inherited money, and old money are not particularly chic, though some people who have this sort of money manage to act as if they are chic. Rockefellers are not chic. Estee Lauder, whose family origins are an impenetrable mystery, is chic. Eugenia Sheppard is chic because of the power of her pen. In her syndicated column she reports on who goes where and with whom wearing what. She and Earl Blackwell, who is her closest friend, constitute a mighty axis of New York social power. Rex Reed is New York chic for similar reasons.

The John Lennons are not chic. It is chic to go around town on a motorcycle, the way Paul Segal does, and it is not chic to travel, old-money style, in chauffeur-driven limousines, the way the Lennons do. The Lennons may think it is chic, or funny, to enter and alight from their limousines in blue jeans, but they can't have it both ways. They merely seem odd. Besides, the Lennons have not done much of anything in recent years, and the man who helped revolutionize twentieth-century music now seems to have settled into the ways of the *haute bourgeoisie.*

Anyone working at a high-paying, exciting job is chic. but the job must be risky. Sculpture is chic, but owning a monument works is not chic. Photographers are always chic. Running a restaurant is chic, but owning a wholesale-food business is not chic. Writing novels and plays is chic, and so is writing advertising copy because of the high-risk factor in the advertising business. Actors and actresses are chic, particularly when they are out of work. Paul Goldberger himself is an example of New York chic. His comments on architecture (a chic subject) are read by thousands of people each week.

If Mr. Greenfield considers the Dakota less "stable" than certain old-money East Side buildings, it is because so many Dakotans have deliberately chosen unstable callings, with uncertain rewards, subject to the whims of an unpredictable economy. And so, if the Dakota is a democracy, it is a democracy of an elite, a democracy of chic. As Wilbur Ross, president of the corporation, a man whose income is subject to the vagaries of the international money market, puts it, "We get some of the most literate crank letters of any company in town." Can such a democracy survive and carry the old building through another troubled century? It has certainly become a more unwieldly democracy—the endless meetings, the proliferating committees—than it was in the days when Gordon Greenfield ran it with a more autocratic hand. And yet it survives.

The Dakota is often compared with London's Albany—like the Dakota, an anomalous island of luxury and privilege in the bustling business heart of Picadilly. (Unlike the Dakota, Albany does not allow children or any pets larger than a budgerigar.) Albany is more than fifty years older than the Dakota, and it has survived.

The Castle of Montmort, rising and falling against the horizon, has survived for hundreds of years under the stewardship of a single ducal family. It would be pleasant to think that the Dakota could also survive as a democracy of chic, a democracy of hard-driving and successful New York egos. But chic is subject to the whim of fashion and change. Perhaps in the end something more than chic or cachet will be required —something quite irrational, like faith—faith in this peculiar address, faith in this peculiar city.

New York remains a city—like London, Paris, Rome and Madrid— where the wealthy still find it pleasant to spend the majority of their time, and where the not-so-wealthy still have faith in the tantalizing possibilities of success and in what E. B. White has called "the queer prize" of privacy. Like San Francisco, New Orleans, Chicago, Philadelphia and Boston, New York is a city where the well-to-do are happy to reside in an urban setting. Interestingly, all these cities are harbor or waterfront cities, and New York has not lost its peculiar harbor mentality. Cities that face the water face risks, for what is more uncertain than the vagaries of the waves? Water is an ancient symbol of trade, and New York is a city of traders and risk-takers—gamblers whose choices are guided by sheer faith.

New York is still a city where success is the main industry—a one-company town in a sense, a city of aspiration. New York is not a city like Cleveland or Detroit, cities which the rich have pretty much abandoned and left to the poor. Nor is New York a city like Houston, Phoenix, Atlanta or Los Angeles, where almost everyone lives in a suburb. In Manhattan, more and more luxury apartment houses keep going up. They succeed, and their towers seem to symbolize the city's constantly renewing faith in itself as a residence. Between the towers the old Dakota snuggles, shoulders hunched against the parade of progress, as though keeping its own particular, private faith.

New York, like the rest of the country, has entered what has been called the Era of the Self, the Me Decade, the laid-back age of laziness and self-indulgence and Looking Out for Number One. This attitude has affected some Dakotans' notions about their property as well, given them a what-the-hell, I own it, why not? sort of stance. There is a perceptible feeling of Nobody's-going-to-tell-me-what to do: This is my house, and I'll do with it what I please, and to hell with what the neighbors think. Considerateness is equated with conformity, and, heaven forbid, nobody wants to be called a conformist. In this mood it is easy to shrug off as inconsequential the systems, like those of the Dakota, that were designed to protect us. In this frame of mind it is easy to ignore—or refuse to acknowledge—the obligations that go with property and position, even though there is something quite self-destructive in this attitude. It is easy to forget that buildings can commit suicide too.

At the Dakota, this problem may be even more acute than in ordinary buildings because the Dakota does not think of itself as an ordinary building. So many celebrities live there that it easy for everyone who lives there to think that he or she is a celebrity or, at the very least, a celebrity *manqué* . . . and is entitled to the full star treatment and perquisites . . . is licensed to display star temperament with foot-stamping, tantrum-throwing shouts of, "Shoot the scene my way or I'll walk off the set." Too much of this sort of thing could spell the Dakota's doom.

The Dakota has always managed to reflect shifting New York attitudes through the generations. It has always been a sign of the times. Today's young New Yorkers are a self-conscious generation, working terribly hard at being genuine and real, at being a part of what is trendy and arty and radically chic. To some people the Dakota today seems to have become a building, as Dorothy Parker put it, of "Authors and actors and artists and such" who "never say nothing and never say much." At a gathering of such young Dakotans, the very air seems jagged with competition and one-upmanship. If this sort of mood were to prevail, the Dakota could easily become what New York City is to some people—a nice place to visit, but one wouldn't want to live there.

At the Dakota today the feelings about the possibilities of the building's future are a curious mixture of concern and blind faith—the kind of faith that leads villagers to live comfortably on the sides of volcanoes, to build houses and swimming pools along the San Andreas fault and in the burning hills above Benedict and Laurel Canyons. The Dakota has always been there, they say. Therefore, it will always be there—though the chances are probably more than fifty-fifty that it won't.

Dakotans, it sometimes seems, live in a kind of dream. In 1970 a novel by Jack Finney called *Time and Again* was published, which used the Dakota as its principal setting. *Time and Again* involved a science-fictional journey backward in time and, in the process, several facts got a bit twisted. (The time of the novel was a year before the Dakota was even built, for example.) To some people the Dakotans today are living in a similar world of fiction, make-believe and magic. At every board meeting new and more fanciful suggestions for "improving" the Dakota are proposed—a rooftop garden with pergolas and trees and shaded walks, a swimming pool, a private night club, and—again and again—the matter of the expensive and much-needed face cleaning. In the end, all the fine notions prove too impractical, too expensive, or both, and nothing comes of them. To the outside observer the building grows darker and dingier as the years speed by.

Of course the kind of rich the Dakota attracts today—that high-intensity, high-profile variety of rich—is not known for fiscal astuteness. These are not Rockefellers or Vanderbilts or Astors who amass huge fortunes and store them away in unshatterable trusts for future unborn generations. The Dakota's rich are the kind who install saunas and Jacuzzi whirlpool baths, buy Rolls-Royces and summer places in the Hamptons and, at the same time, have trouble paying both the maintenance and the milkman. Faith supports them, rather than intelligence or foresightedness.

Every community has its myths, and the Dakota is no exception. Scarsdale and Palm Springs both believe absolutely that their community is the richest-per-capita community in the world. (Neither is.) Philadelphians confidently believe that their city is "the second largest in the United States." (It isn't.) The Dakotans continue to believe that, for one, theirs was the first luxury apartment house in America, though it wasn't, and, for two, that—as the *Daily Graphic* put it—the Dakota is "the most perfect apartment house in the world."

Well, it is if you think it is. That's faith.

Be it ever so humble, there's no place like home.

Index

8-16